SIKH GURUS

Their Lives and Teachings

SIKH GURUS

Their Lives and Teachings

K.S. Duggal

Foreword by Sri Swami Rama

The Himalayan International Institute
of Yoga Science and Philosophy of the U.S.A.
Honesdale, Pennsylvania

© 1987 Himalayan International Institute of
Yoga Science and Philosophy of the U.S.A.
RR 1, Box 400
Honesdale, Pennsylvania 18431

Second Printing 1989

Originally published by Vikas Publishing House, PVT, LTD, New Delhi, India.

The paper used in this publication meets the minimum requirements of American National Standard for Information Sciences—Permanence of Paper for Printed Library Materials. ANSI Z39.48-1984.⊚

ISBN 0-89389-106-1

Contents

Foreword

The author of this book, K.S. Duggal, has done a great service to the modern reader in making available these inspiring stories of the Sikh Gurus. While the stories of their lives are told in a simple, straightforward fashion, the author succeeds in conveying the courage, determination, love, and devotion that their lives represent and inspires the reader to cultivate these qualities in the pursuit of his or her own spiritual path.

Far from being pedants or recluses who isolated themselves from the world, the Sikh Gurus embodied the ideal of a spiritual life lived in the world, yet above the world; they demonstrated the ideals of love, service, and surrender.

The author, Kartar Singh Duggal, a prolific writer, is eminently qualified to write such an account, and has received numerous honors for his work. His dedication shows itself in his beautiful translations of the hymns of the Gurus, which should delight the reader.

I am very happy to write this foreword to the second printing of this beautiful book, and hope that through it, many readers, both Sikh and those of other beliefs, will come to appreciate the essence of the Sikh tradition and the essential unity of all spiritual paths.

Swami Rama

Preface

I belong to a devout Sikh family. My father was deeply religious, having been influenced by the Singh Sabha Lehr, a revivalist Sikh movement in the early part of this century. My uncle used to be an Akali to the core, an ardent admirer of Master Tara Singh, in spite of the fact that he was in Government service. No wonder that he was sacked and put on the blacklist by the white man during the Akali movement. I was brought up in the strict discipline of an orthodox family. Even as a child, I went to the Gurdwara both in the morning and in the evening, said my prayers regularly, wrote poems in praise of the Sikh Gurus, and won prizes on festival occasions.

And yet I was different. I made friends with Muslim boys. I had my midday meal with a Bengali classmate who lived close to our school. For my higher education, I went to Christian mission colleges where attending the Bible class was compulsory.

I read Urdu and Persian and after completing my studies, when I was looking for a job, it was my writings in Urdu and not in Punjabi that fetched me a fairly coveted post.

I was, therefore, not at all surprised that when the time for my marriage came, I chose a Muslim girl. She was so sweet that, more than I, my people were charmed by her.

We have already lived a little over four decades of a blissful married life. We have two children. The son is a doctor; he is married and lives with us. The daughter has also married a doctor who works in the U.S.A. They live in Florida.

In this perfect picture of happiness, of late I had started feeling that something was, perhaps, missing somewhere. I discovered that I had no occasion to introduce my children to the Sikh tradition and the Sikh way of life as such. Educated in public schools outside the

Punjab, they didn't have an opportunity even to learn to speak Punjabi, much less acquaint themselves with the Gurmukhi alphabet letters in which the Sikh scriptures are written.

With this book I do my duty as a father. As I said, my son is a medical graduate and my daughter did her Honours in English literature. I have tried to tell the life and teachings of the Sikh Gurus in their idiom, an account that must not only be convincing but also be acceptable to the modern mind.

The Sikh Gurus were plain people. Excepting Guru Harkrishan, who died very young, all others were married and lived utterly simple lives, exhorting their followers to earn an honest living and share it with others. They had their children, who did not necessarily succeed them. They never made tall promises to gain for their followers heaven or houries (beautiful celestial maidens) or rivers of honey. According to them, all men are born equal; they gave no quarter to distinctions of caste or creed. They started practices like community eating, community singing, and congregational prayers, rejecting rituals and ceremony. A little over five hundred years old, Sikhism is the newest amongst the major religions of the world. At times it appears as if the great Gurus culled the best from all the religions and presented a synthesis that promised to meet the needs of the new society.

Says the Sikh scripture, "My God is like what I see in the mirror." Man is made in the image of God. This is the greatest hope held out by the Sikh Gurus. You need not fast, you need not go on pilgrimage to holy places. You need do nothing except have faith in Him and remember Him day and night. This will lead you to the Guru. And the Guru's grace will get you peace of mind here and freedom from life and death hereafter.

And the Guru, according to the Sikh faith, is the *Holy Granth*— the living Guru. The Sikh scripture is a unique work among those the world has known. It contains hymns of the Sikh Gurus along with the work of a large number of like-minded saints, both Hindus and Muslims, high caste and low caste, princes and plebeians, of their time.

In this book, apart from telling the fascinating life-story of the Sikh Gurus, I have translated afresh selections from their popular hymns. The book opens with a chapter on the time when Guru Nanak was born and closes with an account of the compilation of the *Holy Granth* and its consecration, "the manifest corpus of all the Sikh Gurus." I have spared no effort as a devoted Sikh and lifelong story writer to portray the lives of the Sikh Gurus as faithfully as possible and present their teachings in as simple a manner as I could.

I believe that every generation must reinterpret its preceptors and translate their sayings into its own idiom. This book attempts to meet this need both for the Sikhs and the non-Sikhs, Indians and those living abroad, and most particularly, for those who have missed the opportunity to acquaint themselves with the Sikh tradition through writings in Punjabi in the Gurmukhi script.

Before placing the script with my original publishers I had it read by the late Sardar Ranbir Singh, the celebrated author of *The Divine Masters* and *The Sikh Way of Life* and also Mr. P.R. Kaikini, formerly Editor, National Book Trust, India. They made valuable suggestions, most of which I have gratefully accepted; where I have differed, I take the entire responsibility for it. I am also deeply indebted to my friend, Mr. Keshav Malik, for his valuable suggestions in the translation of the *Gurbani*.

K.S. Duggal

To Swami Rama

The Times

In the black night of deceit
The moon of truth is nowhere to be traced.

—Nanak

It was the worst of times. The Punjab was reeling under Timur's attack. He had pillaged and plundered the country as no one else had ever done. He was followed by no less avaricious marauders than Jasrat Khokhar, Faulad Khan Turkbacha, and Sheikh Ali. Then the Lodi kings tried to outdo them with their fanaticism. In fact, the Muslims, who had converted to Islam the entire population of Arabia, Iraq, Turkey, Egypt, Iran, Afghanistan, and several other countries felt strangely helpless in Hindu India. The Hindu philosophy and the Hindu way of life seemed to defeat the proselytizing Muslim priests and the bigoted Muslim conquerors who styled themselves *ghazis*. Excepting the low caste *shudras* and a handful of the fighting forces, none seemed to accept Islam. The victors felt defeated in their designs.

The Sufi cult among the Muslims tried to resolve, through intuition rather than through reasoned argument, the conflicts of formal religions dividing the people. They had come under the influence of Vedanta and the practices of the yogis. Among the Hindus, the Bhakti movement laid stress on loving devotion to God. They believed that salvation was gained not through knowledge but through the grace of the Guru. Multan and Pak Pattan in the Punjab were the leading Sufi centers. Kabir and Ravidas, Mira and Tulsi, were the leading *bhaktas* of their time. They ignored the distinctions of religion and caste, of the rich and the poor. Ravidas was a Hindu

1

cobbler, Mirabai was a princess, and Sadhna was a butcher by profession.

Yet the Muslims and the Hindus remained completely alienated from each other socially and culturally. The Hindus were divided into various castes; the Muslims had no faith in the caste system. The Hindus believed in many gods; the Muslims worshipped one God. The Hindus looked upon the cow as sacred; the Muslims were non-vegetarians, relishing meat, including beef. The Hindus burned their dead on the funeral pyre, the Muslims buried them in the belief that they would rise on the day of reckoning. The Hindus were passive and introverted, the Muslims were aggressive and overbearing. The Muslims looked upon Hindus as *kafirs*—pagans, while the Muslims were *mlechhas*—brutes, in the eyes of the Hindus. The Hindus felt polluted even by the shadow of a Muslim. The Muslims had no such inhibitions; they had no compunction in taking Hindu women as their consorts.

It was the age of the worst repression. The Hindus were persecuted systematically. They were treated as second class citizens in their own country. Bodhan, a Brahman, was executed because he believed that, if followed with devotion, both Hinduism and Islam were alike and equally acceptable to God. The Muslim ruler, Sikandar Lodi, ordered that Bodhan should either accept Islam or face death. Bodhan accepted death. The Hindus were called *zimmies*. They lived a miserable life, humiliated and discriminated against at every step. They had to pay *jizia*, a tax for being Hindus. They could not build new temples, nor repair old ones. They had to pay taxes to visit places of pilgrimage. If the Muslims so desired, the Hindus could not stop them from entering temples. Any Muslim could stay as a guest for at least three days with a Hindu and they could not object. If a Hindu felt inclined to accept Islam, no one could oppose it. They were not permitted to possess lethal weapons like swords or bows and arrows. They had to dress in a manner that would distinguish them from the Muslims. They could not build houses in Muslim neighborhoods. They were not permitted to purchase Muslim slaves. They were forbidden from mourning their dead too loudly, lest they disturb the peace of the Muslim elite. They had to show respect to all Muslims, and if the Muslims so desired, allow them to join company with them. When asked to describe the status of a Hindu, the *qazi* in the court of Allauddin Khilji said:

> They are payers of tribute and when the revenue officer demands silver from them, they should without question and with all humility and respect tender gold. If the tax collector chooses to spit in the mouth of the Hindu, the latter must open his mouth without hesitation.
>
> (*Guru Nanak and His Times* by A.C. Bannerjee.)

However, in some quarters it is maintained that the conditions in the Punjab during Guru Nanak's time were not so bad. Bahlol Lodi (1451-89) and Sikandar Lodi (1499-1517) were on the lookout for an opportunity to shake off the hegemony of the Delhi Sultan. They could, therefore, ill-afford to alienate the vast majority of their subjects. Rather than style themselves as *ghazis*, they tried to give the impression of being secular. The Hindu aristocracy was befriended. Those who were literate and had proficiency in Persian were given odd jobs. Some of them who came to gain the confidence of the administration were even entrusted with responsible assignments.

In order to get rid of the stranglehold of the Delhi Sultanate, the Lodis also sought foreign intervention. Daulat Khan invited Babar to attack India in 1523. An invader, usually, is no respecter of person or property. The Hindus had a harrowing experience of the conquerors. The Muslim rulers were too weak to defend themselves. It was the people who were the worst sufferers. The Punjab, being the gateway, had to bear the brunt of every attack and suffered most. There was lawlessness. The peasants could not tend their crops, the traders could not carry on their trade undisturbed. The people lost all faith in moral and spiritual values. The successive invaders drained the country of almost all talent and resources. During the course of one of his attacks, Babar observed in his diary:

> Its people have no good looks; of social intercourse, paying and receiving visits there is none; of genius and capacity none, in handicrafts and works, there is no form of symmetry, method, or quality, there are no good horses, no good dogs, no grapes, musk-

melons or first-rate fruits, no ice or cold water, no good bread or cooked food in the bazaars, no hot baths, no colleges, no candles, torches or candle-sticks.

(*Guru Nanak and His Times* by A.C. Bannerjee.)

Such was the havoc the successive Muslim invaders had wrought on the Hindu society and on the economy of the time.

Shahab-ud-din, the king of Ghazni, the first Muslim invader of India (1170-1206), put Prithvi Raj, the sovereign of Ajmer, to death in cold blood. Ibn-i-Asir writes that, after he conquered Benares (Varanasi), he carried out indiscriminate slaughter of the Hindus. None was spared except women and children. The massacre continued until "the earth grew weary of the monotony."

Hasan Nizami Nishapuri observes in *Taj-ul-Maasir* that when Qutbuddin Aibak (1194-1210) vanquished Meerut, he erected mosques, demolishing all the Hindu temples of the town. Similarly, in the city of Kalinjir, 113 Hindu temples were desecrated and mosques constructed on their sites. More than one hundred thousand Hindus were massacred and about fifty thousand were made slaves. It is said the town became pitch-black with dead bodies decomposing all over.

Minhaj-ul-Siraj records in *Tabaat-i-Nasiri* that Mohammad Bukh-tyar, who conquered Bihar, killed one hundred thousand Brahmins and destroyed a highly valuable library of ancient Sanskrit works.

Abdulla Wassaf, the author of *Taziyat-ul-Amsar wa Tajriyat ul Asar*, says that Allauddin Khilji (1295-1316) put to the sword the entire male Hindu population of the city of Kambayat in order to glorify Islam and the rivers were flooded with blood. He sent the women with all their jewelry to his home-town, making twenty thousand young girls his slaves.

The renowned author of *Twarikh-i-Ilahi*, Amir Khusrau, writes that when the Emperor Firoz Shah Tughlak (1315-88) conquered the city of Bhilsa in Madhya Pradesh, he destroyed all the Hindu temples, collected their idols in front of the fort and bathed them daily in the blood of one thousand Hindus.

As many as sixty foreign invasions of India took place between the 11th century and the birth of Guru Nanak. For a long time, more than conquering the country to rule over it, the invaders came to loot and convert the Hindus to Islam. Those who resisted were massacred. The marauders seemed to believe that there was religious sanction for this. They had, therefore, no compunction in committing the worst of crimes against those they called kafirs or pagans.

As a result of such successive attacks, the people were rendered destitute; the villages dirty. The towns were in decay, the jungles encroached upon the city, and robbers and bad characters took shelter in them. The poor were found going about naked. The government did not run any schools or colleges. The Hindu *pathshalas* were maintained by voluntary effort, the Muslim *madrasas* or *maktabs* received grants in cash or in the form of rent-free land. The Hindu libraries had books on religion, philosophy, and medicine. These were in Sanskrit. The foreign invaders made it a point to destroy them. Since young Hindu girls were invariably picked up by the Muslim conquerors or the local rulers, the rich took recourse to infanticide. In order to save their honor, the girls were married early. And then they were given all sorts of dirty jobs to do and encouraged to neglect their toilet, so that they did not attract notice from an admiring eye. Widows were not permitted to marry and more often than not they immolated themselves along with their dead husbands on the funeral pyre. A widow could not participate in any festivity, sing songs, or indulge in merrymaking. A number of them preferred conversion to Islam or took to prostitution, rather than face this dreary prospect. The majority of the people worshipped idols, believed in ritualism and all sorts of superstitions. The essence of religion was forgotten altogether. This was equally true of the Muslims, who had also degenerated. The administration was corrupt at every level. Bribery and unfair means were the order of the day.

Guru Nanak has described his times in a most telling manner:

Kaliyuga is a dagger,
Kings are butchers,
Dharma has taken wings and disappeared.
In the black night of falsehood
The moon of truth is nowhere to be seen.
I am lost in the search,

I find no way out of the darkness.
Afflicted with the ego, I wail in sorrow.
Says Nanak, how do I attain deliverance?

Here is how Guru Nanak reacted to Babar's attack on India and
the affliction it caused the people:

He occupied Khurasan and subdued Hindustan.
God doesn't blame Himself having sent the Mughal like a doom.
Seeing such suffering and wailing, didn't it hurt you, O Lord?
You are the lone creator of all.
If an aggressor were to kill an aggressor, I wouldn't complain.
But when a fierce lion falls on a poor herd of cattle, the master
    must take the blame.
The dogs have ravaged the gems of us; when they die, none will
    ever bother about them.
O God! you alone make and unmake, this is your greatness.
If anyone else were to style himself great and indulge in pleasure-
    making, He is like an insect in the eyes of God, feeding on a few
    grains.
He who dies in life, he alone lives, says Nanak, by repeating the
    name of God.

(*Asa*)

Guru Nanak's heart seems to bleed at the devastation caused, and
the undoing of all that was Indian by the foreign invaders.

Guru Nanak condemned the corrupt ways of the administration as
vehemently:

There is none
    Who receives or gives not bribe;
Even the King distributes justice
    When his palm is greased.

It was, indeed, the worst of times. It is said that when evil exceeds
all limits, God takes pity on His creation and sends a Messiah to show
light to the people. Thus was born Guru Nanak.

Guru Nanak

Baba Nanak, the great man of God
The guru of the Hindus and the *pir* of the Mussalmans
—Popular Punjabi saying

Unlike Mahavira and Buddha, Nanak was not born to affluent parents. He was the son of Mehta Kalian Das, a village *patwari*, at the lowest rung of the revenue hierarchy. His father led a clean life; he was honest and God-fearing. These were rare qualities to come by in those days. He was, therefore, greatly respected by the Muslim headman of the village, Rai Bular.

Born on 15 April 1469 at Talwandi in the Sheikupura district of West Punjab, Nanak was the only son of his parents. Their other child was a daughter called Nanaki born a few years earlier. The son arrived after a long wait. His mother Tripta and his sister Nanaki doted on him. His father, however, was too involved with work to spare any time to be with his children.

Mehta Kalian Das, also known as Mehta Kalu, was a Bedi, a caste that is supposed to be well versed in the Vedas. As a child Nanak was given the name Nanak Rai in the tradition of the Hindus of the day. Talwandi, the village where he was born, came to be known in due course as Nanakana Sahib—the holy city of Nanak. It is located about fifty kilometers to the northwest of Lahore, the capital of West Punjab in Pakistan.

While playing in the company of other children, Nanak was always fair. He made friends with the poor and the so-called low castes. Muslim boys were as good friends of his as were Hindus. He had a melodious voice and was fond of singing devotional songs.

When he sang, he went into a trance, as it were; phrases tripped on his lips and he composed hymns extempore. He was used to taking long walks and would go out of his village into the fields and jungle in both the morning and the evening. There was always a freshness on his face, a soothing light in his eyes. He was genial and gentle, soft-spoken and amiable.

His sister Nanaki was deeply attached to him. She thought it was probably because he was her only brother, but in her heart of hearts she knew it was more than that. Every time she saw Nanak, she felt a tug at her heart. He was indeed unlike other children. When he was asleep, she found a strange glow reflected on his face. It was enchanting to watch him. She continued to look at him for hours on end. Sitting all alone at times, she would suddenly feel that there was a sweet fragrance spreading through the courtyard and turning her face, she would find her young brother enter the house arm-in-arm with one of his playmates. When he sat in the prayer chamber, she would hear the sound of cymbals being beaten and *arti* being sung in praise of God. She remained glued to where she sat. It was like divine music travelling from heaven. She had never heard such melody before. No doubt her brother was no ordinary child, but she dared not talk about it to anyone. It was a closely guarded secret with her.

Nanak, who was to emerge in due course as Divine Master, had his first devotee in his own sister. She found in her brother an evolved soul, a messenger of God.

The second disciple of Nanak was no other than Rai Bular, the Muslim chief of the village. Day after day, week after week, month after month, and year after year, he heard amazing stories about Mehta Kalu's child. His utterances astonished both Hindus and Muslims. They found them bold and meaningful, endowed with a queer charm.

The village school teacher, Gopal Panda, found in a short while that he had nothing more to teach Nanak. Nanak learned reading and writing very quickly. He even composed an acrostic on the Punjabi alphabet. When the teacher tried to teach him arithmetic, he found him equally proficient in figure work. He had little to add to the knowledge of the unusually gifted child. Instead, Nanak told his teacher that without knowing God all other knowledge was meaningless. Without truth, even a cartload of books was of little use:

> Burn worldly love
> Grinding it into ashes to make ink.
> Let your intellect be the fine paper
> On which you should write
> With the pen of divine love,
> As dictated by the Guru.
> Write the praises of his Name
> Write that He is limitless and great.
> Oh teacher, if you were to learn writing this
> The truth of it will stand by you
> Wherever you are called upon to render account.
>
> *(Sri Rag)*

Nanak was then sent to a *madrasa* to learn Persian and Arabic. His teacher was Ruknuddin. The understanding was that after he acquired proficiency in Persian, he might, in due course, succeed his father as the village *patwari*. Rai Bular would be very happy to have him work with him. Nanak surprised his new teacher with the manner in which he picked up Persian and also Arabic quickly. One day he even astonished Ruknuddin with an acrostic composed on the Persian alphabet.

It was time that Nanak was invested with the sacred thread according to a custom prevalent among the caste Hindus. It is a sacrament like baptism amongst Christians, signifying the spiritual rebirth of a Hindu. Hardyal, the family priest, was invited to perform the ritual in the presence of relatives, friends, and neighbors. The ceremony was to be followed by lavish feasting and rejoicing. However, when the presiding priest approached Nanak to invest him with the sacred thread, he refused to wear it. Young Nanak had no faith in the ritual. He would have nothing to do with a thread which must wear out sooner or later. Everyone present was stunned. They tried to argue with the child but none succeeded in persuading him. When the priest persisted, Nanak went into a trance and sang:

Let mercy be the cotton, contentment the thread,
Continence the knot and truth the twist.
O priest! if you have such a thread,
Do give it to me.
It'll not wear out, nor get soiled, nor be burnt, nor lost.
Says Nanak, blessed are those who go about wearing such a thread.

(Rag Asa)

Rai Bular, who had been invited to participate in the feast following the thread ceremony, was thrilled to hear it. He complimented Mehta Kalu on his son's talents. But the devout Hindu in the father would not understand it and was heartbroken.

As he grew, Nanak spent more and more of his time in the company of Hindu anchorites and Muslim dervishes in the thick forest around Talwandi. He was most happy in their company. But the matter-of-fact Mehta Kalu did not approve of it. "If he is fond of wandering about in the forest," he said to himself, "he might as well take the family cattle out for grazing. He could spend his time in the fields as well as look after the cattle." Nanak agreed to this. He liked tending cows and buffalo. Accordingly, he led his cattle out for grazing every morning and brought them back in the evening when it was time to milk them. Before long, the cattle were completely tamed. They didn't bother the cowherd at all. He sat under the trees and sang hymns; the cattle grazed on and frolicked about.

Then one day, an agitated peasant came and complained to Rai Bular that Mehta Kalu's cattle had ravaged his entire crop and that his son, sent to look after the cattle, was found sleeping under a tree. Rai Bular, who understood Nanak better, didn't believe a word of it. He decided to verify the loss himself. Out in the field, he did find Nanak sitting under a tree, lost in deep meditation, but the crop allegedly ravaged by the cattle was intact and not a blade seemed to have been disturbed. The peasant who had lodged the complaint could not believe his eyes. He felt frightfully embarrassed. Rai Bular then walked up to the tree where Nanak sat. He found that there was a halo around Nanak's head. He bowed in reverence and was convinced that Mehta Kalu's son was a blessed soul; he was no ordinary youth born in the village.

Rai Bular made indulgent inquiries about Nanak every day—where he spent his time, what he did, and so on. Even if it meant going out of the way, he would do so to drop in at Mehta Kalu's house and meet Nanak. Every time Rai Bular looked at Nanak, he felt charmed. His head would bow before him spontaneously. Every word that Nanak uttered acquired new significance; it haunted him day and night.

On the other hand, Mehta Kalu did not understand a word of it. In fact, he was irritated at the fuss his daughter Nanaki and his mentor Rai Bular made about his son. He thought Nanak was good-for-nothing, that as the only son, he was being pampered by people and spoiled. He thought Nanak showed little interest in any worthwhile activity. And of late he had developed a strange tendency to keep to himself. As far as possible, he avoided company and was always lost in thought. His eyes were dreamy. He didn't eat for days together. At night when everybody slept, many a time Mehta Kalu saw his young son deeply absorbed in meditation. At times he felt as if he heard his sobs. At others, he saw with his own eyes tears rolling down Nanak's cheeks. It gave a wrench to his heart. Everyone who saw Nanak those days felt that there was something wrong with him. He appeared to be suffering from some ailment. It was therefore decided to have the youth checked. They sent for Hari Das, a leading physician. As the old physician was feeling his pulse, Nanak went into a trance and started singing in his melodious voice. The physician listened to his patient spellbound:

The physician called to diagnose an ailment
Pulls out my arm and feels the pulse.
The simple physician is not aware,
The malady is deep in the heart.

(Rag Malhar)

I suffer the pangs of separation
I hunger for Him and suffer.
I suffer the fear of mighty death.
I suffer from the ailments
That must kill me one day.
And no remedy of the poor physician will help.

It's an eternal agony,
No remedy howsoever potent can cure it.
I forgot God, indulged in pleasure
And thus I contracted many an ailment.
I went blind; I must be punished,
And no remedy of the poor physician will help.

(Rag Malhar)

The physician heard it and his eyes suddenly opened. Certainly it was a malady beyond his capacity to cure.

Helpless, the anxious parents decided to get their son married before it was too late. They thought that, if bound in marriage, Nanak might start taking interest in household affairs. He might take to some profitable pursuit. Accordingly, a suitable match was found in Sulakhni, the daughter of Mula, a Chona Khatri. Mula was also a *patwari* of Pakho di Randhawa. Nanak did not object to this, since he maintained that married life did not conflict with spiritual pursuits; and if anything, it helped.

Nanak was happily married. He loved his wife. They had two sons. Sri Chand was followed three years later by Lakshmi Chand. Now that he had a family of his own, Nanak was persuaded by his father to engage himself in some profitable pursuit, so that in due course he could stand on his own feet. The father's counsel was, indeed, reasonable and Nanak readily agreed to it. The father was most happy at this development. He lost no time in placing a suitable sum at his disposal and deputed Bala, one of his servants, to assist Nanak. It was decided that they should go to Chuhrkana, a wholesale market (in the present day Gujranwala district of West Pakistan) and make some profitable bargain. Nanak did go to Chuhrkana. He made the purchases that could make a profit back home. But during his return journey, he came across a band of holy men who, it seems, had nothing much to eat for several days. They didn't have any clothes either, and winter was fast approaching. Nanak saw their plight and didn't take a moment to decide to feed and clothe them with what he carried. Placing all his purchases at their disposal, he walked back home empty-handed, along with Bala. As he came close to his village, he suddenly realized how his father would react to the peculiar bargain that he had struck. He therefore sat under a tree outside the village instead of going to his house. When his father learned of it, he was wild. Nanak tried to explain to him that he had been sent to make a good bargain and that he could not think of a better deal. Mehta Kalu didn't understand it. As it happened, Rai Bular also turned up on the scene and, listening to Nanak argue with his father the way he did, seemed to agree with every word that he uttered. Nanak was indeed no ordinary youth. Rai Bular became his devoted disciple.

But Mehta Kalu continued to feel miserable. He didn't understand the ways of his son. Neither Rai Bular nor his daughter could make him see the divine in Nanak. The tree under which Nanak sat outside the village fearing the wrath of his father is still there. It is known as Thamb Saheb—the holy trunk. The devout come and meditate under it.

Nanak's sister Nanaki had been married to Jai Ram, a Khatri employed as a steward by Daulat Khan Lodi, the Governor of Sultanpur. He was visiting Talwandi and, finding his father-in-law anxious about his son, he offered to take Nanak along with him to Sultanpur and find a job for him with his master. Everyone approved of it. Nanak, too, didn't object to it. Rai Bular wrote to Daulat Khan recommending Nanak in glorious terms. Daulat Khan met Nanak and was most favorably impressed by the charm of his personality and the transparent honesty of his character. He asked Nanak to take charge of his stores. It was the most appropriate assignment for a God-fearing man like Nanak. A few days later Mardana, one of Nanak's companions from Talwandi also joined him. Mardana was an instrumentalist by profession; he played on the rabab. While during the day Nanak worked in the Nawab's commissariat, they got together both in the morning and in the evening to meditate and sing hymns. Their sessions became longer and longer. More and more people started joining them. Before he left his home in Talwandi, Nanak had promised his wife that he would send her part of his earnings, which he continued to do. With the rest of the money he entertained his companions and the poor and the needy that he came across.

It is said that Nanak remained in the service of the Nawab for about two years. Then early one morning, accompanied by Mardana, he went to the river Bain, close by, for his bath. He did this first thing every day. To Mardana's surprise after Nanak plunged into the water that morning, he didn't appear on the surface. Mardana waited and waited. Then panic-stricken, he ran to the town to seek assistance. Evidently Nanak had either been drowned or washed away by the river, which was in spate. The Nawab, who had become a great admirer of Nanak, got the best divers to scrounge the river thoroughly. But Nanak was nowhere to be found. Then some wicked people started a whispering campaign. They alleged that Jai Ram's brother-in-law had embezzled the stores and, fearing the consequences, he had fled or maybe he had committed suicide by drowning himself. The stores were thoroughly checked and it was found that the inventory and the accounts were absolutely in order.

To everybody's surprise, on the third day Nanak appeared in the town as if from nowhere. There was a great relief in the Nawab's household and rejoicing among Nanak's relatives and friends. But Nanak was no longer his old self. He was altogether a changed man. There was divine light in his eyes and his face was resplendent. A halo seemed to crown his head. People flocked to have a look at him. Nanak wouldn't speak to anybody. He was in a trance. He gave up his job with the Nawab and distributed all that he had to the poor. Accompanied by Mardana, the *rabab* player, he left the town.

When he broke his silence after a few days, his first utterance was: "There is no Hindu, no Mussalman.", He spoke in ecstasy. He was no longer Nanak, the dreamy-eyed youth from Talwandi, he was Guru Nanak, a messenger of God, ordained to propagate His Name and the virtues of truthfulness and clean living. His second utterance was: "One must labor to earn and share one's earnings with others." These were the two cardinal principles of Guru Nanak's teaching when he started his life-long mission. It is said that he was thirty years old when he left Sultanpur.

Before he took his leave, the Nawab asked Guru Nanak what he meant when he said, "There is no Hindu, no Mussalman." Perhaps the Hindus were no longer Hindus but the Mussalmans remained devoted to their faith. At this, Guru Nanak uttered these words:

Let God's grace be the mosque, and devotion the prayer mat.
Let the Quran be the good conduct.

Let modesty be compassion, good manners fasting,
You should be a Mussalman the like of this.
Let good deeds be your Kaaba and truth be your mentor.
Your *Kalma* be your creed and prayer,
God would then vindicate your honor.

(Majh)

The *qazi* in the Nawab's court, however, was not convinced. "If you are not a Hindu," he said, "you must join us in prayers, we who are devout Muslims believing in the unity of God." Guru Nanak was certainly willing to keep company with those who had faith in God. He agreed to join them in prayers. But when the *qazi* commenced the prayers, Guru Nanak stood aside and watched with a smile on his lips. As soon as the prayers were over, the infuriated *qazi* asked Guru Nanak, "Why didn't you join us in prayers after agreeing to do so?" Guru Nanak told him politely, "I did not join you because all the while you were saying the prayers, your mind was on your filly left loose back at your place. You feared that she might drop into the well of your courtyard." The *qazi* heard it and was silenced. "In that case, you could have given me your company," said the Nawab. "Yes, but you were buying horses in Kabul," observed Guru Nanak. The Nawab heard it and fell at the Guru's feet. He was, indeed, a man of God. God spoke through him.

Guru Nanak's times were difficult. The process of communication was forbidding. Messages had to be carried by word of mouth from town to town and from village to village. Guru Nanak undertook long journeys to north and south, east and west. He had with him Mardana, the Muslim *rabab* player, for a companion. Mardana played on the *rabab* and Guru Nanak poured out the inspired word in some of the finest poetry in the language. Not only this, most of it can be sung to music in prescribed *ragas*. With illiteracy rampant around him, Guru Nanak purposely chose this medium to propagate his message. He also endeavored to set up cells called *manjis*, where those who subscribed to his way of life assembled for meditation and recitation of hymns. In due course, there was a network of these cells throughout India and beyond its borders in Sri Lanka, across the Himalayas, and in West Asia.

Leaving Sultanpur, Guru Nanak came to Saidpur, a small town later known as Eminabad (in the present day Gujranwala district of West Punjab). Guru Nanak chose to stay here with Lalo, a carpenter. It so happened that the day Guru Nanak arrived, Malik Bhago, the chief of the town, who had amassed untold wealth, was holding a sacrificial feast to which all the holy men were invited. Guru Nanak decided to remain away and partook of the simple fare of his host. When Malik Bhago came to know of it, he was furious. "How dare an itinerant mendicant refuse my invitation?" said he in vulgar pride. He had Guru Nanak brought to him. When asked why he didn't join in the sacrificial feast which every other holy man in the town had blessed with his presence, the Guru sent for the meal served by Malik Bhago and also for a little of Bhai Lalo's simple fare. It is said that, holding these in separate hands, he squeezed them and, to the utter discomfiture of Malik Bhago, what appeared to be blood drops trickled down from his rich food, and milk oozed out of Bhai Lalo's simple fare. Malik Bhago was put to shame. He didn't have to be told that his riches were amassed by exploiting the poor, while what Bhai Lalo offered was the milk of hard-earned wages. Malik Bhago was a changed man. He distributed all his ill-gotten wealth to the poor and needy, and devoted himself to the service of his fellowmen.

Bhai Lalo craved Guru Nanak's company longer but the Guru had to proceed on his mission. After several days' journeying through jungles and wilderness Guru Nanak, accompanied by Mardana, arrived at a caravanserai. It was maintained by a saintly-looking man called Sajjan. He had tidy rooms for travellers and both a mosque and a temple built for their prayers. All this was, however, a cover for his misdeeds. He was, in fact, a wicked robber and an assassin. He looted those who came to stay with him and if need be, had them killed. Noticing the glow on Guru Nanak's face, Sajjan mistook him for a prosperous trader who was, perhaps, travelling in the guise of a recluse to avoid being waylaid. Sajjan attacked his victims during the night when they were asleep. He waited and waited that night but Guru Nanak would not retire. Late in the night, when everyone else had gone to sleep, Guru Nanak sang, Mardana accompanying him on the rabab:

Bright and brilliant is the bronze.
But the moment it is rubbed its blackness appears.
This cannot be removed even if washed a hundred times.

(Suhi)

Guru Nanak sang this hymn, which was evidently directed towards Sajjan, who was all this while waiting for an opportunity to pounce upon his visitor. Guru Nanak's words touched him. He realized his folly. He came out of his hiding place and fell at the Guru's feet, confessing all his misdeeds. Sajjan's den of assassins was transformed into a *dharmasala*, a seat of *dharma*. It was the first major center that Guru Nanak set up for the congregation of his disciples.

During his sojourn towards the east, Guru Nanak camped in a town. Rains came and he had to stay on in the town longer than he had thought he would. Several devotees came to the Guru regularly. Amongst them were two close friends who lived on the same lane. On their way to see the Guru, one of them came across a prostitute and was allured by her charm. Thereafter, he left his home along with a friend on the pretext of going to the Guru, but instead visited his paramour. A few days later the one who came to pay his homage to the Guru daily was pricked with a thorn, while his neighbor, who visited the prostitute, found a gold coin in the street. The incident bewildered the Guru's devotee, who came every day religiously. He mentioned it in the prayer meeting that morning. Guru Nanak heard it and was amused. He then told the Sikh:

Your friend was destined to come across a treasure but due to his evil ways, it had been reduced to a single coin. While on account of your past karma you were to have been impaled with a stake, but having reformed yourself, you have been let off with the mere prick of a thorn.

When the rains abated, Guru Nanak, accompanied by Mardana, came to Kurukshetra (in today's Ambala district of Haryana State). A big fair was being held at the holy tank on account of a solar eclipse. There were a large number of pilgrims from all over the country. On his arrival at the fair, Guru Nanak asked Mardana to cook meat for them. As it happened, they had been presented with a deer by a shikari on their way to Kurukshetra. Finding a pilgrim cooking meat on the holy premises, the yogis collected for the fair were scandalized. How could anyone defile the sacred premises with the profanity of cooking and eating meat? They gathered around Guru Nanak and started shouting at him. Guru Nanak heard them patiently and then sang thus:

Implanted by flesh, conceived in flesh,
Born in flesh, with mouth, bones, skin, and body made of flesh,
Coming out of the flesh of the womb, he sucks the breasts of flesh,
He grows and marries flesh, bringing flesh to his house,
Flesh is born of flesh.
Fools fight over flesh.
They don't understand truth nor do they meditate on it.
What is flesh? What vegetable?
What is evil? What is it not?
Pandit! You know not how flesh is made.
It's from water,
The source of corn, sugarcane, and cotton,
In fact, of all three worlds.

(Malhar)

The pilgrims collected around Guru Nanak, heard him, and were silenced. The Guru told them to meditate on God alone and address one another with the salutation "Sat Kartar—God is truth," and went on his way.

Guru Nanak's next halt was at Hardwar, a Hindu pilgrim center, on the banks of the holy Ganges. Here the Guru found a large gathering of devotees taking baths in the holy river and offering water to the sun.

"Why do you throw water like that?" Guru Nanak asked a pilgrim.

"It is to propitiate our ancestors," the latter replied.

Guru Nanak heard it and, turning his back, started throwing water towards the west.

"What are you doing?" asked a fellow pilgrim. "The sun at this hour is in the east, not in the west."

"I am not offering water to the sun. I am trying to water my lands in a village near Lahore," said Guru Nanak.

"But my good man, how will the water reach your crops so far away?"

"If your water can reach your ancestors in the region of the sun, why can't mine reach my fields a short distance from here?" observed Guru Nanak.

He had a subtle sense of humor and could at times make his point effortlessly.

Passing through Panipat, where he met a successor of Shaikh Sharaf, who was a disciple of Khwaja Qutbuddin, and then Delhi, where he refused to work a miracle at the insistence of Ibrahim Lodi, the ruling monarch, Guru Nanak witnessed a performance of Ras Lila at Brindaban and rejected it as sheer waste of breath without the spirit of devotion. While journeying towards the east, Guru Nanak is said to have visited Gorakhmata, a temple devoted to Gorakh Nath, not very far from Pilibhit. It is believed that a soapnut tree under which Guru Nanak camped suddenly wore a verdant look. It attracted many an ascetic residing at the center to come and discourse with the Guru. Guru Nanak told them what real asceticism was:

Asceticism doesn't lie in the ascetic robes, nor in the walking staff, nor in the ashes,
Asceticism doesn't lie in the earring, nor in the shaven head, nor blowing a conch;
Asceticism lies in remaining pure amidst impurities.
Asceticism doesn't lie in mere words;
He an ascetic is who treats everyone alike,
Asceticism doesn't lie in visiting burial and cremation grounds.
It lies not in wandering about, nor in bathing at places of pilgrimage.
Asceticism is to remain pure amidst impurities.
On meeting with the true Guru the doubts are dispelled and restlessness of mind resigned.
It drizzles nectar, a steady melody is heard and there is enlightenment within.

Asceticism lies in remaining pure amidst impurities.
Says Nanak, asceticism lies in death in life.
The conch sounds without being blown,
And there is a feeling of fearlessness.
Asceticism lies in remaining pure amidst impurities.

(Suhi)

The ascetics were greatly moved at Guru Nanak's utterances and the center came to be known as Nanakmata instead of Gorakhmata. It is a place of pilgrimage even today.

While passing through Bihar, Guru Nanak is said to have visited Gaya, where Gautama Buddha had obtained enlightenment. Accompanied by Mardana, he then went to Assam. In the Kamrup district of Assam, they encountered Nur Shah, who practiced black magic. When she heard about the Guru's arrival, she sent her scouts to ensnare him with their wiles. They succeeded with Mardana, who happened to have gone to the town in search of food. They charmed and made a lamb of him. They made him bleat and behave like a lamb with their hypnotic power. Guru Nanak was aware of it and he was greatly amused. At last, he went to the rescue of his disciple. The wicked women tried their witchcraft on the Guru also. When her companions failed, Nur Shah herself tried to bewitch Guru Nanak with her charms. She, too, shared the same fate. Nur Shah, who had vanquished many an ascetic in her life, was bewildered at Guru Nanak's spiritual prowess. Having tried all her spells and failed, she accepted her defeat and fell at his feet.

It was again during this journey that Mardana fell into the clutches of a headhunter, Kauda by name. He was about to roast Mardana in a cauldron when Guru Nanak came to his rescue. It is said that every time Kauda tried to kindle the fuel in the oven, it would not catch fire. He tried again and again until Guru Nanak appeared on the scene and showed light to the cannibal.

On his way back from Assam, Guru Nanak returned via Orissa, visiting the famous temple of Jagannath at Puri. This temple is one of the most important places of Hindu pilgrimage. Guru Nanak found that the priests attached more importance to rituals than to true faith in God. They made elaborate arrangements to propitiate the deity in

both the morning and in the evening with trays full of burning
candles, flowers, and all sorts of perfumery. They called it *arati*. Guru
Nanak found that none of the devotees joining the ritual had his heart
in it. At best, people enjoyed the spectacle of it. He left the
congregation, went out of the temple and, sitting in a corner, started
singing his own arati, an ode to God, Mardana accompanying him on
the rabab:

> The sky is the platter,
> The sun and the moon are the lights,
> And stars jewels,
> The sandalwood's fragrance is the incense,
> The wind is the flywhisk
> And all the forests Your flowers.
> What a wonderful arati it is.
> Oh, You destroyer of life and death!
> It's an unending strain—the melody of Your name.
> You have a thousand eyes and yet not one eye.
> You have a thousand forms and yet not one form.
> You have a thousand unsoiled feet and yet not one unsoiled foot.
> You have a thousand noses and yet not one nose.
> Your ways have left me charmed, Oh Lord!
> There is my Lord's light which enlightens everyone.
> By the guru's grace the truth becomes manifest.
> The arati is what pleases God.
> I hunger for the fragrance of your lotus feet day and night.
> Oh Lord! grant a drop of water of Your grace
> To Nanak the thirsty bird,
> So that he finds solace in your Name.

(Dhanasri)

In the meanwhile, the priest and pilgrims had collected around
Guru Nanak and were thrilled to hear him sing the praises of God.
His melody seemed to touch each heart very deeply. They were
delighted to have such an enlightened soul among them. After Guru
Nanak left they remembered him for a long time.

Guru Nanak returned home after a little more than twelve years, because Mardana had started missing his family. He wished to visit his family and provide for them before he accompanied Guru Nanak on his proposed journey to the South. Guru Nanak chose to stay back in the forest and asked Mardana to return after he had attended to his filial obligations. However, when Guru Nanak's parents heard about Mardana's return, the mother in Mata Tripta knew that her son could not be far. Though Mardana, as advised by Guru Nanak, did not reveal to them his whereabouts, they traced Guru Nanak out in the forest and went to him with flowers and fruit, and beseeched him to return home with them. Guru Nanak relented, but he could not be persuaded to take up a job, as his father desired, or involve himself in family affairs as suggested by his mother. He, however, assured his family that he would keep in touch with them, visit them occasionally, and after he had completed his mission, he would come back and stay with them. His old parents were consoled and so was his dutiful spouse.

Before long, Guru Nanak left on his second mission towards the South. At Lahore, not far from Talwandi, he was visited by a rich man, Duni Chand, and his wife. Duni Chand had amassed a lot of wealth and property and lived a luxurious life. He came to Guru Nanak to pay homage to him the way that well-to-do usually propitiate both God and mammon. As he was leaving, the Guru pulled a needle from his sack and gave it to Duni Chand, asking him to keep it safe; he would ask for it in the next world. "But how can one carry a needle to the next world?" remarked Duni Chand. "Then for what have you collected all these riches?" asked Guru Nanak. Duni Chand and his wife heard it and their eyes suddenly opened. They went back and distributed all their wealth to the poor. They became God-fearing and thereafter started sharing their earnings with the needy.

Guru Nanak then visited Ajodhan (Pak Pattan in West Punjab of today), the seat of Baba Farid, the great Sufi dervish of the twelfth century, and met one of his successors, Shaikh Ibrahim. He had a long discourse with him. Shaikh Ibrahim recited the *slokas* of Shaikh Farid, while Guru Nanak composed his own verses extempore to present his viewpoint. They carried on the discourse for a long while until Shaikh Ibrahim was fully satisfied and said, "Guru Nanak, you have indeed found God. There is no difference between Him and you."

On his journey towards the South, Guru Nanak was accompanied by Saido and Gheho. Mardana ultimately stayed behind with his family. As he was crossing the Vindhyachal ranges, Nanak came upon a Jain temple. Its priest, Narbhi, heard about him and came to meet him. He was aware that Guru Nanak did not believe in the exaggerated value of life in every form the way Jains do. He shot a volley of questions at the Guru; "Do you eat old or new corn? Do you drink fresh or boiled water? Do you shake a tree for fruit? Who is your Guru and what power has he to save you?"

Guru Nanak replied:

If the Guru is kind, devotion is perfected.
If the Guru is kind, you know no sorrow.
If the Guru is kind, pains disappear.
If the Guru is kind, you enjoy life.
If the Guru is kind, there is no fear of death.
If the Guru is kind, you remain ever happy.
If the Guru is kind, the nine treasures are obtained.
If the Guru is kind, you get to know the truth.

(Majh ki Var)

The Jain priest heard it and was fully satisfied.

During his sojourn in the South, Guru Nanak went right up to Rameshwaram and Kanya Kumari and also across the sea to Sri Lanka. It is said that there ruled a king by the name of Shivnabh. He had heard about Guru Nanak from Mansukh, a Punjab trader who used to visit his kingdom. Ever since the king had learned about Guru Nanak, he longed to meet the Guru and to do him homage. Mansukh had assured him that if he remembered him from the depth of his heart, the Guru must respond. Learning of the king's anxiety to meet his Guru, many a charlatan tried to cheat the king, pretending to be Guru Nanak. He was sick of them. Then one day his courtiers came and told the king that Guru Nanak had arrived. His prayers had been heard. But the king, who had been deceived many a time, wouldn't believe until he had it verified. Accordingly, he sent two captivating dancing girls to try their charms on the visiting recluse. The moment the girls entered the premises where Guru Nanak was camping, they forgot all about their silly designs. They came and sat in a corner in utter devotion. The king was in the meanwhile waiting impatiently to know what had happened to the girls. When he learned about their submission to the Guru, he rushed to the Guru with his courtiers and fell at his feet. Raja Shivnabh wanted Guru Nanak to accompany him to his palace. Guru Nanak did not go, but, however, had the king put up a dharmasala where the devotees congregated daily and sang hymns in praise of God.

The third time Guru Nanak left home, he trekked towards the North. Penetrating the Himalayas, he went up to Tibet. He was accompanied by Mardana. Guru Nanak's first halt was at Srinagar. The historical *gurdwaras* at Anant Nag and Mattan suggest that the Guru went even to Amarnath.

At Srinagar, Guru Nanak met a Muslim dervish known as Kamal and a Hindu man of learning called Brahm Dass. It is said that Brahm Dass was very arrogant. Wherever he went, he was followed by three camels carrying the ancient works he had studied. He was fond of entering into lengthy arguments with the holy men he encountered. When he met Guru Nanak, in the first instance, he objected to his dress. Guru Nanak happened to be wearing leather shoes and a fur robe as a protection against the Kashmir cold. The Guru ignored it. He then started displaying his learning and asked Guru Nanak about the creation of the world. Guru Nanak's reply was most revealing:

It was all dark billions of years ago.
There was no earth, no heaven except God's supreme order.
There was no day or night, neither the moon or the sun—God
    meditated in a void.
There was no eating, no talking, neither air nor water.
No one was created, no one died; none came, no one went.
There were no continents, no nether world,
Nor were there seven seas; there was no water in the rivers.
There was neither heaven, nor any tortoise underneath the earth.

With His order, the world was created.
It is maintained without any support.

He created Brahman, Vishnu, and Siva.
He created also the love of Maya.
Only a few were blessed with His word.
But He watched and ruled over all.
He set going this world and the other world.
And became Himself manifest.
It is the true Guru alone who gives this understanding.
Says Nanak, those who are truthful live in eternal bliss,
They are blessed with the recitation of God's name.

(Maru)

Hearing this, Pandit Brahm Dass was stunned. He was amazed at Guru Nanak's vision. He became Guru Nanak's disciple and decided to propagate the Word of God. Brahm Dass stayed in the valley and Kamal was advised by Guru Nanak to settle in Kurram, from where he propagated the Holy Word in Kabul, Kandhar, and as far as Tirah.

Leaving Srinagar, Guru Nanak travelled towards Tibet. When he arrived at Lake Manasarovar he came across a large number of yogis who had escaped from the oppression and chaos in the plains and had found shelter in far away abodes in the mountains. The ascetics asked Guru Nanak about the conditions prevailing in the country. Guru Nanak chided them for running away from the hard realities of life the way they had. He, however, told them that the times were not too happy:

Kaliyuga is like a dagger,
Kings are butchers,
Dharma has taken wings and fled.
In the black night of deceit
The moon of truth is nowhere to be traced.
I am lost in the search;
I find no way out of the darkness.
Afflicted with self, I wail in sorrow,
Says Nanak, how may I attain deliverance?

(Majh)

The ascetics called *siddhas* entered into a long discussion with Guru

Nanak. It started with prayers to the Almighty. Then followed a dialogue on how one attains union with God:

> *Siddhas:* Can one find God by wandering in search of Him?
> *Nanak:* Without the True Word, there is no finding Him.
> *Siddhas:* How does one cross the ocean of the world?
> *Nanak:* By living like a lotus or a water bird in water. By meditating on His Name and remaining free from the snare of *Maya.*

Guru Nanak recorded his discourses with various ascetics in "Siddha Gosht," a long composition in the form of a dialogue in verse. It is an interesting record of intricate metaphysical issues discussed by him. Guru Nanak has projected himself, in this long composition, as much a seeker of God as anyone else. He had three major encounters with the siddhas at Gorakhmata (later known as Nanakmata), at Manasarovar, and at Achal Batala.

Guru Nanak's last sojourn, which he undertook after a fairly long stay at home, was towards the West. He was accompanied by Mardana again. Before he left on the journey Guru Nanak donned the blue dress of a Muslim pilgrim, with a staff in one hand and a *lota* in the other. Evidently Guru Nanak's destination was Mecca.

On his way to Mecca, Guru Nanak had an encounter with Wali Qandhari, a dervish who had his abode on a hilltop at Hasan Abdal near Taxila, the ancient Buddhist center. It was midday in a wilderness when Mardana felt thirsty. Guru Nanak explained to him that as it was a barren rocky plateau, there was no water around. But Mardana grew impatient. He was getting old and was like a child in his obstinacy when he wanted something. Guru Nanak looked around and told Mardana that the nearest he could find water was on the top of the hill, the abode of a dervish called Wali Qandhari. Mardana went up and asked for water. But the Muslim dervish, discovering that he was a companion of Guru Nanak, refused to give him any water.

When Guru Nanak heard about it, he advised Mardana to go again and make his request in all humility. "Tell him, 'I am a companion of Nanak, a man of God,'" said Guru Nanak. But Wali Qandhari would not relent. At this, the Guru asked Mardana to go the third time and make a request for water in the name of God. Mardana scaled the hill again somehow, only to be taunted by the arrogant Wali Qandhari, "He styles himself a Guru and cannot get a drop of water for his disciple!"

Mardana was almost dead from exhaustion when he returned. Guru Nanak saw his plight and asked him to lift a slab of stone which lay a little away from them. It is said that the moment Mardana removed the slab, a spring gushed from underneath it. A little later, when he needed water for himself, Wali Qandhara found that his well was emptying fast and that there was a stream of water flowing at the foot of the hill. Evidently the yogi had played a trick on him. In fury, Wali Qandhari rolled a boulder down the hill to crush Guru Nanak and his companion, who sat at the head of the fountain singing the praises of God. It is said that Guru Nanak held the boulder back with his hand, effortlessly. In the course of time, the place came to be known as Punja Saheb, the temple of the Holy Palm. Located in the Attock district of Pakistan, it is one of the important places of Sikh pilgrimage even today.

Arriving at Mecca, Guru Nanak felt tired. It had been a long and arduous journey to the holy city. He fell asleep and it so happened that he slept with his feet towards Kaaba, the holy shrine, instead of his head, which was the accepted practice. At midnight a watchman on his rounds noticed this and was scandalized to find a pilgrim with his feet pointing towards the House of God. "How dare you lie with your feet pointing towards God?" he shouted. He was about to lay his corrective hands on Nanak when the Guru woke up, "Good man, I am weary after a long journey. Kindly turn my feet in the direction where God is not." Jiwan, the watchman, was stunned: "Where God is not!" His head started whirling. "Where God is not!" He saw His abode in all the four directions. He had lifted Guru Nanak's feet and, rather than turning them around, his head fell on them. He started kissing them. He washed Guru Nanak's feet with his tears. In addition to Jiwan, all the rest of the pilgrims and the holy men of the shrine were moved to have Guru Nanak amidst them. They asked him many questions. "I am neither a Hindu nor a Mussalman," said Guru Nanak. "Who is superior of the two?" the pilgrims collected around him wished to know. Guru Nanak replied, "Without good deeds, either is no good." The Guru laid stress on the love of God, on humility, prayer, and truthful living. He, then, recited a hymn in Persian:

I beseech you, O Lord! pray grant me a hearing.
You are the truthful, the great, the merciful, and the faultless Creator.
I know for certain, this world must perish,
And death must come, I know this and nothing else.
Neither wife, nor son, nor father, nor brothers shall be able to help.
I must go in the end, none could undo what is in my lot.
I have spent days and nights in vanity contemplating evil.
Never have I thought of good; this is what I am.
I am ill-starred, miserly, careless, short-sighted, and rude.
But says Nanak, I am yours, the dust of the feet of your minions.

(Tilang)

The high priest of the holy shrine who happened to have arrived on the scene was delighted to hear it.

From Mecca, Guru Nanak proceeded to Medina where he had another debate with the head priest of the shrine. What impressed people was Guru Nanak's emphasis on the unity of God and equality of man. He didn't believe in rituals. According to him only a man's good deeds and the Guru's grace earned him liberation.

At Baghdad, which he visited later, Guru Nanak made one of his most ardent devotees in a dervish who, it is said, sat for sixty long years at the foot of the slab occupied by Guru Nanak during his visit to the town.

On his way back from Mecca Guru Nanak visited Multan. It was an important center of the Sufis in those days. As Guru Nanak was camping outside the town, the dervishes in the city sent him a bowl brimful of milk, indicating thereby that the place was already full of holy men. Guru Nanak put a jasmine flower in the bowl. The bowl didn't overflow while the flower floated on it. Guru Nanak thus spoke to the holy men of Multan in their own idiom, telling that there was still room for a man like Nanak in their midst.

Guru Nanak then visited Saidpur (known as Eminabad in present day Pakistan). By this time, Babar had already entered the Punjab. Guru Nanak advised his devotees in the town to leave the place and thus escape the tyranny of the marauding Mughals. Some listened to him, while others did not. As feared by Guru Nanak, Saidpur was laid waste by the invading forces soon thereafter. Guru Nanak witnessed this heartless killing and the poet in him seems to have revolted against the divine justice. He has left a most remarkable piece of poetry describing the barbarous attack and the sufferings of the people of the Punjab:

> He occupied Khursasan and subdued Hindustan.
> God doesn't blame Himself having sent the Mughal like a doom.
> Seeing such suffering and wailing, didn't it hurt You, O Lord?
> You are the lone Creator of all.
> If an aggressor were to kill an aggressor, I wouldn't complain.
> But when a fierce lion falls on a poor herd of cattle, the master
>   must take the blame.
> The dogs have ruined the gems among us; when they die, none will
>   ever bother about them.
> O God! You alone make and unmake, this is Your greatness.
> If anyone else were to style himself great and indulge in pleasures,
> He would be like an insect in the eyes of God feeding on a few
>   grains.
> He who dies in life, he alone lives, says Nanak, by repeating the
>   Name of God.
>
> *(Asa)*

Guru Nanak was taken prisoner along with Mardana. When the jailor heard him sing the divine hymn, he hastened to report to the king. Babar sent for Guru Nanak to listen to his hymn. He realized that the Guru was indeed an evolved soul. He asked for his forgiveness and offered him his pouch of *bhang* by way of entertaining him as an equal, but Guru Nanak declined it, saying that he was already intoxicated with the name of God. It was during this meeting with Babar that Guru Nanak predicted:

They come in '78 and go in '97
Another hero will also arise.

The prophecy relates to the Mughals occupying India in Samvat
1578 (1521 A.D.) and departing in Samvat 1597 (1540 A.D.). The
monarch who was driven out was Humayun and the "hero" referred
is Sher Shah, who had thrown him out.

Guru Nanak was now growing old. Mardana also had aged. And
then there was such a lot to be done by way of organizing the
community. His devotees all over the country and abroad longed to
visit him and sit at his feet. Accordingly, Guru Nanak decided to settle
down in the Punjab. This was about 1520 A.D.

Guru Nanak acquired a large enough piece of land on the banks of
the river Ravi. Here he set up a new township called Kartarpur—the
abode of God. He left off wearing the garb of a recluse and took to
the normal dress of a Punjabi peasant. He started farming like anyone
else. His wife and sons lived with him. So did Mardana and several
other devotees. It was a sort of community living. Everyone was
expected to work in the fields and share the harvest. There was a
common kitchen. Every visitor, irrespective of caste and creed, must
partake of the meal offered there.

Not many days later, Mardana's end came. Guru Nanak advised
his son Shahzada not to wail and lament the loss of his father because
he had returned to his heavenly home. There is no mourning for
blessed souls. After his father's death Shahzada joined Guru Nanak as
his rabab player.

One day Guru Nanak was working in his fields when he saw a
horserider heading towards him. "I am Lehna," said the stranger,
leaving his horse at a respectable distance and approaching the Guru in
all humility. Guru Nanak looked into his face and observed, "So you
have arrived, Lehna—the creditor. I have been waiting for you all
these days. I must pay your debt." ("Lehna" in Punjabi means debt or
creditor.)

Lehna didn't understand it at all but he was charmed by Guru
Nanak's person. He had heard a great deal about him from one of
Guru Nanak's devotees, Bhai Jodha, who lived in Khadur, the village
to which Lehna belonged. Lehna was the son of a well-to-do

businessman who was a great devotee of Durga. He went to the
Kangra shrine of the goddess every year. The more he heard about
Guru Nanak and his *Bani* from Bhai Jodha, the more he longed to
meet him. At last he could restrain himself no longer and, while
leading a party of pilgrims to the Kangra shrine of the deity, he left
them midway and came to Kartarpur. Once he had met Guru Nanak
there was no looking back. He served the master day and night. Before
long he became the most trusted disciple of the Guru. Lehna's
devotion to Guru Nanak was absolute. He served him as none else
did, not even his two sons.

It is said that once Guru Nanak, accompanied by Lehna and his
two sons, came 'across something that looked like a corpse covered
with a sheet of cloth. "Who would eat it?" asked Guru Nanak
unexpectedly. His sons were astonished to hear these words. They
thought something had happened to their father. "Master, if it pleases
you, I'll do it," said Lehna and, moving ahead, removed the cover to
find that it was a tray of sacred food. Lehna offered it first to Guru
Nanak and his sons and then partook of the leftovers himself. Guru
Nanak was most touched to see this. He said:

Lehna, you were blessed with the sacred food because you could
share it with others. If the people use the wealth bestowed on them
by God for themselves alone or for treasuring it, it is like a corpse.
But if they decide to share it with others, it becomes sacred food.
You have known the secret. You are my image.

Then, Guru Nanak blessed Lehna with his *ang* (hand) and gave
him a new name—Angad. Angad was a changed man. He became a
part of Guru Nanak's body and soul, as it were.

A few days later Pir Bahauddin, a high priest from Multan, visited
Guru Nanak. He said, "My end is near, I have come to seek your
blessings, so that my journey to the next world is smooth." At this
Guru Nanak observed that he, too, would soon follow him.

Then one day Guru Nanak held a special meeting for which
devotees gathered from far and near. Amidst the chanting of hymns,
Nanak invited Angad to occupy formally the seat of the Guru. Thus
ordaining Angad as his successor, he retired. While everyone present

hailed the new Guru, the members of Guru Nanak's family were not happy over the decision. They felt that the sons had been deprived of their right to succession. According to Guru Nanak, hereditary privilege was not what made a Guru; the one who deserved it most was chosen.

One day Guru Nanak was found reciting:

The auspicious hour has been determined,
Come and pour the ceremonial oil.
Bless me, O friends, so that I meet my Master.
Every house gets such tidings, these calls are received daily.
Says Nanak, the Caller must be remembered,
The day is approaching.

(Sohila)

The day had approached. Guru Nanak said his prayers after his bath and lay down, covering himself with a sheet of cloth. The light that showed the path to millions then merged into the eternal flame. It was a day like any other day; having completed his mission, Guru Nanak passed away quietly. It is said that in his memory his Muslim devotees built a mausoleum and his Hindu disciples a *samadhi* on the banks of the river Ravi. Soon both were washed away by the changing course of the river, leaving behind the fragrant memory dear to both Hindus and Muslims. The people of the Punjab remembered him as:

Baba Nanak, the great man of God,
The Guru of the Hindus and the *pir* of the Mussalmans.

He is remembered as such even today by Hindus and Muslims alike.

While there is no definitive biography of Guru Nanak, there had been a number of attempts by his devotees to write the story of his life soon after his passing away. Historians might reject a great many of these writings as sheer adulation born of excessive devotion, but these do provide the essential landmarks and help us structure a fairly reliable picture of the Guru's life and times.

To my mind this outline can be filled in with details by a

perceptive writer devoted to Guru Nanak. He can provide flesh and bones with the help of a large fund of *gurubani* whose authenticity cannot be challenged. Unlike Mahavira and Buddha, Guru Nanak has left a vast treasure of his utterances in verse, carefully compiled in the *Guru Granth*. It is not at all difficult to imagine what sort of a soul the author of these writings must have been. Not only this, the poetical work bequeathed to us by Guru Nanak inevitably contains copious references to his times, to the places he visited, the people he met, and the discourses he delivered.

Guru Nanak's times are not very far removed from us. It is easy to project oneself to them. Unless we wish to indulge in hair-splitting, we have more than enough reliable data. The researcher seems to be missing the historical record—as if all history is always reliable!

I visualize Guru Nanak as being born of simple parents in a small village in the Punjab. As the only son with an elder sister, a great deal of affection was showered on him. He was brought up with abundant care and often pampered by his mother and sister. His father, however, was much too preoccupied with his affairs to devote any time to his son. But he did try to ensure that he received proper education and prepared himself for a respectable avocation in life.

Nanak was an exceptionally precocious child who acquired proficiency in reading and writing earlier than other children of his age. He was sensitive and given to keeping to himself. He was fond of singing and as a child he found poetic phrases came effortlessly to his lips. While he said his prayers regularly and spent long hours in meditation, he made friends with both Hindus and Muslims. He never discriminated against anyone; in fact, the so-called low caste were dearer to him than others. He loved his parents, he loved his sister, he loved life, but he loved God more. He felt that he had a mission in life and that he must fulfill it. While he was always conscious of his duty towards his wife and his children, he treated the whole world as his family and all the human beings as his brothers and sisters. He raised his voice against injustice anywhere and felt unhappy at the sufferings of the people.

He was religious by temperament but he didn't approve of ceremonials, formalities, and rituals. He was genial and amiable. He had a subtle sense of humor. He never hurt anyone. He differed with people and yet did not give them offence. He had a rare spirit of adventure and never avoided undertaking a journey because it involved travelling through difficult terrain and unfamiliar parts. He was always anxious to go on long journeys because it gave him opportunities to meet more and more people. He was large-hearted. He was not parochial or narrow-minded, communal or caste-ridden. He set out for the regeneration of mankind. He undertook long journeys to preach, to teach, to bear witness to the light Divine, to awaken the spiritual consciousness in men, and to bring back erring humanity to God. While he rejected both Hinduism and Islam, as they were practiced in his times, he was humble enough not to style himself as an *avatar*. He called himself a slave of the slaves of God. But he was proud to be a poet. More than once he called himself "Nanak the poet." Almost all his compositions have his name figuring in the last couplet according to the poetic tradition of his time. And what a fine poet he was! The like of him is yet to be born in his language. His writing remains unsurpassed. He has 958 compositions to his credit. They contain also the longer works, like the *Japji*. It is not only exquisite poetry; almost the whole of it can be sung to music. Not only did poet Guru Nanak respect the traditional forms, he also is the most modern among the modernists, even today. His verse at times conforms to the conversational rhythms and varies its pace according to the mood of the text.

As a man, he was sensitive, kind-hearted, but never sentimental. He was fair and correct. Love of his parents, his sister, his wife, or his children did not prevent him from undertaking long travels, at times lasting several years. When the time came for him to lay down his ministry, he chose the most deserving candidate to succeed him. He bypassed his own sons. He did not like to impress anyone with miracles; in fact he did not approve of miracles. He was methodical in his functioning. He decided to settle down towards the close of his stewardship, so that he had time to consolidate and give proper direction to his movement. And he succeeded in it eminently. He didn't believe in the false barriers of religion and the stupid rigidities of caste. He was an ideal Muslim among Muslims and a model Hindu among Hindus. He believed in the fatherhood of God and the brotherhood of man and he practiced them vigorously in his day-today life. All men were equal in his eyes. No one was big and no one was small. It is deeds, not birth that determine the status of a man, he said.

Dr. Hari Ram Gupta in his book, *A Life-Sketch of Guru Nanak,* says:

At the time of Guru Nanak's advent, both the prevailing religions—Hinduism and Islam—had become corrupt and degraded. They had lost their pristine purity and glory. The Vedas were unintelligible to the people and had been replaced by Tantric literature . . . Caste had grown rigid and had split into numerous subcastes . . . Similar was the state of affairs in Islam . . . . Political conditions were much worse.

Men with vision were worried about this state of affairs. They attacked the rot that had set in their society from various angles. There was the Bhakti movement, there was the Sufi cult, and there was the Sant tradition. All the three had dedicated men from among the Hindus and the Muslims to give them direction. They attempted a synthesis of the Hindu and the Muslim ways of life, though their nature remained different with different sets of people. However, they placed first things first. Rather than engage themselves in the political and economic issues, they devoted their attention to social problems, trying their best to restore man's faith in God. They believed that once man turned his face towards God, the rest of the maladies from which society suffered would be easy to cure.

By and large, Guru Nanak can be said to belong to the Bhakti movement. Bhakti is loving devotion. In the case of Guru Nanak, this devotion is towards God, the Supreme Being. Its expression is strictly through meditation and through living a life in the image of God.

The Bhakti movement in Northern India was a revolt against the ritualism, castism, and the formalism of the Brahmins among the Hindus, and the *Qazis* among the Muslims. It had its roots in the cult of *Vaishnav bhakti* which came from the South, the ancient tradition of Tantric yoga as practiced by the Nath sect of yogis and the Sufi orders of Islam. It rejected all exterior forms, ceremonies, pilgrimages, ritual bathing, etc. No importance was attached to celibacy or asceticism. Guru Nanak himself married and had two sons. Towards the close of his life, he came to settle down at Kartarpur, where he tended his crops and ran a community kitchen shared by high and low, rich and poor.

The poets of the Bhakti movement rejected Sanskrit as well as Persian, the languages of the elite, and chose to communicate in the language of the people to whom they belonged. Namdev, Raidas, and Kabir, some of the predecessors of Guru Nanak, belonged to the so-called lower classes of their society. Namdev was a washerman, Raidas was a cobbler, and Kabir was a weaver. Guru Nanak himself was a Khatri (Kshatriya), and not a Brahmin.

The protagonists of the Bhakti movement not only evolved a link language (called *Sadhukkari*) spoken and popularized by the saint-poets in Northern India, they also adopted the poetic forms that were popular with the common people. Their meters and measures followed the folk songs and folk ballads with which the common people were familiar. They drew their similes from the everyday life of the common man. They employed familiar symbols, though with a freshness of their own. Almost all the poetry that Guru Nanak wrote can be sung to music. The text conforms to specific ragas prevalent in the Hindustani music of the day. Where Guru Nanak followed better-known musical forms of folk ballads, he made it a point to mention in the beginning of the composition the fact that it was designed to be sung in such and such tune in the style of such and such ballad. For instance, in the opening of *Asa di Var,* a longish work sung by the Sikh community every morning as a divine service, it is stated:

"The *Var* with *slokas* is written by the First Guru (Nanak) and should be sung to the air of Tunda as Raja."

Faith is the prerequisite of all devotion. Without faith love does not happen. The devotee must not question the will of God. He must carry out His dictates. In comfort he must not feel elated, and in trouble he must not get depressed. The ways of God are inscrutable.

The Guru's words in the heart are the earrings of the yogi
And humility the garb of the recluse
Acceptance of His will is the eternal bliss.

(Asa)

Devotion also entails complete surrender to God, an unconditional submission. The devotee is like a bride who must surrender herself completely to her lord to enjoy the bliss of married life. God is the bridegroom and the whole world is a bride.

> Go and ask the bride, how she won her lord's heart.
> Do as he desires and shake off all cleverness.
> He who bestows the bliss of loving devotion,
> He alone should be adored.
> Carry out his commands,
> Surrender to him body and soul
> Says the bride, this is how you win your lord.
>
> *(Tilang)*

Love of God is not possible without the fear of God. One fears him most whom one loves best. The *bhakta* must recognize the immensity and the authority of God absolutely. The entire world created by God lives in His fear.

> In fear the winds ever blow.
> In fear millions of rivers flow.
> In fear the fire does its job.
> In fear the earth is buried under its weight.
> In fear the moon moves on its head.
> Even the god of death is in fear.
>
> *(Asa)*

Real devotion is God's love. It can be of two types: outward (*laukik*) and inward (*anuraga*). Guru Nanak rejected outward devotion. He laid stress on inward devotion, or pure love. He did not believe in dancing and jumping and other antics of the yogis and the sufis of his time.

> The devotees play on the accompaniments and the gurus dance.
> They move their feet and shake their heads.
> The dust rises and settles on their hair . . . people see it and laugh.
> They do this only to earn their livelihood.
>
> *(Asa)*

The bhakta must sing God's praises day and night. By singing His praises, one can hope to be like Him. By singing His praises, one can hope to find a place in the Lord's court.

There is no end to God's praises
To those who praise Him there is no end.

(The Japji)

There are nine forms of bhakti accepted in the spiritual order. These are: 1. listening (*srawan*), 2. music (*kirtan*), 3. remembrance (*simuran*) 4. following in the footsteps of the master (*padsevan*), 5. service (*archan*), 6. singing praises (*vandana*), 7. obedience (*dasbhav*) 8. friendship (*mitrata*) and 9. self-surrender (*atma nivedan*). Guru Nanak subscribed to all these but the best form of bhakti according to him, is *prema bhakti,* loving devotion to God.

According to Guru Nanak, the love of God follows the love of man. Only those who love their fellowmen can love God. At times it is through the love of men that one finds the love of God.

Guru Nanak broke the barriers of caste. In his eyes, there was no higher or lower caste. He rejected the privileges acquired by birth. He fraternized with the poor and the downtrodden; the peasant and the worker. The whole world was one family for him. He respected other religions. He spoke many languages. He dressed like Turks and Pathans while visiting their countries; in his own country, he clad himself like *Udasis* at times, and in the saffron robes of the yogis or the ordinary dress of a Punjabi Khatri or a Sufi mystic at others.

Guru Nanak never made promises of paradise and heavenly luxuries as a reward for ritualistic practices. He did not offer future bliss as a bait for religious living. No *houries,* no rivulets of honey, no springs of milk. He assured people peace and harmony in this world for a truthful life and correct social behavior.

Excepting, of course, the places of pilgrimage that he visited as a seeker of truth, Guru Nanak never cared to stay in temples, mosques, or other shrines while visiting a town. He did not prefer the conventional places of worship for preaching his message. The blue dome of the sky was his cover and he talked about his new way of life in the open. His meetings were free for anyone who cared to come to him. If he had to choose he went and stayed with people like Sajjan, the cheat, who needed him to show them light and put them on the path of righteousness.

Guru Nanak combined in himself a recluse, an ascetic, and a family man who married and had children. He was the fond brother of a loving sister. He was a dutiful husband. He was a loving father. And yet he was unduly attached to none. For years, he would go out towards the East, West, North and South, but every time he came back to his home. He promised his sister Nanaki that he would come to her whenever she remembered him. It is said that once, when the sister in Nanaki had the better of her, and she wished in her heart of hearts to have a glimpse of her brother, to her joy, Guru Nanak did keep his promise. He ensured that his wife was suitably provided for and his sons were brought up properly. His parents took a little longer to appreciate the unconventional ways of their only son.

During the last twenty years of his life, Guru Nanak made an experiment that was unique for his times. He had one of his well-to-do devotees part with a large enough piece of land and had a new town built thereon. It was called Kartarpur, the abode of the Creator. It was the first experiment in community living in our part of the world. The land was common, the farming was common, and there was a common kitchen. Guru Nanak insisted on the common kitchen, so that the curse of the caste system could be removed from his society. The Hindus of the day were obsessed with the caste system, which had acquired rigidity over the ages. The Muslims had also acquired it to some extent from the Hindus. Nobody could see him unless he had eaten in the common kitchen. It is said that Guru Nanak did farming in the fields along with the rest. He attached great importance to manual labor. Before long, Kartarpur became a flourishing town with lush, green fields laden with rich crops. Guru Nanak's devotees came from far and near to pay homage to the Master. Here Guru Nanak lived with his wife and two sons.

When the time came for Guru Nanak to nominate a successor, he felt neither of his sons was up to his expectations. Here was the greatest test of his life. His sons aspired to become the Guru. One of them had never married and lived the life of an ascetic. Guru Nanak did not approve of it. He attached greater importance to normal family life. He, therefore, ordained one of his followers who had come to stay with him as the next Guru. This put off the two sons of Guru Nanak, one of whom started his own sect. But the stewardship of the Sikhs remained with Guru Angad, who is known as the second Sikh Guru.

Guru Nanak's three important precepts are: There is neither Hindu nor Mussalman; one must work and share one's earnings; and, an active life is superior to contemplative life.

It is no wonder that his followers have weathered many storms and have continued to remain in the forefront of the progressive forces. They are a hardworking people, devoted and self-sacrificing.

Selected Hymns of Guru Nanak

1. He was here in the beginning
   And before the beginning.
   He is here today;
   He will be here hereafter.

   (Japji)

2. If you were to think Him out
   You may not succeed
   Even if you tried a hundred thousand times.
   If you tried to take to silence
   You may not succeed
   Even if you concentrated on Him ever and ever.
   A hungry man's hunger is not satisfied
   Even if he were to collect the entire world's wealth.
   You may try a million ways,
   Not one will see you through.
   Then how can one be truthful?
   How can the wall of falsehood be broken?
   You must do as He wishes you to do.
   Says Nanak, it's been given to man to do so.

   (Japji)

3. He is the true Lord
   His Name is true.
   His language is endless love.
   They ask and ask and ask
   The giver always gives.
   What should I offer
   To behold His court?
   What prayer should I make
   Hearing which He should take kindly to me?
   In the ambrosial hour of the morning
   Remember and adore Him.
   You are born in the image of your Karma
   But salvation is His gift alone,

Says Nanak, this is the way to know Him
The True One is everywhere.

                                                                    (Japji)

4. Hearing His Name
    One becomes truthful, contented, enlightened.
    Hearing His Name
    Is like bathing at sixty-eight places of pilgrimage.
    Hearing His name
    Is reading and reading and gaining glory.
    Hearing His name
    Is composing the mind and meditating Him.
    Says Nanak, the devotees are ever in bliss.
    Hearing His Name
    Destroys the sufferings of evil deeds.

                                                                    (Japji)

5. Those who believe in Him
    Get to the gate of salvation.
    Those who believe in Him
    Are saved with their kin.
    Those who believe in Him
    Swim across and help other Sikhs to swim.
    Those who believe in Him
    Don't have to beg of others.
    Such is the Name of God the Pure,
    Those who believe in Him
    They alone get to know Him.

                                                                    (Japji)

6. What is the gate like,
    What is the house like
    Where You sit and watch over all?
    Where countless instruments are played,
    Where numerous singers sing?
    There is no end of musical measures
    Presented by fairylike faces.
    The air, the water, the fire
    Sing Your praises.
    Dharmaraj adores You standing on Your threshold.

The scribes of Dharmaraj sing Your praises,
And those who keep just record.
Ishar, Brahma, and Devi sing Your praises
Those who have been blessed by You.
Indra sings Your praises
Sitting on his throne
Along with other gods waiting at Your gate.
Siddhas sing Your praises sitting in meditation.
The holy ones sing Your praises
While contemplating on You.
They sing Your praises
Who are continent, truthful, contented,
Those who are mighty heroes.
Sing the pandits and the learned yogis
Who have read the Vedas for ages.
Your praises are sung by the charming beauties
Who beguile heaven, the nether, and middle worlds,
All the gems of men created by you
Sing your praises at sixty-eight places of pilgrimage.
Your praises are sung by warriors and great heroes
Together with all those born from the four sources of
    creation.
The entire world, its continents and the whole universe
Created and maintained by You
Sing Your praises.
They sing Your praises whom You love.
Those who are Your disciples and devoted to You.
And several others sing Your praises
Whom I cannot recall.
They are beyond Nanak's reckoning.
He is the eternal True Lord, His name is true.
He is there; He will be there.
He doesn't go; nor will He ever go,
He who has made this world,
He who has created several species in various forms.
As it goes with His greatness
He looks after His creation.

He does what He pleases,
No one may order Him about.
He is the King, the King of Kings.
Nanak does as He desires.

(Japji)

7. Continence is the smithy,
   Patience the goldsmith,
   Understanding is the anvil,
   And divine knowledge the tool.
   God's fear is the bellows
   And penance the fire,
   Love is the crucible,
   Where nectar is distilled.
   God's Name is forged in this true mint.
   Those who are favored
   They alone can do it.
   Says Nanak, a graceful glance
   Blesses and makes one happy.

(Japji)

8. Riches, youth, and flowers are a day's guests
   Like the leaves of an herb that withers away without water.
   You may enjoy your life as long as you are young and fresh.
   But your days are numbered; the body must grow old and
       tired.
   My loved ones have gone to rest in the graveyard.
   I grieve in my heart for I must also follow them.
   Don't you hear the call, O fair one?
   You must go to the in-laws.
   No one ever lives at her parents' house.
   Says Nanak, the bride who remains at her parents'
   Her house is broken in daylight.
   She loses the treasure of virtues
   And continues to be loaded with sins.

(Sri)

9. You are the all-knowing, the all-seeing river
   I am a fish, how can I measure you?
   Wherever I see, it is You I find

The moment I get away I die.
I know neither the fisherman nor the net . . .
Whenever I am in trouble, I remember You.
You are everywhere and yet You appear so far away.
Whatever I do is in Your knowledge.
You know it and I deny it.
I follow You not, I remember You not
And yet I eat whatever You offer,
There is no other door to which I could go.
You are the only one Nanak can make a prayer to.
I owe this body and soul to You.
You are close, You are far, You are in between.
You see, You hear,
You create the universe in Your own way.
Says Nanak, whatever happens is under Your orders,
Which I must accept.

                                                    (Sri)

10. Man! You should love God the way the lotus loves water.
    It is knocked down by waves and yet it blossoms and
        continues to love.
    Born out of water, it dies without water.
    Man! How can you be saved without love?
    God lives within you and blesses you with the gift of
        devotion.
    Man! You should love God the way a fish loves water;
    The more the water the happier she is in her heart and soul.
    She lives not a moment without water,
    God alone knows the agony of her heart.

                                                    (Sri)

11. You are a recluse amongst recluses.
    You indulge in pleasure amongst the pleaure-loving.
    Nobody has been able to know You
    Neither in heaven, nor on earth, nor in the nether world.
    I am a sacrifice to You and Your Name.
    You have created this world
    And made everyone an assignment.
    You have thrown the dice and you watch the game.

You can be found in the world around.
Everyone hungers for Your Name;
That can't be obtained without the true Guru.
The world is pitched in *maya,*
I am a sacrifice to the true Guru.
A meeting with him earns salvation.
He whom the angels and ascetics look for
The true Guru has made me know Him:
I look for the company of holy men
Where I may remember His Name.
My true Guru has made me understand
That remembering His Name is one's only life-mission.

(Sri)

12. The night is gone in sleep and the day in feeding,
    The gem of a life is lost like a cowrie.
    You have not remembered God,
    Fool! You will regret it.
    He who keeps on amassing untold gold
    Knows not the Limitless
    Has no use for limitless wealth.
    If it could be got by one's own effort
    Everyone would be rich.
    It depends upon one's deeds
    Not upon one's wishes.
    Says Nanak, He takes care,
    Who has created the world.
    No one knows the ways of God,
    On whom He bestows His honor.

(Bairagan)

13. Had I been a doe I would live in a dale
    Eating leaves and grass,
    With Guru's grace I would find my Lord,
    To whom I am a sacrifice.
    I deal in His Name;
    God's Name is my goods-in-trade.
    Had I been a *koel*
    I would live on a mango tree

And ever meditate on His Word.
I would meet my Lord one day,
He who is most charming to behold.
Had I been a fish
I would dwell in water
That sustains all living creatures.
My Lord who lives on both the banks,
I would meet Him by stretching my hands.
Had I been a snake
I would live under the earth.
Lost by the Guru's Word,
I would shake off my fear.
Says Nanak, they are happily married
Who have merged themselves into God.

(Asa)

14. He is called great by hearsay;
    He who has seen Him can say how great He is.
    He can neither be described nor evaluated;
    Those who've tried, have failed.
    O my great Master, deep, profound, and virtuous,
    No one knows how great You are.
    All the thinkers got together to think about You.
    All the evaluators got together to evaluate You.
    The master thinkers and master divines
    Could not measure a fraction of Your greatness.

(Asa)

15. I remember You and I live;
    I die if I forget You.
    It is not easy to remember You.
    I hunger for your true Name;
    Satisfying this hunger kills all pain.
    Mother, how can I forget Him!
    He is the true Lord, His name is true.
    Measuring a fraction of His greatness
    Many have tried without success.
    If everyone got together to do it
    He'll neither be bigger nor smaller,

He never dies nor is He mourned.
He is always giving,
There is no end to His favors.
His only quality is
That there is none like Him,
Neither was there ever
Nor would there ever be.
His gifts are as great as great He is.
Those who pass their nights like day
(They get to know Him).
He who forgets the Master is a wretch.
Says Nanak, without His name one remains defiled.

                                                                        (*Asa*)

16. You may read and read and load yourself like a cart.
    You may read and read and equip yourself fully.
    You may read and read and bind yourself.
    You may read and read and dig pits around you.
    You may read for years and years,
    You may read for months and months,
    You may read for as long as you live,
    You may read as long as you breathe.
    Says Nanak, only one thing will be reckoned in the end
    The rest is all vanity and vexation of spirit.

                                                                        (*Asa*)

17. Suffering is the remedy, comfort the malady;
    Where there is comfort You are not.
    You are the Creator; I dare not do anything.
    If I were to try I may not succeed.
    I am a sacrifice to You whom I see in Nature;
    Your limit cannot be known.
    Your light is seen in the Universe;
    The Universe is sustained by Your light.
    You are found all over, as a whole and in parts.
    You are the true, praiseworthy Master.
    He who adores You finds salvation.
    Says Nanak, you must surrender to Him.
    He does what pleases Him.

                                                                        (*Asa*)

18. He himself makes vessels,
    Himself He fills them.
    Some contain milk,
    Others are put on fire.
    Some have peaceful sleep,
    Others keep their vigil.
    Says Nanak, blessed are they
    To whom He takes kindly.

                                                                (Asa)

19. The peahen sings,
    It's the rainy season,
    I feel a stab in my heart.
    Your charm is irresistible,
    I die without seeing you,
    I am a sacrifice to Your Name.
    When You are mine I feel proud,
    Without You what pride can I feel?
    O bride! you should break the set of your bangles;
    You adorn your arms, the whole of them,
    You adorn yourself no end
    While your Lord loves others.
    Neither the bangle-maker nor the bangles seem to help
    Let the arms burn that don't entwine the Master's neck.
    All my friends have gone to please their lords,
    Where should I go, the blasted one?
    Friends! I am done up well
    And yet I am not endeared by my Lord.
    I do my hair and fill the parting line with bridal powder.
    But when I present myself to Him,
    I am not accepted.
    I die pining day and night.
    I cry and the whole world cries with me.
    Woods and birds shed tears
    Excepting my wretched heart that has alienated me from my
        Lord.
    I saw Him in a dream and He disappeared.
    I cry, my eyes swimming in tears.

Lord! I cannot come to You.
Nor can I send anyone.
Come the fair sleep, may I see my Master again!
Says Nanak, what should I offer him
Who comes and gives me tidings of my Lord?
I offer him my beheaded head for seat
And I serve him without my head.
Why should not one die and lay down one's life
If one's Lord is found estranged?

(Wadhans)

20. Let mind be the peasant that does the farming.
Hard work be the water and the body the field.
Let Name be the seed and contentment the cover.
You must don the dress of humility,
Then alone will love be born with His favor.
Such a one is blessed.
Man, wealth doesn't accompany you.
Wealth has charmed the world.
Not many understand this secret.
Let every breath of your life be your shop
And the true Name the goods you deal in.
Let your contemplation be rows of vessels,
Let His Name be contained in them.
You must deal with holy men
And gain profit to your satisfaction.
Let listening to the holy books be your trade.
Let your houses be the true Name.
Let your good deeds be the investment.
Don't put it off till tomorrow.
If you arrived in God's kingdom like this
You will find a place in the palace of bliss.
Let the service you take be devotion.
And God's name the effort.
Let your labor be eschewing evil deeds
Only then will the people commend you.
Says Nanak, if He were to be gracious
Man flourishes in life manifold.

(Sorath)

21. I am a foul sinner, an inveterate dissembler,
    You are clean, blemishless, God!
    Those who come to You for protection
    Taste nectar and are intoxicated with eternal bliss.
    God, You are the pride of the humble.
    Those who are devoted to the true word
    Are proud possessors of Your Name.
    You are perfect; I am poor and mean.
    You are great, I am small.
    I remember you day and night.
    My tongue utters your Name time and again.

    (Sorath)

22. The corporeal body is lost to *maya* complete.
    It's dyed in avarice;
    My Lord doesn't like such garments.
    How can I go to His bed?
    I am sacrifice to him, I am sacrifice to him,
    I am sacrifice to him who remembers Your Name.
    He who remembers Your Name
    I am sacrifice to him a hundred times.
    Let your body be the container
    And put the fast color of Name in it.
    If the Great Dyer were to dye it
    No one would know such a color.
    The Lord is with them
    Whose dress is red-colored.
    Nanak prays for the dust of their feet.
    He creates, He dyes, He blesses.
    Says Nanak, she who is acceptable to the Master
    He makes her remember His Name.

    (Tilang)

23. He is kind, my Master is kind.
    Indeed my Master is kind.
    He bestows favors on all those living.
    Why be worried, O man?
    The Creator will protect you.
    He who has created you,

He will sustain you.
He has made this world,
He maintains it.
He is the Master of every soul, the true Creator.
No one can know His greatness.
He is too big to bother about anything.
Man! as long as you live
You must remember Him.
God, You are all-powerful, indescribable, unknowable.
My life is dedicated to You.
Nanak has always prayed to You
And gained peace with Your grace.

(Tilang)

24. What scale, what measure, and who should be the evaluator?
    Which Guru should guide me?
    How should I determine Your status?
    My Precious One, You are beyond my reckoning
    You are all over, in water and on earth, in every living
        creature.
    Let my mind be the scale, my heart the measure and Your
        service my evaluator.
    Let me reckon You in the heart of my heart.
    This is how I would like to go about it.
    You are the scale, You the measure, You the evaluator.
    You watch Yourself, You assess Yourself, You are the trader.
    Nanak lives in the company of the blind, the petty, those
        who are strangers to You.
    He remains restless.
    How can such a foolish one get close to You?

(Suhi)

25. My Beloved has come to my house.
    The True One has brought about this union.
    Having met in *Sahj* I have endeared myself to Him
    All my five senses are at rest.
    I have obtained what I longed for.
    I live with Him day and night,
    I am happy at heart.

The temple of my house is pleasing.
There is an ever-resounding symphonic melody of the five
    notes
My Beloved has come to my house.

(Suhi)

26. Come, my Loved One, I long to see You;
    Excited, I wait on my threshold.
    O Lord, listen to my prayer,
    I long to see You,
    You are my support.
    A glimpse of You and I am cleansed.
    I am freed from the agony of birth and death.
    Your light is seen in every living creature.
    You are found when You so desire.
    Nanak is sacrifice to the Lord.
    Meeting the True One is like arriving at one's destination.

(Suhi)

27. You are called Sultan, O Master!
    You are beyond my praise.
    I have what You give.
    The simpleton, I know not what to ask.
    Grant me the understanding that I sing Your praises
    And I live a truthful life as ordained by You.
    Whatever happens is under Your orders.
    You are known everywhere.
    O, Master, I know You not fully,
    What virtue can a blind man possess?
    How can I sing Your praises,
    Sing them and measure You?
    I cannot sing, I am incapable of it.
    Whatever You say, I say the same
    And it is a small praise of You.
    There are so many seekers
    I am a novice among them.
    I crave for myself alone.
    But if I am devoid of devotion

I'll bring a bad name to Him
Whose servant I am.

(Bilawal)

28. My Lord God has come to my bed
    I am at peace now.
    With the Guru's grace I have found my love
    And I enjoy Him to my heart's content.
    The bride is fortunate,
    Her head is held high in pride.
    Meeting the Lord is true union.
    This is what Nanak longs for.

29. Nothing happens unless You allow it.
    You do what You desire.
    What should I say? I can't say much.
    Whatever is there is according to Your wishes.
    If I have to ask for anything
    It is You I ask.
    To whom else should I make my prayer?
    I read about You and listen to Your Word.
    You the greatest of all, know Yourself.
    You do Yourself.
    And make others do as You desire.
    Nanak sees his maker and destroyer thus.

(Bhairo)

30. If one is lucky, one finds the true Guru.
    Without good luck he is not to be found.
    Meeting the true Guru, one becomes gold,
    But only if God so desires.
    O man! Remember God with devotion.
    God is found through the true Guru.
    And one remains merged in God.
    The true Guru helps one gain knowledge
    And the doubts are removed.
    The true Guru makes one realize God
    And frees from the cycle of birth and death.
    With Guru's grace, the dead become alive

And the reborn devote themselves to God.
He alone attains salvation
Who gets rid of his ego.
He controls the uncontrollable,
Gains the knowledge of good and evil
And merges into the ultimate.

(Malhar)

Guru Angad

Angad had the sacred mark on his forehead
And the hallowed umbrella over his head.
He ascended the throne of Guru Nanak,
The Guru's spirit had entered the disciple.

—*Bhai Gurdas*

At Khadur near Taran Taran in the Punjab, there lived a prosperous trader called Pheru. His son Lehna was an ardent devotee of Durga, the Hindu goddess. He led parties of pilgrims to her temple and Jwalamukhi every year. They went singing and dancing all the way.

Early one morning while meditating on the goddess, Lehna heard a neighbor called Jodha recite a hymn and it touched his soul. He tried in vain to forget it, the melody echoed and re-echoed in his ears:

There is but one God,
His name is Truth,
He is the Creator,
He fears none.
Nor does He nurse ill will for anyone,
He is immortal.
Neither is He born nor does He die,
He is self-existent.
He is reached by the Guru's favor.

(*Mool Mantra*)

At dawn, Lehna went to Jodha, his neighbor, and anxiously asked him whose hymn it was that he was reciting. Jodha told him all about Guru Nanak, who lived at Kartarpur. Lehna decided in his heart of

56

hearts to visit Guru Nanak on his way to Jwalamukhi a few days later when he led the pilgrims' party.

However, when he mentioned it to his companions, they did not approve of it. They worshipped the goddess and they would not pay homage to anyone else, particularly on their way to the deity. Lehna was helpless. Had he not been leading the party, he could have opted out, but as the leader of the group, how could he desert them? He longed to see Guru Nanak.

Lehna prayed to Guru Nanak with folded hands day and night. The hymn had caught his imagination. He must see the Guru. Then one night he mounted his horse and left for Kartarpur without telling anybody. Early next morning, he was with the Master, his head on his feet.

From the day he met Guru Nanak, Lehna served him day and night like a bond slave. When he went to the fields, Guru Nanak found Lehna working with the peasants, at mealtime he was found serving in the kitchen, at the time of prayers he was among the devotees singing with complete abandon.

Then Lehna wished to be initiated formally as a Sikh and stay with the Guru. Guru Nanak advised him to go to his people for a few days and settle his household affairs before he joined him permanently. He had a wife and children awaiting him. Accordingly, Lehna went home and made adequate provisions for his family, and in no time he was back. The day he arrived he was wearing the rich silken garments of a well-to-do trader's son. Finding Guru Nanak not at home, he went to the fields looking for him. The sun was setting as he reached the fields. Guru Nanak had three loads of fodder collected and tied up to be carried home for the cattle. Since it had rained in the afternoon, the fodder was wet and muddy. When Guru Nanak found the peasants unwilling to carry the bundles home, he asked his two sons. They, too, declined, saying that they would send a servant from the house who would carry them. At that moment Lehna appeared on the scene. He picked up the bundles one upon the other and carried them home, all three of them. Lehna's rich dress was completely soiled.

Guru Nanak's wife, Mata Sulakhni, was unhappy to see a guest treated thus. Guru Nanak told her that the load was carried by one who was fit to carry it. She didn't seem to understand. "See how his clothes have been dirtied," she protested. "It's not dirt, it's saffron," remarked Guru Nanak. And for a moment Mata Sulakhni didn't believe her eyes. It was indeed saffron splattered all over Bhai Lehna's dress. It is said that the three bundles that he carried represented the spiritual, the temporal, and the stewardship of the Sikhs, which were to fall on his shoulders shortly.

One night, a portion of the compound wall in Guru Nanak's house collapsed. It was during a spell of winter rain. Guru Nanak desired that the wall be erected immediately, that very night. His sons thought it was the job of the masons, who would attend to it the next morning. Lehna volunteered to raise the wall as desired by the Master. Lehna had hardly completed the job, when Guru Nanak turned up and remarked, "It's all uneven." Lehna demolished the wall and started doing it all over again. This time, too, Guru Nanak was not satisfied. The wall was pulled down again. Guru Nanak's sons advised Lehna not to heed "the crazy old man." But Lehna would not listen to them. He obeyed his Master and started doing the wall afresh.

Guru Nanak was extremely pleased with Lehna's devotion. The more Lehna endeared himself to the Master, the more jealousy he created in the household. His worst enemies were the two sons of the Guru—Lakshmi Chand and Sri Chand. Since Guru Nanak didn't wish any unpleasantness in the house, he advised Lehna to go back to Khadur and look after his family. Guru Nanak had once stayed at Khadur and there was a nucleus of his devotees who needed guidance that Lehna could provide. Lehna heeded his Master's instructions in all humility and left for Khadur.

At Khadur, Bhai Lehna lived in the style of his Master. He spent his time in the service of the people and in meditation. Every day his wife cooked food that was distributed to the poor and the needy. Whenever he found time, Lehna went out of town and, sitting by the side of a tank, meditated on the Master. Though physically he was at Khadur, Bhai Lehna's thoughts were always with the Master. He longed to see the Guru. And then his prayers were heard and Guru Nanak paid him a visit. He was extremely happy about the way Bhai Lehna had collected the devotees around him. Congregations were held both in the morning and in the evening. Guru Nanak blessed

Lehna and, after staying at Khadur for a little while, got ready to leave for Kartarpur.

Lehna wanted either the Guru to stay with him or himself to accompany him to Kartarpur. Moved by his devotion, Guru Nanak agreed to take Bhai Lehna along with him to Kartarpur. At Kartarpur Bhai Lehna again plunged himself into the service of the Master. His humility and devotion won for him the worst hostility in the household. Guru Nanak was greatly pleased with him and one day, placing his hand on his head, blessed him and gave him the name of Angad—a part of his *ang* (body). He was no longer Lehna the son of Pheru, the trader of Khadur.

All indications were that Angad was to succeed Guru Nanak. He was the closest to him. But Guru Nanak must prove it to the fullest satisfaction of other aspirants, and humble their pride.

Guru Nanak made several tests, the last being one in which he asked his sons to eat what appeared to them to be a corpse. They scoffed at the suggestion, while Angad obeyed the Master blindly. Not only this, but when he found it to be the sacred food, he brought it first to Guru Nanak and his sons to partake of it and he would eat only the leftover.

Before long, Guru Nanak ordained Angad as the Guru and invited Bhai Budha, a trusted Sikh, to anoint him. After his succession, Guru Angad shifted to Khadur. Bhai Gurdas, the noted Sikh bard, has described it thus:

Angad had the sacred mark on his forehead
And hallowed umbrella over his head,
He ascended the throne of Nanak,
The Guru's spirit entering the disciple.

(Var 1-46)

Though he had come away from Kartarpur fully blessed and anointed by the Guru, the disciple missed his Master. Day and night he remembered his mentor and wished to have a glimpse of him. One day he came across a Jat girl called Nihali, who had heard about him and longed to pay homage to him. She was making cowdung cakes for fuel when she saw the Guru pass by the side of their house. She flung herself at his feet and wished to entertain him with fresh milk. Guru Angad was moved by her devotion and asked if they could place a room at his disposal where he could live in hiding as he wished. What more did Nihali want in life? They vacated a room for the Guru and placed it at his disposal. It is said the Guru would have nothing but a little milk twice a day and meditated in the room for six long months, unknown to the world from which he had disappeared.

In the meanwhile, the Sikhs became panicky. They looked for the Guru everywhere. A deputation comprising Bhai Lalo, Bhai Saido, Bhai Ajita and others went to Bhai Budha, who was greatly respected by Guru Nanak, to have him help them locate Guru Angad. Bhai Budha was a man of great insight, he had been particularly blessed by the great Guru. He led the anxious Sikhs to Khadur to Bibi Nihali's house, where in a secluded room Guru Angad was found in deep meditation.

The Sikhs were astonished to find that their Guru appeared to be the very image of Guru Nanak. The same glow in his eyes, the same resplendence on his face, the same halo around his head. His words were poetry. He was compassion incarnate. Still Guru Angad seemed to long for Guru Nanak. When he saw Bhai Budha, he said:

> He whom you love, die for him.
> Accursed is the life lived without the beloved.
> The head should be sliced that does not bow before the Master.
> O Nanak! the body should be burnt that suffers not the agony of
> separation.
>
> *(Sri Rag)*

By using the nom de plume Nanak, Guru Angad testified to the fact that he was Guru Nanak himself. The great Guru's spirit had entered into him. He was no longer Lehna, trader Pheru's son.

Bhai Budha and his companions persuaded Guru Angad to come out of his hiding-place and meet his disciples, who were yearning to have a glimpse of him.

It was difficult to refuse Bhai Budha. Guru Angad asked Bhai Budha how he happened to come so close to Guru Nanak and be favored by him. Bhai Budha told him that as a child he was once watching his mother make a fire. He was surprised to see that the small pieces of firewood lighted more easily and were consumed faster than the larger pieces. He was convinced that death was a reality and it was no respecter of age. One could die any time. He had not yet recovered from this perception when one day the king's soldiers passed through their village mindlessly ravaging the crops. Bhai Budha ran home to report to his father, who said, "Child, you can do nothing with the king's soldiers." Bhai Budha realized that if his father couldn't protect his own crops from the king's men, how could he save his child from the clutches of death? This realization led him to Guru Nanak, who showed him the light and freed him from the fear of death.

"We have now come to you. You are Guru Nanak incarnate. Kindly show us the path of liberation," said Bhai Budha and his companions.

At this, Guru Angad uttered these words in utter humility:

He who has been blessed by Guru Nanak
Is lost in the praises of the Lord.
What could one teach those
Who have Divine Nanak as their Guru?

(Majh)

Guru Angad followed Guru Nanak in his daily routine. He woke up long before daybreak and went into meditation. At dawn, the recitation of *Japji* was followed by *Asa di var* sung in a congregation with the Sikhs joining from far and near. Satta and Balwand, the two local musicians, were particular favorites and they led the singing of hymns daily. Guru Angad also followed Guru Nanak's practice of maintaining a free kitchen for all those who came to visit him, irrespective of caste and creed. He also took a keen interest in physical exercise and watched wrestling matches in which his devotees participated. Guru Angad came to be known as the healer of incurable ailments like leprosy, and poor patients came to him in large numbers.

Once Malu Shah, an orderly in the Mughal army, came to Guru Angad for spiritual guidance. The Guru was aware that the Mughals were in a bad way those days. He advised Malu Shah to remain loyal to his master and serve his King devotedly, more so in his adversity.

Humayun had succeeded Babar on the Mughal throne but he was soon overpowered by Sher Shah. As he was being hounded out of power he came to Khadur to seek Guru Angad's blessings. It so happened that, when he came to the Guru, he was sitting in a congregation listening to hymns being sung by the devotees. The Mughal king had, therefore, to wait for a while. Humayun felt slighted and, losing his temper put his hand on the hilt of his sword, threatening to attack the Guru. Guru Angad was unmoved by this threat. He chided Humayun, "When you should have used the sword, you did not, rather you ran away from the battlefield like a coward. Here with a dervish, you show off, threatening to attack unarmed devotees engaged in prayer!" Humayun heard it and was embarrassed. He wished to be pardoned. Guru Angad then reminded Humayun about Guru Nanak's prophecy. He must leave the country in his own interest and, as foreseen by the great Guru, he would return to his throne shortly thereafter. History is witness that Humayun attacked India in due course and regained his throne.

A certain Sikh, Mana by name, used to serve in the Guru's kitchen. He was a good cook and became a great favorite of the Guru. This turned his head. He would listen to no one and was rude to everybody. He said that he would serve only the Guru and none else. It so happened that one day a few Sikhs visited the Guru at an odd hour. When asked, Mana was reluctant to attend to them. He insisted that he would obey the Guru and listen to none else. At this, Guru Angad sent for him and told him to go into the jungle, make a funeral pyre, and burn himself. Mana must obey the Guru's orders. He went to the jungle and collected firewood and erected a funeral pyre. But when it came to setting fire to himself, he wavered. At that very instant, a robber turned up in the jungle and asked Mana what he was going to do. Mana told him all about his Guru. When the robber heard it, he was so much moved that, handing over the pot in his hand to Mana, he decided to honor the Guru's word. The robber burned himself to death, while Mana carried the pot, which was full of jewelry and precious stones, to the town to sell it. As he was negotiating the sale of his fortune, he was arrested by the police for having committed a robbery and was then hanged.

Similarly, Satta and Balwand had also become swollen-headed. They had come to believe that all the popularity of Guru Angad was due to their excellence as musicians. They started making all sorts of fantastic claims. Guru Angad put up with them, but then came a stage when he felt that he had to take some action. He asked them to quit service and advised his followers to have nothing to do with them. At this, they started their independent service. It was indeed very rude and Guru Angad ordered that, far from having anything to do with them, none may mention even their names in his presence. He who spoke about them to the Guru would have his face blackened, be mounted on a donkey, and taken through the town. They were not only rude to him, they were disrespectful even to Guru Nanak. They believed that since they sang the Guru's praises, the Sikhs came to him. Without them, no one would visit the Guru. They continued holding musical sessions at their own place. They sang both in the morning and in the evening but no one ever went to them. On the other hand, the Sikhs in Guru Angad's congregation started singing hymns on their own and were highly popular. Before long, Satta and Balwand realized their folly and started looking for someone who could arrange for their reconciliation with the Guru. But in view of the Guru's condemnation of their conduct, no one dared give them any quarter. They tried their best but they failed miserably. At last, they went to Lahore to see Bhai Ladha, who had considerable influence with the Guru. Bhai Ladha was aware of their misbehavior but, as a true Sikh of the Guru, he decided to do good for evil and intercede on their behalf. He, therefore, had his face smeared with ash, and riding on a donkey he went through the entire town of Khadur and then, presenting himself before Guru Angad, begged his favor to pardon the erring minstrels. The Guru was greatly moved at Bhai Ladha's spirit of self-abnegation and dedication to the lofty ideal of mercy and compassion upheld by Guru Nanak, and took Satta and Balwand back in his fold.

Guru Angad was fond of children and took great interest in them. He gathered children, organized games for them, and distributed prizes. He devoted equal attention to their proper education. He insisted that children should be taught in their mother tongue and to that end he is said to have simplified and codified the Gurmukhi script and popularized its use amongst his Sikhs. This, perhaps, is the most important contribution of Guru Angad.

Guru Nanak once had an encounter with the siddhas at Atal Batala. The debate lasted for several days and was bitterly contested. Guru Nanak had ultimately won over the siddhas. A yogi called Daya Nath, who did not happen to be in Batala at the time, wondered how anyone could vanquish Bhangar Nath and the Yogi Superior of Batala in argument. He therefore came looking for Guru Nanak and, finding that he had his successor in Guru Angad, he entered into an argument with him. He advocated that mental purity could be obtained only through the observance of rituals, introspection, suspension of breath, contemplation, trance, etc. By practicing yoga, longevity, material wealth, and supernatural powers are obtained. Guru Angad attached little importance to such things. Guru Nanak had taught a simple way to realization, finding God by living a truthful life, remaining pure amidst impurity. Daya Nath felt convinced in his heart of hearts and, in view of his being senior in age, asked Guru Angad if he could do anything for him. Guru Angad asked to be blessed. The yogi was nonplussed by Angad's humility. He realized he didn't have that humility. He went into meditation and found that humility had been bestowed only on Guru Nanak and his successor Guru Angad, and that even demi-gods didn't possess it. Daya Nath fell at Guru Angad's feet and was cleansed of his arrogance about learning and asceticism.

One evening there was a severe and almost blinding dust storm. No fire could be lit or food prepared. Jiva the cook was worried that if the storm did not abate, he would not be able to prepare food for the devotees. He came to Guru Angad seeking his intercession to quell the dust storm. The Guru, rather than oblige him, told him to accept the will of God.

The Khahiras Jats of Khadur had a headman who was extremely proud of his wealth and never cared to visit the Guru. He, in fact, lost no opportunity to mock the Guru's teachings. His young son followed his father and took to drinking and evil ways. Before long, he was stricken with epilepsy and many other diseases. They tried all sorts of medicines but the young man was going from bad to worse. They went to the local *tapa* (ascetic) who said that it was due to evil spirits and that he would exorcise them with his spiritual power. He tried his best but the patient did not get any relief. When he was almost on his deathbed, they brought him to Guru Angad. The Guru told the young man to abstain from liquor, repeat God's name, and serve holy men. Following the Guru's instructions, the young man fully recovered. However, during the rainy season, when there were clouds in the sky and the easterly winds brought torrents of rain, the young man forgot the Guru's words and, sitting on the terrace of his house, started drinking. He had a relapse of epilepsy and fell down from the top of the house and died in the street. The rich father wailed and begged the Guru to revive his only son, but Guru Angad told him that God's will must be done; no one could ever interfere with His ways.

One Amar Das, a Vaishnav by faith, used to observe regular fasts. He visited the holy Ganges every year for a ritual bath. While on his way back after his twelfth pilgrimage to Mother Ganges, he felt frustrated. He was as empty-handed as ever. He was still in search of truth that seemed to elude him. On his return journey this time, he met a monk and they became great friends. They travelled together for several days. Then one day his companion asked Amar Das, "But who is your guru?" "None," replied Amar Das. The monk was shocked to hear it. He had been friendly with a man who had no guru! It was a great sin. He must return to the holy Ganges for another bath. He therefore left the bewildered Amar Das and made his way back.

Amar Das now started seeking a guru. One day while he was sitting all alone on his terrace with an aching emptiness in his heart, he happened to hear Bibi Amro, the daughter of Guru Angad, who was married recently to his nephew, recite hymns of Guru Nanak. It was her practice to get up early in the morning and recite the *Japji* and then sing slokas from *Asa di Var*. Amar Das started listening to her every morning without anyone knowing about it. Every word of the hymns that she recited seemed to sink deep into his heart. The melody seemed to haunt him. He was enchanted. He went over to the young bride next door and fell at her feet. It is never done. He was like her father-in-law. But Amar Das was paying homage to the Divine Word uttered from the lips of the devotee in her. Bibi Amro told him about Guru Nanak and promised to take him to her father Guru Angad. But Amar Das could not wait even for a moment. He must meet the great Guru and offer himself to him. Since they were related to each other, Guru Angad got up from his seat on his arrival to embrace him. But

Amar Das would have none of it. He fell at his feet, and felt strangely elevated.

Forgetting his age, his status, and his relationship, Amar Das started serving Guru Angad day and night. He looked after his person with the devotion and humility of a slave. One day the Guru was partaking of a meat dish and, realizing Amar Das's embarrassment, since he had been a Vaishnav all his life, he sent for a vegetarian dish for him. Amar Das was deeply gratified at the consideration shown to him. The Guru, however, wished to rid Amar Das of his prejudices and told him that what one should abstain from was temptation, slander, covetousness, and ego. There is life in everything; even fruits and flowers have life. Whatever is eaten while remembering God is like nectar itself. Amar Das was an enlightened man.

One of Guru Angad's disciples, Gobind by name, was involved in litigation with his relatives. He prayed for the Guru's blessings and vowed that, if he won the case, he would have a new township built in his honor on the banks of the river Beas. As luck would have it, he won the case and started building the promised township. However, he was told that whatever the masons put up was found demolished the next morning. It was believed that it was the doing of evil spirits. Accordingly, he went to Guru Angad and sought his intervention. It was, in fact, his enemies who were doing all the mischief. Guru Angad sent Amar Das with him and advised him to stay there personally and supervise the construction of the township. When the town was completed, it had a stately palace for the residence of the Guru. But Guru Angad did not agree to leave his ancestral home. He, however, asked Amar Das to go and live in the new township called Goindwal. In due course, Amar Das had his family shifted from Basarke and settled in Goindwal permanently. He would get up early in the morning, carry water from the river for the Guru's bath, and remain in attendance on him during the day, and return to Goindwal in the evening.

The ascetic, called tapa, in Khadur bore an eternal grudge against Guru Angad, whose followers visted him in large numbers from far and near. He indulged in magic and superstitious practices. Once it so happened that the rains failed Khadur and the adjoining region. The people waited and waited, but not a drop of rain fell from the empty skies. The crops started withering. The peasants became panicky and went to the tapa to work a miracle and have the rain brought for the parched crops. The tapa had indeed the opportunity of his life. He taunted the village folk, "You go to Guru Angad day and night for spiritual guidance, why can't he get rain for your dying crops?" The village folk heard it and came to Guru Angad and reported what the ascetic had said. Guru Angad smiled as usual and told the people that there was no interfering with the ways of God. The rains would come when God willed. The peasants were getting impatient. They went to the tapa again and pleaded for his intervention. He agreed to work the miracle provided they turned Guru Angad out of the village. The entire village was desperate. They came and started shouting slogans against the Guru, demanding that he quit the village so that the tapa could bring them rain. Guru Angad left the village and, having been refused shelter in any village in the vicinity, he settled in a forest, south of Khadur.

When Amar Das came to know of it, he reproached the villagers. They were ignoring the sun and seeing light from a puny lamp. But they would not listen to him. In the meanwhile, the tapa tried his best, he read *mantras* and observed fasts but the dry spell continued. The villagers now realized their folly and went in a group to Guru Angad, soliciting his forgiveness and bringing him back to the village with due honor. There was great rejoicing when the Guru came and with the rejoicing came the long-awaited rains. The people went mad with joy.

It was Guru Angad's practice to distribute robes of honor to his devotees for meritorious services every six months. Amar Das had earned six such robes, more than anyone else had. He would wear them one above the other on his head as his turban since discarding any one of them would be disrespectful to his Master.

Evidently, Amar Das was most deserving among his disciples and most dear to the Guru. When the time came for Guru Angad to name his successor, he was inclined towards Amar Das in preference to his own sons, Dasu and Datu. He was still to announce his decision when an incident took place that decided the issue.

It was a practice with Amar Das to fetch fresh water for Guru Angad's bath every morning, long before daybreak. One winter

morning, it was blowing cold, there was lightning, and it threatened
to rain. Yet undeterred, Amar Das came with a pitcherful of water on
his head. When passing through a colony of weavers, his foot struck
against a peg of a weaver's loom and he was about to tumble down,
but somehow he saved himself and the pitcher of water. The
disturbance in the street at that unearthly hour upset the weaver, who
was inside his house, and he started shouting, "Thief, thief." However, his wife, who knew better, said, "It must be the old Amru, the
homeless, who carries water for his Guru daily, early in the morning.
He slaves day and night for a good-for-nothing man." When Amar
Das heard her say this, he observed, "Woman, you have gone mad!"
He couldn't bear anyone speaking ill of his Guru. It is said that the
weaver's wife became mad that very instant. No remedy could cure
her. At last, she was brought to Guru Angad. When he heard the
story, he pardoned her in his grace and said, "Amar Das is not
homeless, he is the shelter of the unsheltered. He is the strength of the
weak and the emancipation of the slave!"

Realizing that his end was near, Guru Angad sent for Bhai Budha
and revealed to him his decision to make Amar Das the next Guru.
Accordingly, he had Amar Das installed as the third Sikh Guru. Guru
Angad's two sons didn't like the decision. They had their own
ambitions. Guru Angad told them that the honor would go to one
who deserved it, and who was most devoted and humble.

Guru Angad left this world in 1552, after having administered as
the guru for twelve and half years, six months, and nine days.

Guru Angad is the instance of a seeker who, by the very intensity of
his search, finds what he seeks. Son of a prosperous trader, he was
God-fearing, and given to spiritual quest from his early age. A searcher
for truth at heart, once he came in touch with Guru Nanak, he found
his way to the highest position by dint of devotion and dedicated
service. He became the spiritual son of Guru Nanak and yet he was
humble and self-effacing. Perhaps the most remarkable trait of his
character was his complete surrender to the Master. He was utterly
obedient and carried out his Guru's instructions devotedly. After he
had been installed successor to Guru Nanak formally, he understood
the delicacy of the situation, and rather than continuing to stay with
his mentor, he shifted to Khadur. He did not wish to embarrass Guru

Nanak's sons and Mata Sulakhni, who were evidently unhappy at the decision regarding the succession. At Khadur he suffered pangs of separation from the Master but would not hurt anyone if he could help it. During his stewardship of the Sikh community, though he had the spirit of Guru Nanak, not once did he try to consolidate his own position by working miracles or charming people with occult practices. In fact, he condemned such practices and, as far as possible, proved the futility of it all.

Here was a spiritual leader who was also practical-minded. He took care of the physical and mental health of his flock. He encouraged the Sikhs to take interest in sports and also send their children to the *pathshalas* where they were imparted education in their own mother tongue, in a simplified Gurmukhi script. And in the end, he lived up to the tradition of his Master in choosing as his successor the most deserving of his disciples in preference to his own sons, who did aspire to succeed him. Like Guru Nanak, he encouraged Guru Amar Das to set up his headquarters at Goindwal rather than Khadur, where he had come to live permanently. The intention, perhaps, was to not deprive,the legal successors of their rights to property and also to save them the embarrassment it might cause. Guru Amar Das was much too senior in age. He was already in his seventies when he first met Guru Angad and yet, when the time came, he succeeded Guru Angad because he was considered most suitable among the devotees. It was due to his humility and devotion to Guru Nanak that he used the nom de plume Nanak in his *Bani*, the practice which was followed by the rest of the Gurus succeeding him. Guru Angad was an extremely sensitive soul. There are poignant references to his separation from Guru Nanak and it must have been he who suffered the most at Guru Nanak's final departure. He yearned to be at his bedside to see his Master leave, abide by his instructions not to cry and yet shed tears of blood in his heart to see his beloved depart forever and ever.

Guru Angad's times were as bad as Guru Nanak's. There was political unrest. The people were given to evil ways and corruption was rife:

The beggar is called the king,
And the blockhead pandit,

The blind are the judges,
Such are the ways of the world.
Those given to evil are headmen,
And falsehood acceptable.
Nanak, these are the ways of the Kaliyug.
How can one arrive at truth?

(Malhar)

While Guru Nanak says time and again that he was ordained by God, Guru Angad owes everything to his Guru. He is attached to his person, he cannot bear separation from him:

Nanak, spring is for her
Who has her spouse at home.
She whose master is away
Suffers day and night.

(Suhi)

He believes in complete surrender to the Guru, utter obedience to his instructions, and fond emulation of his ways.

I have a nose-string,
It's in the hands of the Master.
He drives me where he likes
Verily, O Nanak! what God gives man eats.

(Sorath)

One must obey the Guru. It is obedience to the Guru that earns for one the reward of spiritual uplift:

The Guru has the key;
The heart is the treasure-house
And the body its cover.
Nanak! the door of the heart can't be opened
Without the Guru
Who alone has the key.

(Sarang)

Obedience begets devotion and penance and everything else,
All other efforts are in vain.
Nanak, obey him who himself has obeyed God;
He is known by the Guru's grace.

(Ramkali)

The Guru is pleased if one lives a virtuous life, does good deeds, and devotes one's life to remembering God and serving his people:

They are blessed who remember God
During the fourth watch in the morning.
They are fond of visiting rivers
With true Name on their lips and in their hearts.
The rest of the seven watches of the day
It's good to speak truth
And live in the company of the learned.

(Majh)

It is the love of God and not ascetic practices and the like that bring God's favor:

God is not won with asceticism
Howsoever you may try.
O Nanak! God is attained with love and truth
And the understanding of His word.

(Suhi)

While the origin of the Gurmukhi script continues to be disputed, there is no doubt that Guru Angad gave a lead in making an extensive use of the script in his time. He got a number of copies of Guru Nanak's *bani* made out in the Gurmukhi script, consisting of thirty-five letters culled from the various scripts prevalent at the time. It is amazing how much Guru Angad could achieve in the short time at his disposal.

Selected Hymns of Guru Angad

1. Seeing without eyes,
   Hearing without ears,
   Walking without feet,
   Working without hands,
   Uttering His Name without tongue,
   And dying while living,
   Says Nanak, meeting the Master
   Is accepting His will.

   (Majh)

2. He is seen, heard, and known
   And yet He is not my own.
   How can one without feet, hands, and eyes
   Go and cling to the Lord?
   With the feet of fear, hands of love, and eyes of
      understanding,
   Says Nanak—O wise woman!
   This is how you meet the Master.

   (Majh)

3. Air is the guru, water the father, and earth the great mother,
   Day and night are the male and female nurses making the
      world to play.
   Dharamraja watches good and bad deeds sitting in his court.
   In keeping with your karma you are close or away from the
      Lord.
   Those who remember His Name, their effort is rewarded.
   They come out beaming with success and obtain deliverance
      for others.

   (Majh)

4. The nose-string is in the hands of the Master
   And a man's deeds drive him along.
   Says Nanak, the truth is
   One has to be what happens to be one's lot.

   (Sorath)

5. Those who know, they have to go;
   They don't involve themselves here.

Those who know not the truth of death,
They attach themselves too much here.
They collect wealth during the night
And depart as the day dawns.
Says Nanak, nothing goes with them
And they repent and repent.

(Suhi)

6. He who does his work unwillingly,
   He does good neither to himself nor to others.
   Only that job is worth doing
   Which is done with pleasure.

(Suhi)

7. Those who fear Him, they fear none.
   Those who fear Him not, they are afraid of everyone.
   Says Nanak, this truth is known
   Only when one enters His court.
   He who walks meets one who is walking;
   He who flies meets those who fly.
   He who is living lives with those who are alive.
   He who is dead remains with the dead.
   Says Nanak, praise be to Him
   Who has created the Universe.

(Suhi)

8. Everyone has someone;
   This humble one has none but You.
   Why shouldn't I die crying
   When I can't remember You.
   I remember You in pleasure
   I remember You in pain.
   Says Nanak, O wise one
   This is how you meet the Master.

(Suhi)

9. Says Nanak, worry not,
   All worries are His.
   The creatures in water He has created
   He feeds them.
   There are no shops,

Nor does anyone labor there.
There are no goods,
Neither one buys nor one sells.
They feed on each other
Those created in the ocean.
This is how He looks after them.
Says Nanak, worry not,
All worries are His.

(Ramkali)

10. It's the rainy season, O my playmate!
And I long for my Lord.
Says Nanak, dies pining
The accursed one who loves other than her Master.
It's the rainy season, O my playmate!
It pours and pours.
Says Nanak, she sleeps in peace
The blessed one who loves her Lord.

(Malhar)

Guru Amar Das

The community was delighted to see
Guru Nanak's umbrella over Amar Das' head.

—*Satta*

He was seventy-three when Amar Das was ordained the Guru. A mere devotee, who prided himself on being the humblest servant of Guru Angad; living where the Guru desired him to live, doing what the Guru ordained him to do, he was raised to the supreme status of Master who had to provide leadership to a new resurgent community. He felt that he must equip himself for it. In humility and in a spirit of thanksgiving, the first step he took was to retreat to the attic of his house at Goindwal and meditate day and night praying for God's grace, Guru Nanak's blessings, and Guru Angad's guidance for the heavy responsibility placed on his shoulders. Satta, the minstrel, has described Guru Amar Das' taking over as the third Sikh Guru thus:

The community was delighted to see
Guru Nanak's umbrella over Amar Das' head.
The grandson was as revered as the father and the grandfather.

The Sikhs started flocking to him from far and near. However, Datu, one of Guru Angad's sons, was not reconciled to his father's decision. He had set himself up as guru at Khadur, as successor to his father. But, to his utter dismay, nobody cared to visit him. Before long, he lost his patience and, accompanied by some of his followers, he came to Goindwal to assault Guru Amar Das. In a fit of temper he said, "You were a mere menial servant of the house until yesterday

75

and how dare you style yourself as the Master?" He is said to have kicked the revered old soul. Rather than get annoyed, Guru Amar Das held Datu's foot and started caressing it, as if it might have been hurt while hitting the stiff bones of an old man.

As desired by Datu, Guru Amar Das left Goindwal for an unknown destination, and Datu established himself as the successor to his father. However, no one paid any reverential attention to him; he was held in contempt instead. In the meanwhile, Guru Amar Das went to his ancestral village, Basarke, and shut himself up in a small room with a notice on the door saying, "He who opens this door is no Sikh of mine, nor am I his Guru." Days passed, and the Sikhs grew impatient, looking for the Guru. At last, they went to Bhai Budha.

Bhai Budha closed his eyes in contemplation. After a while he opened his eyes, and suggested that the Guru's mare should be let loose and the Sikhs should follow her. She would lead them to the Guru's hiding place. The Sikhs did exactly as they were told. They had Bhai Budha also accompany them. And as observed by the great sage, the mare led them unmistakably to the hut where the Guru had hidden himself. But the instruction on the door was forbidding.

Bhai Budha came to their rescue again. He suggested that they should break open the back wall and enter the hut. They would, in this way, not be violating the Guru's injunction. The Sikhs did accordingly and entering the hut, Bhai Budha remonstrated with the Guru: "Guru Angad had tied us to your apron, where should we go now if you are not to show us the way?" This brought tears in the eyes of Guru Amar Das. Unable to disregard his disciples, he mounted the mare and accompanied them to Goindwal. The opening in the wall at Basarke is still intact and has since become a place of pilgrimage. Datu, in due course, understood how mistaken he was in arrogating to himself the title of Guru. Nobody took him seriously now, and he returned to Khadur. It is said that at a little distance from Goindwal, he was intercepted by robbers who looted all that he had on his person and beat him severely.

On his return to Goindwal, Guru Amar Das attended to the various needs of his Sikhs. He set up a free kitchen where everyone, irrespective of caste and creed, was welcome. In fact, the Guru made it obligatory of all those seeking his audience to first eat in the *langar* and then go to see him. This helped in ridding Hindu society of the evil of the caste system, brought the Hindus and the Muslims closer, and fostered communal harmony. The Guru also tried to eradicate social evils like *sati,* requiring a Hindu widow to burn herself on her husband's funeral pyre or remain unmarried all her life after the death of her husband. With a view to spreading Guru Nanak's message far and wide, Guru Amar Das trained a band of 146 apostles, of whom fifty-two were women, to go to various parts of the country and attend to the spiritual needs of the Guru's followers. It is said that he also set up twenty-two *manjis* (dioceses) presided over by devout Sikhs.

As the message of Guru Nanak spread, more and more people visited Goindwal. Some of them decided to settle there to benefit by living in the Guru's proximity, attending his darbar morning and evening. It was felt that the town, having expanded out of all proportion, was going through a shortage of timber for construction. When the Guru was apprised of this situation, he deputed Sawan Mal to go to Haripur in Kangra district, arrange for the felling of pine and cedar trees, and float them down the Beas river. Sawan Mal sought the local Raja's help, which expedited matters. The Raja of Haripur then came to pay homage to the Guru accompanied by his queens. The king also had to partake of food in the *langar* like everyone else before he could see the Guru. One of the queens insisted on wearing a veil in his presence. He called her jhalli (crazy) for being so self-conscious and she, it is said, became insane instantly, tearing at her clothes and running away into the jungle.

By now Goindwal had become a flourishing town and a number of Muslim dignitaries came and settled there. As members of the ruling community, they tended to be overbearing. They harassed the non-Muslims on one pretext or another. Even their children were unruly. They pelted stones at the Sikhs who went to bring water for the Guru's household and broke their earthen pots. When the matter was reported to the Guru, he counselled forbearance and suggested that his Sikhs bring water for the household in metal pots. Now, the unruly Muslim youths started aiming arrows at them. A band of sanyasis happened to pass through Goindwal one day and the Muslim youths, spoiled as they were, also misbehaved with them. A scuffle followed, in which a number of them lost their lives. This taught them a lesson and there was peace in the town for some time. However, it did not last long. After a few days, the Muslim youths started their old practice of harassing non-Muslims. Every time it was reported to the Guru, he advised his disciples to be patient. They must not take the law into their own hands. They should have faith in God, who must do justice sooner or later. So the Sikhs could neither retort nor strike back.

A little later, a detachment of the Mughal force was carrying the imperial treasure from Lahore to Delhi. While passing through Goindwal, one of their mules was lost. The mule was carrying the state treasure. The soldiers searched for it high and low. The leader of the detachment had a proclamation made in the town but no one seemed to know where the mule could have disappeared. Eventually, the mule, which had been hidden in the Muslim quarters, started braying in captivity. The matter was duly reported to the Nawab who was already aware of the Muslims in Goindwal harassing the Sikhs and of their scuffle with the sanyasis. He ordered demolition of their houses, confiscation of their property, and their imprisonment.

Once the Guru, along with some of his disciples, was passing along a street. It had been raining for several days and it seemed the wall was about to collapse. The Guru hurried his steps and advised his companions also to do likewise. When they came out of the street, his disciples wanted to know why the Guru behaved the way he did. Was he afraid of death? The Guru smiled and observed, "Human life is a blessing that many a demi-god yearns for. One should preserve life as long as possible. A healthy, smiling face is pleasing even to God."

The working of miracles is not looked upon with favor in Sikhism. A number of miracles are attributed to Guru Nanak and other Sikh Gurus, but it is also a fact that Guru Nanak and the Gurus following him scoffed at miracles as mere gimmickry. A couple of times when Guru Nanak was asked to work a miracle, he declined. Guru Tegh Bahadur specifically forbade his envoy to the Mughal court to work a miracle. Later, rather than deviate from his principle and work a miracle for the king, he chose to give up his life. And yet miracles are said to happen and men of God are believed to have worked them. Accordingly, a number of miracles are attributed to Guru Amar Das.

While Angad refrained from them, even when it meant hardship to his person (he left his town rather than bring rain to a rainless region), Guru Amar Das seemed to have worked miracles from time to time, maybe because he had launched a massive reformation movement trying to spread Guru Nanak's message to the people and it is always easier to impress people with something unusual and seemingly supernatural. Among spiritualists, miracles are never deemed to be an achievement. Even novices on the spiritual path are said to have worked miracles.

Some of the miracles attributed to Guru Amar Das are:

Haripur Raja's mad queen, who was roaming the jungle, assaulted a Guru's Sikh who called himself Sachansach. He had gone to the forest to collect firewood. The next day the Guru sent Sachansach armed with one of his slippers. When the mad woman came to assault him, Sachansach shielded himself with the slipper. It is said that the moment the slipper touched the queen, she regained her sanity.

A goldsmith in Goindwal married an elderly lady. They naturally didn't have any children. This made them unhappy. They had a well dug and a temple built for travellers. The Guru was pleased and blessed them. They had two sons. Since the mother was too old to bear children, people started calling the babies *maipotre*—Mummy's grandsons. The family continues to be known as *Maipotre* even today.

With a view to providing his Sikhs a place where they could have a holy dip when they visited Hardwar, Varanasi, and Kasi, Guru Amar Das decided to have a *baoli* dug in Goindwal. This is a sort of open water reservoir with wide steps approaching the surface of the water. Rather than employing labor, the Sikhs joined hands after prayers on the day of the full moon in the month of *Kartik* and in a few days dug deep enough to strike water. However, they found that there was rock that hindered their progress. The Sikhs were at a loss to know what to do. They went to the Guru for advice. Guru Amar Das contemplated for a while and then told the Sikhs, "The slab will have to be blasted, but my fear is that the one who does so, if he cannot be brought out instantly, might be overpowered by the gushing water and drowned." Now who was there to take this risk? The Sikhs looked at one another. Then suddenly Manak Chand of Vairowal volunteered to go down the baoli and do the needed task. As observed by the Guru, the moment the slab cracked, the water gushed forth with such force that Manak Chand was overpowered and drowned! The next morning his body was found floating on the surface of the baoli. Manak Chand's mother saw it and lamented the loss of her son. His widow shed tears of blood. The Guru took pity on them and called out to Manak who, it is said, opened his eyes in response to the Guru's call. The baoli in due course, was provided with *pucca* steps. The Guru declared that he who recited *Japji* once at every step would be free from the cycle of eighty-four lakh lives destined for every living being in creation.

Prema, a devout Sikh, lived in a village at some distance from Goindwal. He was lame in one leg and yet he carried a pot of milk for the Guru's langar every morning. He walked with a crutch. Once it rained incessantly and the road to the town became slushy. He was advised by the villagers not to go to the town. But Prema was determined to do his daily duty to his Guru. When he left the village in rain and storm, slipping at every step, the passersby made fun of him, "Your Guru heals all and sundry, why can't he cure you of your limp?" Prema paid no attention to what they said. But when he reached Goindwal, he was sent for by the Guru, who seemed to know what the villagers had said to his devotee. The Guru asked Prema to go to a Muslim dervish, Husaini Shah, who lived on the bank of the river and he would cure the limp in his leg.

Prema went over to the dervish and told him about what had come to pass. The recluse was scandalized to hear it. He picked up a stick to chastise Prema. Prema got frightened and ran as fast as he could. He had forgotten his crutch! It is only after he had come a good distance that he realized what had happened. It was, indeed, a miracle. He went back to the dervish and fell at his feet. Husaini said, "Your leg had become all right when the Guru sent you over to me. He has only given me the credit for working miracles."

Amongst a band of devotees who had arrived from Lahore one day, Guru Amar Das spotted a handsome youth called Jetha. There was a strange spark in his eyes. He was never idle, always busy at one thing or another, whether it was cleaning utensils in the kitchen or helping in the digging of a baoli or attending to the Guru's personal needs, such as giving him a massage, pressing his legs, or running odd errands for him. He had endeared himself greatly to the Guru. His real name was Ram Das. And he was truly a slave of God. Humble and helpful, he made friends with everyone with his fine looks and pleasant manners. In the meanwhile, Bibi Bhani, the Guru's younger daughter, had come of age and her mother Masa Devi was keen to have her married. Once, sitting with her husband, she asked the Guru to look for a suitable match for their daughter. "What sort of a match would you like to have for Bhani?" asked the Guru. "He should be a young man like him," said Mansa Devi pointing to Jetha, who happened to pass by, absorbed in some household chores. "Then why not Jetha himself?" the Guru asked spontaneously. The decision was made. A date was fixed and Bibi Bhani duly married Ram Das. Though married to the Guru's daughter, Ram Das, rather than taking his bride away as is customary, continued to live with the Guru and serve him as devotedly as ever.

During one of his visits to Lahore, Emperor Akbar was crossing the river Beas. And he decided to make a slight detour and visit Goindwal to pay homage to Guru Amar Das, about whom he had heard a great deal. To see the Guru, even the Emperor had to partake of food in the langar like any other visitor. It is said that the Emperor sat with the lowliest of the low and ate with them and then had an audience with the Guru. Akbar was highly impressed at the meeting and wished to grant a *jagir* to the Guru for the maintenance of the free kitchen. The Guru would not agree to it. "The rations are brought by the devotees daily and are distributed among them every day," said the Guru. "We start afresh every morning. Nothing is saved for the next day." The Emperor insisted on making the grant in appreciation of the great humanitarian work being done by the Guru. Since the Guru would not accept any favor from the king, Akbar thought of a way out. "I can, at least, present a few villages as a wedding gift to your daughter, Bhani, who is as much my daughter." The Guru could not decline it and the king had his way. After a few days when the headman of the town brought the formal papers of the endowment and other bounties from the king, the Guru sent for his son-in-law, Bhai Jetha, and handed them over to him.

Once a rich devotee brought a necklace of pearls and offered it to the Guru. He wished to put the costly necklace around the Guru's neck. "I am too old for it," said Amar Das. "You may put it on one who is most like me." The banker did not understand what the Guru was trying to convey. He handed over the precious necklace to the Guru and requested him to give it to anyone who he thought had been cast in his image. The Sikhs sitting around the Guru started making their conjectures. It could be either of the two sons of the Guru, Mohan or Mohri, they thought. To their utter astonishment, the Guru sent for Jetha and put the necklace on his neck. It was a clear indication of what the Guru thought regarding a successor.

Consistent with the practices of Guru Nanak, who had advised Guru Angad to settle down at Khadur after his appointment as the second Guru, and Guru Angad, who had encouraged Guru Amar Das to reside at Goindwal, a time came when Guru Amar Das sent for Jetha and suggested that he set up a new township for himself. He had been endowed a *jagir* by the Emperor and it was the best way to make use of it. Accordingly, Jetha decided upon a vacant tract of land at a little distance from Goindwal and built a house for himself. He then started the digging of a tank. In due course, a big village grew around it.

When Guru Amar Das felt that his end was drawing near, he sent for Bhai Budha and other prominent Sikhs, including his two sons, Mohan and Mohri, and declared: "According to the tradition established by Guru Nanak, the leadership of the Sikhs must go to the most deserving. I, therefore, bestow this honor on Ram Das, known as Jetha." Everyone present, excepting Mohan, bowed his head in reverence. As the custom was, Bhai Budha was then asked by the Guru to apply the *tilak* on Guru Ram Das's forehead and the spiritual sovereignty passed on to the fourth Guru. Guru Ram Das became the image of Guru Amar Das, as Guru Amar Das was the image of Guru Angad, and Guru Angad was the image of Guru Nanak himself. It was the same spirit passing from one Guru to the other. Guru Ram Das was appointed the fourth Sikh Guru in 1574.

There was great rejoicing. Everyone was happy except Mohan, the Guru's son, who felt that he had been denied his birthright. In the meanwhile, Bibi Bhani, too, created a complication. In a moment of fatherly exuberance, the Guru once told Bibi Bhani, "Ask anything you desire and it shall be given unto you." The mother in Bibi Bhani said, "If you are kind, the spiritual leadership should now remain in my family." The Guru hesitated, but he had given his word. He told Bibi Bhani, "Your progeny will be revered by the world. You will be the mother of a universal savior but, since you have plugged the free flow of Guru's light, there will be unpleasantness and heart-burning at every step."

Considering that it was at the ripe old age of seventy-three that Guru Amar Das had become the Guru, his achievements during his tenure are considerable. By this time the Sikhs had emerged as a distinctive community. Amar Das sent out his emissaries to various parts of the country with a view to consolidating Guru Nanak's followers into a well-knit brotherhood. Those who came to pay homage to him were properly looked after. The free kitchen, called *Guru da Langar,* became a permanent feature of the Guru's head-quarters. He provided the pilgrims a baoli and other amenities. He ensured that timber was available in the town for those who wished to settle in Goindwal permanently. The mischievous elements amongst the Muslims in the town, who harassed his Sikhs, were left to God for punishment. Similarly, when the orthodox Hindus complained to the king that Guru Amar Das was violating their time-honored practices by rejecting Sanskrit and decrying their rituals and religious practices, he listened to the kings' suggestion and agreed to visit Hindu places of pilgrimage, since he found God everywhere. The king, on his part, went out of his way to exempt the Guru and whosoever followed him, from the pilgrim tax. It is said that wherever the Guru went, he attracted large crowds. The Guru's slogan *Sat Nam Sri Wahguru* resounded all over. He lived a simple life, eating two frugal meals a day, though it is said his langar offered all sorts of dainties for pilgrims. He spoke Punjabi and propagated his message in the language of the people. In view of his age, he didn't do much travelling excepting a brief visit to Hardwar and other Hindu pilgrim centers, but he visualized the setting up of a premier Sikh center with a holy tank at Amritsar. A beginning towards this was made in his lifetime, though the main project was left to his successor, Guru Ram Das, to complete.

His teachings were as simple as his way of life.

Mere reading of the Vedas, the Shastras, and the Puranas can lead one nowhere, it is the Guru who can show the way.

The Smritis and the Shastras talk about good and evil.
But they know not the truth,
They know not the truth,
Without the Guru they know not the truth.

Pilgrimages, penance, or the rituals of the Hindus were all right for
the three ages—Satyug, Dwaparyug and Tretayug; they would,
however, not do for the Kaliyug. It is the Name alone that can earn
salvation in this age.

The Guru helps those who have endurance. God rewards patience.
If anyone ill-treats you, bear it once, twice, thrice. God will Himself
intervene on your behalf the fourth time.

A yogi does not become holy by donning garb and wearing
earrings:

Wear the rings of humility on your ears,
And let compassion be your ascetic's garb,
The fear of death be your ashes.
This is how you'll conquer the three worlds, O Yogi!

There is no place particularly pure or impure. Where God is
remembered, the place becomes sanctified:

The fire, the wind, and the water are impure,
Impure is whatever is eaten,
There is impurity in rituals and in worship,
Only he who remembers God is pure.

One must serve God alone. It is the service of the men of God that
brings liberation. After one has prepared food, one must feed the holy
men and then eat it himself:

Serve God and none other.
His service alone will get you your heart's desire.
All other service is of no avail.

The Guru counselled the Sikhs on the day-to-day problems that they brought to him. Those who used to consult astrologers before undertaking any new venture he advised that the most favorable time is when a Sikh prays to God. One must invoke God even before starting to eat meals. Women must not wear veils; they are in no way inferior to men. One must not look at another's wife with covetous eyes. One must avoid evil company. One must not be conceited and should not glorify oneself. One should forswear slander and false-hood. One should eat and work according to one's capacity; over-eating is bad, equally bad is not doing one's duty. One must give a little of one's earnings in charity. One should associate with virtuous people and should help and entertain strangers.

Though a number of miracles have been attributed to Guru Amar Das, there are also instances to show that he did not approve of them. He wished his Sikhs to accept the will of God and not to interfere in His ways. It is said that one Girdhari, a rich Sikh from the South, who had been married for many years, came to the Guru and wished to be blessed with a child. He had been married for many years and didn't have progeny. He took a second wife but remained childless. The Guru heard him and said, "No one can undo what's written in one's fate." The Guru advised him to do good deeds, remember God, and obey His will. Girdhari's eyes were filled with tears. Evidently, his prayer had not been heard. As he was leaving the Guru's *darbar* he happened to meet a Sikh by the name of Paro. He was a great favorite of the Guru. Taking pity on him, Paro said, "If you have faith, you should have five children." It is said that, in due course, Girdhari had five children. He brought them to the Guru. When the Guru came to know how he had been blessed with five children, he sent for Paro and reprimanded him. Bhai Paro, who had done so out of compassion for a Guru's Sikh, asked Guru Amar Das's forgiveness.

But then, as the Guru himself had said, saints are unaffected by joy and sorrow, as the lotus remains unaffected by water.

Like Guru Angad, Guru Amar Das had more copies of Guru Nanak and Guru Angad's *bani* made, to which he added his own for use at the various *manjis* he had set up all over the country.

In Guru Amar Das we have another major step towards the consolidation of the Sikh community by inculcating in the Guru's followers the virtues of clean living and service of the people in a spirit of humility and devotion to God.

Selected Hymns of Guru Amar Das

1. If one were to look for the hour
   At what hour should one say one's prayers?
   Remembering Him day and night
   You become truthful and get to know the True One.
   If the lover is forgotten for a moment,
   No prayer avails.
   With the mind and heart devoted to Him in earnest
   Not a breath goes to waste.
   Man! Meditate on Him,
   True prayer is possible only
   If God dwells in one's heart.

   (Sri Rag)

2. Listen, O cupid-smitten maiden!
   Why do you flaunt yourself the way you do?
   You haven't cultivated your own spouse,
   With what face will you go to Him?
   Those who know their Master
   I bow before them.
   I would like to be like them,
   Meeting them in the company of godmen.
   O you thoughtless one! Lost in falsehood and untruth
   The truly charming Lord one finds alone with the wisdom of
      the Guru.

   (Sri Rag)

3. Passion is killed by controlling the mind.
   He who kills it not cannot attain God.
   Not many know how to control the mind.
   He knows it who kills it with the Word.
   He who is blessed is honored.
   With the Guru's grace, God dwells in one's mind.
   The man of God does good deeds.
   This is how he understands the mind.
   The egoist is like an intoxicated elephant,
   The Guru revives him with the driving rod.
   The mind is uncontrollable, not many control it.

He who controls the uncontrollable
Cleanses himself.
The man of God disciplines his mind
By shedding vanity and vice.
Those who have been blessed with the union
Part not; they are absorbed in the Word.
God alone knows His ways
Says Nanak, the man of God knows Him by meditating on
   Him.

(Gauri)

4. Serve God, serve none other than God.
Serving God fulfills one's heart's desire.
Any other service is a waste of time.
God is my tradition of love,
God is the story of romance.
With God's grace I am absorbed in Him.
This has become my way of life.
God is my Smriti, God is my Shastra.
God is my friend, God is my brother.
I hunger for God and God's name satisfies my hunger.
God is my relation who'll help me in the end.
Without God everything else is false,
While leaving, it doesn't go with one
God is my riches that accompany me,
They go where I go.
He is false who is devoted to false values.
Says Nanak, it's all God's pleasure
None else may interfere with His ways.

(Gujri)

5. Neither going on pilgrimage to Kasi makes one
     knowledgeable,
Nor not going on pilgrimage to Kasi leaves one ignorant.
Knowledge comes only by meeting the true Guru,
And the man is enlightened.
O man! Listen to what God says with devotion.
When you meditate on Him, all wavering ceases.
With the memory of his feet in your heart

All sins are washed away.
He who controls the five temptations
Finds himself residing in a place of pilgrimage.
The egoist is foolish who understands it not.
He remembers not God's Name and repents in the end.
The mind is Kasi, other places of pilgrimage are smritis.
The True Guru has revealed it to me.
The sixty-eight places of pilgrimage are within him
Who remembers God.
Says Nanak, meeting the true Guru
One starts understanding God's ways.
And God alone dwells in his heart.
Whatever pleases Him is right,
He who is devoted to the True One.

(Gujri)

6. Maya is like the snake—It has ensnared the world.
    He who serves her
    She bites him in return.
    The holy one knows the antidote,
    He cleans the dirt sticking to the feet thoroughly.
    Says Nanak, only they are evolved
    Who remain devoted to truth.

(Gujri)

7. Vanity and God's Name are opposites,
    Both can't dwell at one place.
    The vain cannot serve God,
    His heart remains empty.
    Man! You must remember God.
    And meditate on the Word.
    He who listens to God gets close to Him.
    His vanity vanishes from within him.
    This world is all vanity.
    It's born out of vanity.
    Vanity is like pitch darkness;
    No one can see anything in vanity.
    One cannot pray in vanity.
    The vain don't understand God.

Vanity is a blind spot of the mind.
God's Name won't dwell in it.
Say's Nanak, meeting the True Guru vanity goes,
And understanding of truth is gained.
He who is true lives truthfully,
He is given to the service of the True One.

(Wadhans)

8. Finding the world on fire
   I ran for God's protection.
   I prayed to the Great Guru
   To save me with His grace
   And take me in His charge,
   And bless me with the honor of His Name.
   There is none like God.
   Those who serve Him are blessed.
   They get to know God who is Eternal.
   Without the Guru's help,
   Controlling passions, good deeds, truthful and moderate
       living
   Fail to obtain salvation.
   Says Nanak, only he understands the Word
   Who seeks refuge in God.

(Wadhans)

9. God! You protect the man of God ever.
   You have done so ever and ever.
   You have saved men like Prahlad
   And destroyed Hiranyakashya.
   The men of God alone get to know you.
   The egoist is misled by false beliefs.
   God! You are known for Your greatness.
   Master! give protection to Your devotees.
   Those who came to You for favors
   Let them not be plagued with death.
   Let the god of death not stare at them.
   Remembering the Name they attain salvation,
   They attain power to work miracles,
   With the Guru's abiding grace.

(Sorath)

10. O fool! You are collecting false wealth,
    You are conceited, misled, and blindfolded.
    Worldly wealth is always painful;
    Neither can one keep it nor can one carry it away.
    True wealth is gained by the Guru's guidance,
    False wealth comes and goes.
    Those who are conceited go astray and die a wretched death.
    They drown in the ocean,
    They are neither here nor there.
    Fortunate are those who adore God,
    Who are devoted to truth, and who long for Him day and
        night.
    The ambrosial Name is true in the four ages.
    A man meditates on the Name with good luck alone.
    Those who work miracles and the ascetics yearn for Him.
    He is obtained only with good luck.
    He who understands the great Brahma
    He becomes truthful and finds truth everywhere.
    It is the True One who inculcates Truth.
    Says Nanak, He sees Himself and fosters truth Himself.

    (Bilawal)

11. Forgive my past sins and show me the path now,
    Killing my ego, I should remain in God's service.
    Man of God! You should remember His Name
    Remain in His service always
    Loving Him alone, devoted to Him alone.
    I have neither high caste nor honor,
    Neither a dwelling nor a shelter.
    Understanding the Word many doubts are resolved.
    The Guru has inculcated His Name in me.
    The mind is greedy and lost in greed.
    He is involved in evil deeds
    And perishes in the town of death.
    Says Nanak, He is all-powerful
    There is none other like Him.
    He blesses with the gift of prayer
    And the devotee is ever happy.

    (Maru)

12. It is good karmas alone that lead to the true Guru.
    He is not attained without good karma.
    A meeting with the True Guru purifies one;
    It takes place if ordained by God.
    Man! You should meditate on God.
    The True One is reached with the help of the Guru.
    And one identifies oneself with Him.
    The True Guru gives the understanding and dispels doubts.
    The True Guru reveals God and saves from transmigration.
    He who is blessed by the Guru lives in death,
    Meditating on the Word he attains immortality.
    He reaches the gate of deliverance
    Who annihilates his ego.
    With Guru's blessings he is born in God's own house.
    He is free from all temptation.
    He controls what is not controllable with superior wisdom.
    He meets God with the help of the Guru.

    (Malhar)

13. I sin a lot, there is no end to my misdeeds.
    God! Save me with Your grace, I am a great sinner.
    God! According to my karma, my turn will never come.
    It must be Your grace that can lead me to You.
    The kind Guru led me to God
    Washing all my sins and evil deeds away.
    Those who remember God—Says Nanak, they are honored.

    (Shloka)

Guru Ram Das

Guru Ram Das, a beloved of God, went to God's own city.
He gave him a throne and seated him on it.

—*Mathura*

"You are Nanak, you are Lehna, you are Amar Das . . .," Satta
the minstrel sang when Guru Ram Das succeeded as the fourth Guru
of the Sikhs. The same spirit moved from Guru Nanak to his
successors, so that to not a few, they appeared to be one another's
images. When Baba Sri Chand, one of the two sons of Guru Nanak
who had turned an *Udasi* (a recluse) and roamed all over the country,
came to see Guru Ram Das, he was supposed to have been struck by
the Guru's close resemblance to his own father. He looked at the
saintly beard of Guru Ram Das and observed, "Why do you have such
a long flowing beard?" Guru Ram Das knew it was the old grouse
and not curiosity that prompted Baba Sri Chand to ask this question.
He replied in all humility, "It's to wipe your feet with." Sri Chand
felt embarrassed. He realized that it was humility that had won for
the devotees, one after the other, the high honor that had been denied
to him.

Guru Ram Das was the son of Hari Das, a Khatri of Sodhi
subcaste, and Anup Devi, known as Daya Kaur, who lived in Chuna
Mandi in Lahore. They were God-fearing and led a simple life. After
twelve long years of prayers, they were blessed with a son in 1534. He
was formally given the name of Ram Das, though he was popularly
known as Jetha—the first born. Jetha was fair of complexion and
extremely handsome. When he grew up, he was always found in the
company of holy men. His parents were keen that he should take to
some worthwhile avocation, so that he could earn his living like

92

everyone else. Accordingly, at the instance of a neighbor who used to peddle roasted gram, Daya Kaur prepared a bagful of roasted gram and gave it to Jetha to go out and sell. Jetha went to the bank of the river Ravi and fed the gram to a band of yogis who had eaten nothing that day. He then came across a party of Sikhs who were proceeding to Goindwal to pay homage to Guru Amar Das, the third Sikh Guru. Instead of going back home, Jetha joined the Sikhs and came to Goindwal.

Guru Amar Das at once noticed this young man with his pleasant bearing and his sense of devotion. "If you have come seeking, then true sovereignty awaits you." The Guru gave him spiritual assurance. And while the rest of his companions returned to Lahore, Jetha stayed back to serve Guru Amar Das. He unfailingly attended to the Guru's personal comforts. Besides, he was always willing to give a helping hand wherever it was needed, be it in the kitchen or at the baoli among those engaged in the excavation. He won every heart with his hard labor and godliness, including Guru Amar Das himself. It was his devotion that earned him the hand of the Guru's younger daughter, Bibi Bhani. Even when he became the Guru's son-in-law, he continued to be as devoted to him as ever. He stayed back at Goindwal and served the Guru as a humble slave. When Akbar invited Guru Amar Das to his court, the Guru deputed Jetha and he acquitted himself most creditably at the Mughal court. With his knowledge of Hindu mythology and Vedic lore, he convinced the Emperor that Guru Amar Das never had any intention to malign the Hindu faith; he was only trying to make people understand the true meaning of life. Only the body is cleansed when one bathes in sacred rivers like the Ganga, the Jamuna, or the Godavari. For the mind to become pure, one has to be with saints and men of God. The Hindus believed in the caste system; according to them, some are born high while others are born low. The Guru believed that all are born equal. It is only our deeds that determine whether we are high or low, good or bad. The Emperor was convinced that the Guru stood for a healthy approach to life and he did not malign any particular religion. Akbar, who was an exponent of Din-i-Ilahi, a new religion trying to combine in itself the best of Hinduism and Islam, found in the Guru's teachings something essentially close to his way of thinking.

After he had been ordained as the Guru, Ram Das started building a new township on the *jagir* gifted to Bibi Bhani by Akbar. But till Guru Amar Das' death, he stayed in Goindwal most of the time. This new township is what came to be known as Amritsar.

The name Amritsar, by which the premier seat of the Sikh community is known even today, is derived from the holy tank called Amritsar—the pool of nectar, around which the township grew. There is an extraordinary story about how people discovered the miraculous powers of this tank, which, it is said, used to be a small neglected pond near Patti, an old settlement. The *kardar*, or revenue collector, of Patti had five daughters, all five of them charming and talented. The youngest one was deeply religious—devoting a great deal of her time to prayers. She enjoyed meeting holy men. Her father, an arrogant government official, scoffed at her piety.

In due course, her elder sisters were married. For the youngest one who always said, "God is the Cherisher of us all," a suitable match was yet to be found, and the father didn't seem to be bothered about it. Whenever her mother reminded him about it, he reacted in anger and scorn, "Let God cherish her."

The father, however, could not deflect his daughter from her belief. In a fit of temper the father married her to a crippled leper. The girl, instead of feeling broken, accepted her fate patiently. When they had to travel, she even had a basket made to carry her husband in. On their way once, they came to the pond near Patti. The young bride, wanting to collect food for herself and her husband, put her husband under a tree and went away to the nearby village. The leper, to his great amazement, saw a pair of crows come and dip down into the pond and turn into swans and fly away. He, perceiving what had happened, struggled out of the basket, and crawled to the pond. The moment he dipped into the water, he was no longer the leper he had been. When his wife returned from the village, she was most disturbed by this new presence. She wouldn't believe a word of the story of his transformation. She thought the young man standing before her had maliciously done away with her husband to grab hold of her. She wailed and protested and went to Guru Ram Das who was, at the time, supervising the digging of the tank on the other side of the pool. Even when the Guru explained the miracle to her, she would not believe. As it happened, the young man had not dipped one of his fingers in the pond water. This finger remained stricken with leprosy. At the Guru's instance he dipped the finger in the pond and at once it became normal, and as healthy as the rest of the young man's body. The girl went away with her husband a happy bride.

Bhai Gurdas, the noted scholar and poet, came to Guru Ram Das seeking his blessings and requesting his formal initiation as a Sikh. Greatly moved by his devotion and humility, the Guru asked Bhai Gurdas to proceed to Agra and look after the spiritual needs of the Sikhs there. Before he left, the Guru prescribed the following routine for his followers there:

> He who calls himself a Sikh of the True Guru
> He must get up in the morning and say his prayers.
> He must rise in the early hours and bathe in the holy tank.
> He must meditate on God as advised by the Guru.
> And rid himself of the afflictions of sins and evil.
> As the day dawns, he should recite scriptures
> And repeat God's name in every activity.
> He to whom the Guru takes kindly is shown the path.
> Nanak! I seek the dust of the feet of the Guru's Sikh
> Who himself remembers God and makes others remember Him.
>
> *(Gauri)*

In the meanwhile, the Sikhs were busy day and night completing Amritsar—the holy tank of nectar. Pilgrims came from far and near and joined in the work. The small hut that the Guru built close to the tank was expanded in due course. It is known as the Guru's Mahl (palace) now.

Though the Sikhs did not spare any effort, the construction of the holy tank needed a large contingent of hired labor, which meant lots of funds. The Guru sent out his agents to various parts of the country to collect contributions for the construction of the holy tank and maintenance of the free kitchens. These agents came to be known as *masands*. The Guru was called *Sacha Padshah*—the true king. The *masands* returned with a large fund and the completion of the holy tank was expedited.

An aged couple came to the Guru and prayed to be blessed with a son. The Guru told them that nobody could change the course of destiny. The old couple persisted, saying that they knew they were not destined to have a son. They wanted the Guru to intercede. Touched by this unshakable faith, Guru Ram Das said, "Well, I was to have had four sons, I'll give one to you and I shall have three instead." And soon a son was born to the old couple. He was named Bhagtu.

Along with the holy tank, a settlement came up rapidly and it was called Ramdaspur—the abode of Ram Das. Later this acquired a new name, Amritsar—the city of the holy tank, as it is still known.

One of the Guru's cousins, Sahari Mal, came to invite him to visit Lahore in connection with the marriage of his son. The Guru was much too preoccupied with the construction of the holy tank. It was an assignment made to him by Guru Amar Das and he wished to complete the work in his lifetime. He therefore called his eldest son Prithi Chand and asked him to go with Sahari Mal to Lahore. Prithi Chand feared that his father was, perhaps, trying to eliminate him in order to install his youngest brother Arjan as Guru. Arjan was a great favorite of his father. Also, once it so happened that while the grandfather was eating, Arjan crawled into his room as a baby and tried to share his meal. The Sikh attending the Guru carried the baby away but he reappeared after a little while. He was again forbidden by the Sikh and removed from the Guru's chamber. When the baby persisted in entering the room the third time, the Guru said, "Here, you may have the tray that you must inherit one day." The Sikhs attending the Guru heard this and picked up the baby in reverence. Evidently, it was an indication that the baby would grow up to become the Guru one day. Prithi Chand, who knew all this, refused to go to Lahore.

The Guru then called his second son Mahadev. He, too, declined to oblige on some pretext. At this, Arjan, the youngest son, was summoned and apprised of the problem. He took no time to make up his mind to go to Lahore and participate in the wedding as desired by his revered father. As he was leaving for Lahore, the Guru told Arjan to take charge of the Dharmasala at Lahore and not to return until he was sent for. During one of his earlier visits to Lahore, Guru Ram Das had converted his ancestral house into a Dharmasala and he was keen that it should become popular with the Lahore Sikhs who congregated there for meditation and prayer.

Arjan had been gone to Lahore for several months and the Guru seemed to have forgotten all about him. There was no news from the Guru. As days and weeks passed, Arjan started feeling intensely homesick. He had already spent more than two years waiting for a call. At last he composed a poem and sent it to his father through a servant:

> I long to see the Guru
> My heart cries like a Chatrik bird.
> Its thirst is not quenched nor is it still
> Denied the sight of the beloved Saint.
> I am sacrifice, I am sacrifice again
> For a glimpse of the beloved saint.
>
> *(Majh)*

When the messenger reached his destination, the Guru happened to be resting. However Prithi Chand, recognizing the servant from Lahore, inquired what brought him there. The messenger innocently told him that he had a letter from Arjan for the Guru. Prithi Chand took the letter and, assuring him that he would pass it on to the Guru, dismissed the servant. He opened and read the letter. Fearing that the moment the Guru saw the letter he would send for Arjan, Prithi Chand decided to withhold it and sent word to Arjan on behalf of his father that he should continue to stay at Lahore a little longer.

Several months passed and still there was no news. Arjan then composed another poem and sent it to his father:

> You've a charming face, the melody of your word is enchanting.
> It's ages that the *Sarang* bird has seen water.
> Blessed is the place where you dwell,
> My dear friend and lord.
> I am sacrifice, I am sacrifice again to my friend and lord. (2)
>
> *(Majh)*

Prithi Chand, who was on the lookout for the messenger from

Lahore constantly, intercepted this letter also. He returned the messenger again with a message purported to be from the Guru that Arjan
should continue to stay at Lahore and that the Guru would himself
come to Lahore shortly, when he could accompany him on his return
journey.

Again for several months Arjan waited for the Guru's promised
visit to Lahore but there was no news about it. In the meanwhile, he
was feeling desperate. He longed to have a glimpse of his father, the
Master. Arjan composed yet another piece and sent it to the Guru,
making sure that the message this time was delivered to him personally by the messenger and to no one else:

A moment's separation and it was like an age.
When do I see you now, my beloved Lord?
My night doesn't pass, nor do I get sleep
Without seeing the Guru's darbar.
I am a sacrifice, I am a sacrifice again to the true darbar of the
    Guru (3)

(Majh)

Since it was the third letter, this fact was duly indicated at the end
of the composition by the figure 3. When the Guru read it, he wanted
to know about the earlier two compositions. The messenger said that
he had been delivering these to Prithi Chand. The Guru summoned
Prithi Chand immediately. He, however, denied having any knowledge about the earlier communications. At this, the Guru sent an
attendant to Prithi Chand's quarters asking him to fetch the papers
lying in the pocket of a garment that hung from a peg in a particular
room.

Prithi Chand was humiliated for his treachery. He had no excuse to
offer. Guru Ram Das sent for Bhai Budha and asked him go to Lahore
to bring Arjan with all honors back home. On arrival, Arjan recited
the following composition in gratitude:

I am blessed having met the Saint Guru.
I find God Immortal in my own house.
I serve Him and won't be separated again.

Nanak! I am your slave.
I am a sacrifice, I am a sacrifice again to
Nanak whose slave I am. (4)

(Majh)

Everyone present was thrilled to hear the song. The Guru embraced his son. He then ordained Arjan as the next Guru, inviting Bhai Budha to apply the *tilak* on his forehead. As one candle is lighted with another, the divine light travelling from Guru Nanak to Guru Angad, from Guru Angad to Guru Amar Das, and from Guru Amar Das to Guru Ram Das, it now came to Guru Arjan, the fifth Guru of the Sikhs.

Prithi Chand didn't accept Guru Arjan as the Guru and continued to misbehave and abuse the Guru and everyone else for denying him what he considered to be his birthright. Since he would not see reason, Guru Ram Das had to condemn him publicly.

Shortly thereafter, Guru Ram Das felt that his end was not far. He sent for his family and his Sikhs, and taking their leave, closed his eyes not to open them again. It was in the year 1581.

Guru Ram Das was barely forty-seven years old when he left this world. He had been the fourth Sikh Guru for barely seven years when he chose his youngest son Guru Arjan Dev as his successor.

It is a mark of his humility that, apart from the 679 hymns in which he sang of his devotion to his Guru, he has left little record about his own person.

Efforts had been afoot since Guru Nanak's time to rid Hindu society of the rituals and the stranglehold of the priestly classes. The mass of people were soaked in superstitions and the privileged classes exploited their ignorance. Guru Ram Das introduced social reforms, particularly in the wedding ceremony, making it a simple affair and endowing it with the sacrament of the holy word. He composed a long poem in four parts to be recited at the time of the ceremonial perambulation:

At the first round I dedicate myself to the Lord
To Whom I am a sacrifice!
I accept the word as Brahma and truth as the Vedas.

I remember dharma and meditate on the Name:
Repetition of Name leads to meditation.
Devotion to the True Guru helps wash away sins.
I have attained the spiritual stage of Sahj
And have started relishing His Name.
Nanak! This is how I have made a beginning in the first round.

With the second round, I meet the True Lord
To Whom I am a sacrifice!
I have become fearless and cleansed of the filth of ego.
I fear God the Pure, I sing His praises and feel His presence.
My Master is omnipresent and I see Him everywhere.
He is alone in and out, I meet him and I hail Him.
Nanak! With the second round I enjoy the bliss of ecstasy.

Excited at the third round, I care not for worldly love,
O Lord to whom I am a sacrifice.
With good luck I have found the saint who has led me to God.
I've come to God, the Pure, I sing His praises, I speak His language.
With good fortune I've found the saint.
I can now tell the tale that couldn't be told.
The melody has started sounding in my heart
And I repeat His Name, lucky that I am.
Says Nanak! With the third round I have shed all worldly
    attachments.

At the fourth round my spiritual stage of Sahj
Has led me to the Lord to Whom I am a sacrifice!
Blessed by Him I've become a *Gursikh*.
I love God from my heart and soul.
I love God, God loves my loving Him.
I meditate on Him day and night,
I've attained my heart's desire by singing His praises.
God Himself has made the beginning.
The bride is delighted remembering Him.
Nanak! with the fourth round, I've found God the ever-loving!
                                                    (Suhi)

Guru Ram Das could neither complete the holy tank nor start constructing the Golden Temple on its present site, because he left this world rather early in life.

Hymns of Guru Ram Das

1. Father! I am married;
    The devotee has found the Lord.
    The darkness of ignorance is dispelled;
    The Guru's wisdom has kindled the radiant light.
    The radiant light of the Guru's wisdom is kindled,
    And darkness is driven away.
    I have found the priceless jewel.
    The curse of ego is cured.
    No more do I suffer.
    The Guru's wisdom has killed my ego.
    I have found the Eternal Bridegroom.
    He never dies, He never departs.
    Father! I am married.
    The devotee has found the Lord.

    (Sri Rag)

2. God projects Himself in the world.
    He Himself gives life and takes it away.
    He Himself misleads and Himself shows the way.
    Not many devotees are blessed with the light of His
        knowledge.
    I am a sacrifice to them
    Who have found the Lord with the Guru's wisdom.
    Says Nanak, the lotus of their heart has blossomed,
    And the Lord comes to dwell in it.
    They remember God day and night.
    Man! You should hurry to receive God's protection,
    All your sins and sufferings will vanish.

    (Sri Rag)

3. The Pandit reads the Shastras and the Smritis,
    The Yogi shouts—Gorakh! Gorakh!
    I am unlettered, I repeat the Name of God.
    I know not what's in store for me.
    I repeat the Name of God
    To swim across the ocean of life.
    The ascetic besmears himself with ashes,

The celibate has little to do with women.
I am unlettered, God is my only hope.
The Kshatriya wins laurels with his exploits,
The Shudra and the Vaishya serve others.
I am unlettered, God's name alone can save me.
God! Yours is this creation,
You are everywhere.
Says Nanak, the devotee is glorified,
Eyeless that I am, God is my only support.

(Gauri)

4. The mother likes to see her son eat.
The fish likes to swim in water.
The true Guru likes to feed the devotee.
Lord, give me the company of men of God,
Meeting whom my sufferings end.
The way it pleases the cow to meet her calf,
The wife when her husband is at home,
The devotee is pleased when he sings God's praises.
The sarang likes it when it rains,
The sovereign likes to see riches around him,
The man of God when he can repeat His Name.
The man of the world likes it when he gathers wealth,
The Guru's Sikh likes it when he meets God in an embrace.
Nanak likes it if he can kiss the feet of the man of God.

(Gauri)

5. This township (of my body) is full of passion and choler.
It can be tidied in the company of godmen.
Good karmas alone lead one to the Guru,
And the man lives in the resplendence of God.
It's a great gift saluting Him with folded hands
It's a great gift prostrating before Him.
Those separated from God know not the joy of His presence.
They have the thorn of the ego pricking them.
As they walk it pricks more and more.
And they are tortured,
At the time of death they are lashed with a stick . . .
The men of God are lost in God's Name.

They are free from the agony of life and death,
And they cross the ocean of life.
I am a poor and humble slave of Yours,
You are the mighty God,
Please do protect me.
Says Nanak, he who has the support of His Name
Obtains all comforts from the Name.

(Gauri)

6. He who calls himself the Sikh of the Guru
    He must get up early and meditate on Him.
    He must be active in the morning
    And should take a dip in the pool of nectar.
    He must listen to the Guru's advice and remember God.
    All his sins and misdeeds are thus washed away.
    As day dawns, he should read scriptures
    And repeat His Name every moment of the day.
    The Guru likes the Sikhs who remember God every breath of
        their lives.

(Gauri)

7. He who nurses ill will for anyone,
    To him no good ever comes.
    No one listens to him,
    He cries all alone in the wilderness.
    He who is given to talking ill of others
    All his good deeds go to waste.
    Every time he indulges in running down his neighbor
    He fouls his mouth, he can't show his face to anyone.
    Karmas are the seeds sown in the field.
    Man reaps what he sows.
    No amount of talk helps.
    He who swallows poison must die.
    The true Creator does justice.
    As you do so is done to you.
    Guru Nanak had the knowledge of it,
    He talked to the world about the ways of God.

(Gauri)

8. You are pure, without a blemish
   Beyond understanding, beyond reach.
   Everyone remembers You.
   You are the True Creator.
   It's all Your creation.
   You maintain everyone,
   The saints remember You.
   You are the killer of pain.
   God Himself is the master.
   Himself He is the slave.
   Nanak, the poor is nobody.
   You live in every heart and mind,
   You are everywhere.
   Some are donors and others beggars.
   All these are Your manifestations.
   You are the giver and You are the taker.
   I know none other than You.
   You are the great Eternal Brahma.
   I fail to recount Your virtues.
   Those who serve You,
   Nanak is a sacrifice to them.
   Those who remember You
   Live a peaceful life.
   They attain salvation who dwell on You.
   Their noose of death is snapped.
   Those who remember the Fearless
   All their fears are shed.
   Those who remember my Lord
   They become one with Him.
   Blessed are they who remember You.
   Nanak is a sacrifice to them.
   God, the treasure of Your prayer is vast,
   It is limitless.
   Your devotees sing Your praises,
   There are many; there is no end to them.
   Many are there who worship You,

Undergo penance,
And meditate on You, the limitless.
Many are there who read the Smritis and the Shastras
And do good deeds, all six of them.
Says Nanak, the devotees are blessed
Who are dear to God.
You are the Endless Original Maker
There is none like You.
You remain the same from age to age.
You are the Eternal Creator.
What You like happens.
What pleases You takes place.
It's You who created the Universe,
It's You who destroys it after creation.
Nanak sings praises of the Creator
Who is the Knower of all.

(Asa)

9. To the True Guru and the Creator
The slave makes a prayer.
I am a humble creature come to You
Take pity and bestow on me the light of Your Name.
My well-wisher, my Guru,
Bless me with Your Name.
God's Name is the sustenance of my life,
My prayer is singing His praises.
Those who thirst for Him are blessed.
Their thirst is quenched with His Name.
They become virtuous in Godmen's company.
Those who have not attained God's Name
They are unfortunate,
They live in the neighborhood of death.
Those who do not come to the Guru or to the company of
    the holy ones
Are accursed and their life is accursed.
The devotees who seek the company of Godmen
Have it written in their lot from the beginning.
Blessed is the company of the men of God

Where one enjoys God's presence,
Says Nanak, it helps enlighten the mind.

(Gujri)

10. Where does one meet You, my Love?
    Men of God, pray, show me the way I should follow.
    I cherish the sayings of my Lord.
    This is the golden path,
    And I have found favor with the Master.
    Humbly, I have met my charming one.
    There is only one Lord.
    All of us belong to Him.
    She meets Him whom He favors.
    What can poor Nanak do?
    He only treads the path that pleases God.

(Devgandhari)

11. I am defeated everywhere
    And I come to You, my Lord.
    I seek Your protection.
    You may save me or destroy me.
    I have consigned to the flames
    Worldly wisdom and honor.
    People may talk good or ill of me.
    I have handed myself over to You.
    Those who come seeking Your protection
    You accept them in Your grace.
    Nanak has now come to You
    Lord, save his honor.

(Devgandhari)

12. He who brings me the message of my Lord
    I am a sacrifice to him, heart and soul.
    I serve him daily, fanning cool breeze and fetching water for
       him.
    I serve him day and night who talks to me about God.
    Blessed is the great Guru,
    Says Nanak, who fulfills my desires.

(Wadhans)

13. The man of God sings God's praises.

If someone were to talk ill of him
He is not bothered.
Whatever happens is ordained by the Master.
He does everything Himself:
He shows the path,
He teaches how to talk.
He created the Universe out of the five elements.
Himself He inducted the five passions in it.
Says Nanak, the True Guru arranges the union.
It is He who settles all argument.

(Bairadi)

14. When you call Him
God comes to your help like a friend.
With the Guru's grace, He lives in your heart.
He is not attained in any other way.
Man, you should collect the riches of His Name
So that He helps you in the hour of need.
God's Name is earned in the company of men of God.
There is no other way to gain God's Name.
He who trades in God's Name profits by it.
Those who deal in false goods
They never attain God.

(Suhi)

15. All our efforts and all our triumphs flow from Him.
I would do if I could do.
I cannot do anything on my own.
I act as God wishes me to act.
God! everything is in Your hands
I dare not do anything.
Let me live in Your grace, the way You please.
You gave me body, You gave me soul,
You made me work.
I do as You desire,
The way You have written in my lot from the very
    beginning.
You created the universe with five elements.

There are some whom You show the way under Your
    guidance.
There are those who are full of ego and they cry.
It's not in my lot to sing God's praises.
I am foolish, stupid, and mean.
Says, Nanak, pardon me, O God!
I seek Your protection.

(Suhi)

16. I crave to see my Lord,
    Like an arrow the Guru's Word has pricked my heart.
    It is He Who knows the agony.
    Who else would know the affliction of others?
    I am enamoured of my Guru,
    I am helpless, I can't restrain myself more.
    I search for Him the world over.
    I love to see my Lord God.
    I would make an offering of my heart and soul
    To him who could show me the way to my God.

(Bilawal)

17. Lord! Pardon my past sins and show me the way.
    I come to You for protection, shedding my ego.
    The man of God must remember God
    And remain in His protection forever and ever
    With single-minded devotion.
    I have no respect, I belong not to a high caste,
    I have no home, no place to go to,
    The Word has removed all my doubts.
    The Guru himself has bestowed this upon me.
    One who is avaricious dies in avarice,
    He is lost in false promises
    And is punished in the town of death.
    Says Nanak, He is everywhere
    There is none like Him.
    He bestows the gift of devotion on men of God.
    And the Guru's Sikhs are ever happy.

(Maru)

18. With good karmas alone one meets God,
    Without good karmas He can't be met.
    One becomes gold if one meets God
    But then it is ordained by God Himself.
    Man! You must devote yourself to God.
    You reach the True One through the true Guru;
    This is how one merges in Him.
    The true Guru gives the light
    And doubts are dispelled.
    The true Guru gives the understanding
    And one attains salvation.
    With the Guru's grace one does good deeds.
    He who is reborn meditates on the Word
    He is free from life and death and gives up his ego.
    With Guru's grace is one born in the house of God.
    Killing all the temptations of the world,
    He controls the uncontrollable and gains sovereign
        knowledge.
    And man merges into Eternal Man.

                                        (Malhar)

Guru Arjan

This grandson of mine
Will cruise people
Across the ocean of life.

—*Guru Amar Das*

Guru Arjan was born at Goindwal in 1563. He was the youngest son of Bhai Jetha (later Guru Ram Das) and Bibi Bhani. It is said that there was unusual rejoicing at his birth. It surprised not a few since the newborn was only the third son of the Guru's daughter, whereas his two sons Mohan and Mohri had also been married and not much notice had ever been taken when they had their children. Guru Amar Das was extremely fond of Arjan, who as a child was always hovering around him. It is said that once when the Guru was having his siesta in the afternoon, young Arjan quietly slipped into his room and woke him up. Nobody ever disturbed the Guru during his afternoon nap, since he got up very early in the morning for his meditation and prayers. The attendant was nervous and ran to pick up the child from the Guru's chamber. The Guru forbade him and observed, *"Eh mera dohta bani da bohta hovega*—This grandson of mine will cruise people across the ocean of life."

As predicted, when the time came for Guru Ram Das to retire, Arjan was ordained the next Guru.

However, Prithi Chand, Guru Arjan's eldest brother, did not accept him as his father's successor. On the passing away of Guru Ram Das, according to a custom prevalent among the Khatris of the time, when Mohri invested Guru Arjan with the turban, Prithi Chand objected to it vehemently. As the eldest son of Guru Ram Das, he maintained it was he who ought to have been offered the turban.

111

When Guru Arjan came to know of it, he lost no time in presenting the turban to him. Not only this, he also left Goindwal for his new township to avoid any further irritation.

But Prithi Chand was not reconciled. He started intriguing and conspiring against the Guru. Guru Arjan didn't take much notice of him; he was busy completing the holy tanks of Santokhsar and Amritsar and other jobs left unfinished by Guru Ram Das. It is said that while the excavation at Santokhsar was in progress, the diggers chanced upon a tiny hut in which they found a yogi squatting in deep contemplation. He was brought out immediately and given a massage. After a little while, he regained consciousness and was delighted to meet Guru Arjan. He said that ages ago he had pleased his guru, who had blessed him and said, "You will meet Guru Arjan in the Kaliyug and attain deliverance at his hands." He had been in meditation ever since then.

Santokhsar was completed in 1588. Guru Arjan then devoted his attention to the completion of Amritsar, the tank of nectar. He had the foundation stone of Harimandir—later known as the Golden Temple—also laid. The Sikhs desired that it should be the tallest building in the town. The Guru, however, thought otherwise. He reminded his followers that there was no virtue like humility. The temple was, therefore, built on as low an elevation as possible. He also decided to have the new temple open on all four sides. Anyone could enter it from any side. No one might be discriminated against. To lay the foundation stone of the temple, the Guru invited Mian Mir, a Muslim divine from Lahore. With the resources and dedication of the Sikhs, the construction of the holy tank and the temple made rapid progress. The Guru sang in joy:

God Himself came to participate
And gave His hand in Godmen's task.
He poured nectar in the blessed tank built in the blessed land.
He poured nectar and completed the job,
A dream has come true.
The whole world is hailing.
All fears are set at rest.
He is all-powerful with ever-living presence;

The Vedas and the Puranas sing His praises.
God has blessed His devotee Nanak
Who meditated on His Name.

(Suhi)

When the holy tank was completed, with his characteristic humility, Guru Arjan gave the entire credit for it to Guru Ram Das:

A dip in the tank of Ram Das—
All my sins are washed away.
A dip and I am clean all over
I've been blessed by God Himself.

(Sorath)

Prithi Chand continued to pester the Guru. He therefore decided to leave Amritsar and go out on an extensive tour and meet his disciples in various towns of the Punjab. He visited Khadur, Goindwal, Sarhali, Bhaini, Khanpur, Taran Taran, Lahore, Dera Baba Nanak, and several other places. During his tour, he laid the foundation stone of Kartarpur, a new township near Jullundur. He had also a well, called Ganga Sagar, dug in the town. It is said that a man called Baisakhi came to see the Guru while on his way to Hardwar, which he visited every year on pilgrimage. The Guru told him that taking a bath with the water of the well recently dug in the town could also clean him if he cared. Water anywhere comes from the same source.

Baisakhi would not listen to it. He had been going to Hardwar annually for several years and he didn't want to miss the pilgrimage that year. The Guru kept quiet. However, after some months when the pilgrim returned, he complained that the day he was leaving Hardwar his pilgrim's vessel was lost in the Ganges so that he couldn't bring the holy water for the Guru. At this, it is said, the Guru walked up to the new well and pulled out Baisakhi's vessel which had slipped from his hands and had been lost in the Ganga. Baisakhi was astonished to see the vessel, his name etched on it. He realized the true meaning of pilgrimage.

Guru Arjan returned to Amritsar after several months. Prithi Chand was still bitter and the Guru was at a loss to know how to

appease him. Arjan had no son. Prithi Chand hoped that his own son
Mehrban would have a chance to succeed as guru. But disappointment
was in store for him here also. Finding his wife keen to have a child,
Guru Arjan asked her to go to Bhai Budha for his blessing. Bhai Budha
was revered by the Sikhs and the Guru alike.

It was a tremendous expression of humility on the part of the Guru
to send his wife to ask the blessing of a Sikh but she did as she was
advised. Accompanied by her attendants, she went in a procession to
Bhai Budha, who lived in a jungle outside the town. It is said that
Bhai Budha didn't approve of all the fanfare. Far from blessing the
Guru's wife, he didn't even touch the delicacies she had brought as an
offering to him. She was utterly disappointed. When the Guru came
to know of it, he told her to go again with simple food cooked with
her own hands and with the humility of a devotee. The next day she
did accordingly.

Bhai Budha was delighted to partake of her simple fare and, while
crushing the onion with his fist, said, "The son that you will have will
crush the enemies the way I have crushed the onion. He will be a great
sportsman, fond of hunting; he will ride royal horses and wear two
swords. He will possess both spiritual and temporal powers."

Prithi Chand in the meanwhile cultivated Sulhi Khan, a revenue
officer of the Mughal court, and instigated him to raid Amritsar on
the pretext of collecting tax dues. Guru Arjan's wife was expecting a
baby now. He therefore retired to a village close by, leaving Amritsar
to Prithi Chand to settle accounts with Sulhi Khan. During his stay at
Wadali, Guru Arjan found that due to scarcity of water the people of
the village were put to a great deal of inconvenience. He had a huge
well dug with the voluntary help of the Sikhs. It was large enough to
accommodate six Persian wheels. The place has since come to be
known as Chhehrata—the town of six Persian wheels. It was at
Wadali that a son was born to Guru Arjan in 1595. There was great
rejoicing in Amritsar at the happy event. To commemorate Bhai
Budha's blessings, a fair is held every year in the forest where he used
to live. Childless women who come to participate in the congregation
held on the occasion of the fair are believed to be blessed with
children. The more the Sikhs rejoiced on the birth of Hargobind—
that was the name of the child—the more unhappy Prithi Chand

became. Even his wife Karmo lost her peace of mind. The only hope left to them was to have the newborn killed somehow. Accordingly, they took an old family nurse into confidence and, promising her a rich reward, sent her to Wadali. She had her nipples smeared with poison. Obviously she was looking for an opportunity to suckle the newborn and poison him to death.

However, the moment this woman took the child in her lap, she fainted. The poison applied on her nipples seemed to have affected her. The Guru had her immediately attended to and her life was saved. When she came to her senses, she confessed her guilt.

Prithi Chand was still undeterred. After some time, he got a snake charmer to release a poisonous serpent in Guru Arjan's courtyard where the child normally played. The toddler, it is said, picked up the snake and started playing with it.

Devotees came from distant places to Amritsar to pay their homage to the Guru and, not finding him there, were greatly disappointed. The Sikhs of the town, therefore, came to the Guru in a delegation and persuaded him to return to the holy city, ignoring what Prithi Chand continued to do.

After a while Hargobind was stricken with a severe attack of smallpox and Prithi Chand's hopes were revived. Prithi Chand was sure that the child would not survive. But Hargobind recovered from the malady, once again disappointing his uncle.

The only hope for Karmo's son to succeed Guru Arjan was the elimination of Hargobind, and Prithi Chand was persistent in his design. He now bribed a domestic servant in the Guru's household to poison the milk the child took. Once again Prithi Chand failed. The child refused to take the milk the servant offered. When the servant insisted, Hargobind took the bowl of milk and threw it away. It is said that a dog who tried to lap it up died instantly. The domestic servant was questioned and he confessed the truth. Guru Arjan was greatly distressed by his brother's misdeeds.

Hargobind was fairly grown up now and his father sent him to Bhai Budha so that he could be trained for the responsibilities he was destined to shoulder.

Before long, another situation developed in Guru Arjan's life. Reports came that Prithi Chand was composing his own hymns, and was passing them to the Sikhs visiting Amritsar as the compositions of Nanak and other Sikh Gurus. If this was allowed to continue, Guru Arjan feared, it would be the undoing of the Sikh faith. He therefore decided to take immediate steps to stop this confusion.

He sent his trusted Sikhs like Bhai Piara and others all over the country and went personally to Goindwal, Khadur, and Kartarpur to collect the authentic texts of the *Bani* of the four Gurus preceding him. Mohan, Datu, and Sri Chand were the three who helped him most in this pursuit. He then had a special camp set up by the side of Ramsar tank and started compiling what subsequently came to be known as the *Holy Granth*. Consistent with the tradition of the Sikh faith, Guru Arjan had some of the spiritual verse of other Indian saints, both Hindus and Muslims, also collected and included in the compilation. The hymns were arranged under the specific musical measure, or *raga*, in which they were originally written by Guru after Guru—in chronological order. The compositions of saints outside Sikhism figured after these. It is said that several poets or their admirers approached the Guru to have their verses included in the *Holy Granth* under compilation. A few among these were Chhajju, Shah Husain, and Pilu. But it seems their writings did not qualify for inclusion in the *Holy Granth*.

Bhai Gurdas undertook to prepare the master copy of the compilation. He was also invited by the Guru to contribute his own verses for inclusion in the *Holy Granth*, but his modesty as a disciple would not permit it. The compilation of the *Holy Granth* was completed in 1604. After the monumental work had been completed to his entire satisfaction, Guru Arjan added by way of epilogue, in utter humility:

I can't measure Your grace.
You've made me worthy of You.
I am full of blemishes;
I have no virtue.
You have been compassionate.
Compassionate You have been and kind.
Thus I met the True Guru.
Nanak, I live on the Name alone.
It pleases my heart and soul.

(Sloka V)

A large number of miracles are associated with Guru Arjan.

It is said that a Sikh called Triloka, who was employed in the army at Kabul, once killed a female deer. The deer happened to be pregnant. It pained Triloka to see the two unborn young ones of the deer also die before his eyes. He pledged not to indulge in hunting any more. Not only this, but rather than carry a proper sword, Triloka started donning a sword with a wooden blade. This was unheard of in the fighting forces of the day. Someone complained about it to his commandant, who came for a surprise check of Triloka's arms. Triloka remembered the Guru and prayed for his help in his hour of distress. To his delight, when he pulled out the blade from the scabbard, it was shining like steel. Those who had complained against him were put to shame.

Similarly, Katara, another Sikh from Kabul, happened to be in trouble. Someone wanting to do him harm had replaced his weights and complained to the authorities that he was using short weights. His premises were raided by the police for inspection. The innocent Sikh invoked the Guru's help in his hour of peril. It is said that at the same moment, Guru Arjan was made an offering of some coins at Amritsar. He held the weight of the coins for a while on the right hand palm and then on the left hand palm. He shifted the coins from one palm to the other again and again. When asked by the devotees why he did this, he told them about Katara, who was in trouble in faraway Kabul involved in a false case, accusing him of using short weights, and that was how he vindicated his integrity. The next time the Sikhs visited Amritsar he corroborated every word that the Guru had told them.

Chandu Shah, a Hindu banker of Delhi, who wielded a lot of influence at the Mughal court, was looking for a suitable groom for his daughter. He was originally from the Punjab and was keen that it should be a Punjabi youth. His emissaries went all over the Punjab without finding an eligible match. Eventually, on their way back, they happened to visit Amritsar and saw Hargobind, the young son of Guru Arjan. Besides being handsome and healthy, he was to succeed his father. The agents hurried back to Delhi to inform Chandu Shah. He, however, had the ego of a spoiled rich man. He couldn't imagine giving his daughter in marriage to anyone below his status. "At best,

he lives on the offerings of his followers," he objected, "he has no
social or political position. A brick baked for a palace cannot be used
for a gutter." The agents were silenced. The proposal was accordingly
dropped. In the meanwhile, the Sikhs of Delhi came to know of
Chandu Shah's remarks and they conveyed them duly to the Guru. As
it happened, the agents continued to search everywhere but they
couldn't find a suitable hand for Chandu Shah's daughter. The
marriageable daughter became the source of grave anxiety to the
mother. She couldn't wait any longer. Chandu Shah's wife felt that
Hargobind was an excellent match for their daughter and that they
should not have turned down the proposal. Before long, Chandu Shah
also realized his mistake and, sending for the agents, asked them to
finalize the proposal. The agents went to Amritsar. But the Guru,
who was aware of Chandu Shah's earlier remarks, declined to accept
the offer. He said that the daughter of a rich man like Chandu Shah
will not fit into the house of a dervish. Chandu Shah could not
imagine that the hand of his daughter could be refused by anyone. He
was wild to see the proposal gifts returned to him. In a fury of temper,
he decided to avenge himself on the Guru for the indignity hurled on
him.

Soon an opportunity came his way. Prithi Chand, the Guru's
eternal enemy, complained to him that the *Holy Granth* compiled by
the Guru had derogatory references to Muslim and Hindu prophets
and saints. Chandu Shah lost no opportunity to bring this fact to the
notice of the King. Akbar ordered the Guru and the *Holy Granth* to be
brought to him. Guru Arjan sent Bhai Budha and Bhai Gurdas to the
Mughal court with a copy of the *Holy Granth*. When the Holy Book
was opened, the first hymn that was read was:

From clay and light God created the world.
The sky, the earth, trees, and water are made by Him.
I have seen men pass away.
Forgetting God in avarice is like eating carrion,
The way the evil spirits kill and devour the dead.
One must restrain oneself;
Hell is the punishment otherwise.
The miracle man, the riches, brothers, courtiers, kingdoms,
    and palaces,

None will come to your rescue at the hour of departure,
When the messenger of death comes to carry you away.
God the Pure knows what's in store for me.
Nanak, my appeal of a slave is to You alone.

(Tilang)

The Emperor heard it and he was fully satisfied. He had always
looked upon the Sikh Gurus as social reformers and believers in the
unity of God and the brotherhood of man. And all this was close to
his heart.

However, Chandu Shah, who had considerable influence in the
court, was too wicked to be satisfied. He said that Bhai Gurdas, who
had read the hymn, had done so from memory and had not read the
text from the *Holy Granth*. He therefore, got one Sahib Dyal from the
town and made him read for them another piece from a page of his
own choice. The hymn read out this time was:

You don't see God who dwells in your heart,
And you carry about an idol around your neck.
A nonbeliever, you wander about churning water,
And you die harassed in delusion.
The idol you call God will drown with you,
The ungrateful sinner!
The boat will not ferry you across.
Says Nanak, I met the Guru who led me to God,
He who lives in water, earth, nether region, and firmament.

(Sulhi)

The King was delighted to listen to the hymn. It was as nobly
inspired as the earlier piece. Far from finding anything that could be
construed as maligning anyone, he felt that the hymn inculcated love
and devotion, and strove to rid both the Hindus and the Muslims of
the communalism that was tearing them apart. This is exactly what
he wished to project through Din-i-Ilahi, a new religion he advocated.
The King was happy to be acquainted with the highly inspiring
volume compiled by the Guru. He bestowed robes of honor on Bhai
Budha and Bhai Gurdas, and sent one for the Guru along with

numerous gifts. He also promised to pay his respects personally to the
Guru when he visited Lahore next.

The Emperor kept his promise and came on pilgrimage to
Amritsar. He was greatly impressed with the activities of the Guru.
He made rich offerings and sought the Guru's blessings for the peace
and welfare of his kingdom. At the Guru's intervention, the King
exempted the region from land revenue, as it had suffered a severe
drought that year. When the cultivators came to know of it, they were
deeply grateful to the Guru.

Unfortunately, a monarch of vision like Akbar did not live long.
He was followed on the throne by his son Jehangir. Akbar had,
however, nominated his grandson Khusro to succeed him.

Jehangir was pleasure-loving. He was given to drinking. He left the
administration of the kingdom to his Queen and his courtiers. While
on his way to Kashmir, the Emperor summoned Guru Arjan to meet
him in Lahore, mainly at Chandu's instigation.

When the Guru received the King's summons he knew what was in
store for him. He called Hargobind and had him installed as the sixth
Guru in the presence of prominent Sikhs. As usual, Bhai Budha
applied the *tilak* on Hargobind's forehead. The Guru then took leave
of his Sikhs and, bidding farewell to his beloved city of Amritsar, left
for Lahore.

The Emperor levied a fine of rupees two lakhs and asked the Guru
to revise the *Holy Granth*, deleting all references to Islam and
Hinduism figuring in it. The Guru told the King that his money was
the sacred trust of the Sikh community and the hymns in the *Holy
Granth* were a revelation in praise of God: no one dare alter them.
The King was on his way to Kashmir. He was in a hurry and in no
mood to involve himself in arguments. He asked Murtza Khan to deal
with the Guru the way he considered best and proceeded on his
journey. It was exactly the opportunity Chandu Shah was looking for.
He approached Murtza Khan and poisoned his ears, urging him to
extract the fine levied by the King.

The moment the Sikhs of Lahore came to know that the Guru had
been put in prison for non-payment of the fine, they started collecting
funds. When Guru Arjan heard of it, he forbade them to do so. He
had done no wrong for which he should pay a fine. In the meanwhile,

the *qazi* gave an injunction ordering the Guru to be tortured to death if he didn't agree to expunge the so-called derogatory references to Islam and Hinduism in the *Holy Granth.*

It is said that the Guru was made to sit on a red hot iron sheet. They poured burning hot sand on his body. He was given a dip in boiling water. As the Guru was being persecuted thus, Mian Mir, the Muslim divine of Lahore, who had laid the foundation stone of the Holy Temple at Amritsar, came and begged the Guru to allow him to use his mystic power to undo those who were responsible for the suffering inflicted upon him. The Guru heard Mian Mir and counselled patience. He told him that one must accept the will of God; not a leaf moves if God doesn't ordain it. When Chandu's daughter-in-law heard about it, she bribed the jailor and came to the prison with sherbet and other delicacies to serve the Guru. The Guru declined to accept anything from Chandu's house but blessed the lady for her faith and devotion.

The Guru was tortured for five long days. When the tyrants found him bearing all the agony with perfect equanimity, they became helpless. They were at a loss and didn't know what to do. At this the Guru asked for a bath in the river Ravi by the side of the Mughal fort in which he was imprisoned. Thousands of his followers watched the Guru walk to the river with tears in their eyes. His bare body glistened with blisters. There were blisters on his feet and he couldn't even walk properly. "Sweet is Your will, O God; the gift of your Name alone I seek," said the Guru again and again. As he reached the river, he bade farewell to the bewailing multitude and walked into the water as serene and as calm as ever. It is said that it was the last glimpse his devotees had of the Guru. He never came out of the river. The tide bore him in her longing lap and he was gone forever. Guru Arjan was only forty-three years old at the time of his supreme sacrifice on 30 May 1606.

Thus a magnificent life was brutally cut short by the hands of tyranny. The way in which Guru Arjan gave his life for the values that he cherished is of tremendous significance. With his martyrdom the attitude of the Sikhs toward life changed. Emulating their Guru, they would readily give their lives for any cause dear to them, whether it was a fight with the bigoted Mughals for the protection of their faith, or with the British for the freedom of the country, or even the Congress after Independence for the Punjabi-speaking state.

Guru Arjan's humility is almost unparalleled.

There was no trace of self; he emphasized with actions that more important than the Guru, were the Guru's Sikhs. What they decide as a congregation must hold good. Since the Delhi Sikhs did not want the Guru's son to be married to Chandu Shah's daughter because of his arrogance, the Guru respected their wishes, even when his life was at stake.

Guru Arjan has left a massive volume of 2218 hymns marked for their musicality and richness of imagery. They have continued to be popular with the Sikh musicians generation after generation. He wrote in a simple, conversational language, reflecting the various stages of the spiritual journey of the human soul. His magnum opus, the *Sukhmani*, the Psalm of Peace, is a long poem, ranking next to only the *Japji* of Guru Nanak in popularity with the devout. Though it doesn't form part of the essential set of five hymns enjoined upon the Sikhs to be recited every day, the *Sukhmani* is recited by a large number of devotees every morning and also at the hour of anxiety in the family.

In Guru Arjan we have the culmination of all that Guru Nanak and the three Gurus following him stood for. They combined in themselves the best of Islam and Hinduism. Rather than alienating anyone, they strove for mutual understanding. Venerated equally by the Muslims and the Hindus, they were peace-loving, devoted to meditation and prayers, and service of their fellow-beings. In Sikhism we have only the universal truth. All rites, rituals, and worship of gods and goddesses have been dispensed with. Sikhism comprises love of God and service of humanity only.

The Sikh Gurus established places of worship called *dharmasalas* and promoted projects of general welfare like the digging of wells, baolis and tanks. They set up new villages and townships. With a view to fighting social evils they encouraged common kitchens and community living. They were poets and music lovers. They patronized arts and artists. While Mardana, the rabab player, was a constant companion of Guru Nanak, Satta and Balwand, and a number of other professional musicians, were attached to the gurus following

Nanak. They would have indeed been happy if they were left alone to pursue their mission of propagating the love of God and the love of man to the people of the world.

But this was not to be. The rulers of the day became suspicious of their growing popularity and power. This unfortunate distrust was fed by petty jealousies and intrigues cropping up at every succession. While Guru Arjan represents the best in the way of life led and propagated by Guru Nanak, we also find him standing at the crossroads, as it were. There were tensions brewing; the Sikhs were to face forces of reaction, and the bigotry and arrogance of the rulers of the day.

Guru Arjan's martyrdom precipitated the issues. It gave a new complexion to the shape of things in the Punjab and the Sikh polity. While Guru Arjan's non-violence and the way he made the supreme sacrifice reflects the best in Guru Nanak, the training he gave to his successor Hargobind was a signpost of the long-drawn-out conflict that followed, culminating in a momentous turbulence during Guru Gobind Singh's life and times.

To a student of Guru Arjan's life, the Guru's martyrdom was an inevitability. The forces of evil and hatred were relentless and the events moved with calamitous inevitability. The Guru had attended to all his major assignments. The completion of the holy tank called Amritsar, and the *Harmandir*, known as the Golden Temple, gave the Sikh community a sense of solidarity. The town which came up around the Holy Tank grew into a metropolis of Sikhs from all over the world. The *Holy Granth* not only preserved the Holy Word; it has served as a spiritual lighthouse ever since its compilation. In his not too long life of forty-three years, Guru Arjan's achievements are monumental. He could accomplish all this, perhaps, because he was groomed for his mission by his maternal grandfather, and then by his own father. His predecessors, Guru Angad, Guru Amar Das, and Guru Ram Das, did not have this advantage.

Though a man of letters and a poet of eminence, Guru Arjan was highly organized and practical. Since he undertook massive construction works, he set up brick kilns to bake bricks. With a view to making Amritsar a self-sufficient town, he invited skilled workers of all crafts to settle there. Traders from Kashmir and Kabul were encouraged, so that Amritsar became an important commercial center in the Punjab.

A soldier once came to the Guru for spiritual advice. Guru Arjan told him that as long as he served in the army, he must remain loyal to the king and fight his enemies. A soldier's *dharma* is to live for peace and die fighting.

Similarly, he was against the renunciation of the world. He said that it was like a soldier running away from the battlefield. One must live in the world and yet, as a lotus remains above water, remain above it.

Guru Nanak had rejected the caste system of the Hindus. "There is no higher caste," he said, "and there is no lower caste. It is one's deeds that determine whether one is good or bad, high or low." Guru Arjan sought to abolish the distinction between the haves and the have-nots, the caste system that permeated the economic field; those who labored and those who exploited them. He didn't attach any great importance to contemplative life if it had to be sustained on the sweat of the neighbor's brow. He advised that one must work and earn and share one's earning with others.

The Hindu theory of karma upholds that what we are is of our own making. We suffer because of misdeeds committed in our previous life. So even the indignities and atrocities inflicted by the rulers were borne by the Hindus with stoic indifference. Guru Arjan said that evil must be resisted, even if one has to give one's life for it. He underlined the virtues of self-sacrifice. According to Guru Arjan, one must fight evil and injustice, evn if it means giving away one's life.

Guru Arjan was highly practical in day-to-day conduct. Once, a village headman called Chuhar came to him for his blessings. He believed that the nature of his duties was such that he had to resort to falsehood. He was anxious to know how he was going to find his deliverance. The Guru asked him to maintain an account of his good and bad deeds and bring it over to him at the end of the month. When Chuhar came after a month, it was discovered that he had done hardly any good deeds, whereas he had a large number of bad deeds to his credit. The Guru asked him to read them out and confess his sins in public. The next month his performance was better. It improved consistently in the following months, until the village headman had only good deeds to his credit and not one bad deed.

Accepting the Will of God, Guru Arjan gave up his life suffering inhuman atrocities. Yet the last message he sent to his son was to arm himself fully and prepare for the struggle ahead, which was to be a long-drawn-out war against tyranny.

Selected Hymns of Guru Arjan

1. Depending upon Your indulgence
   I whiled away my time in filial love.
   I am an erring child,
   You are the gracious parent.
   It's easy to boast
   But difficult to belong to You.
   You are my pride, You are my power.
   To You I come.
   You are amidst us; You are outside us.
   You depend upon none.
   Father, I know not Your ways.
   You are the deliverer of Your devotees.
   You must protect me, my Lord.
   With God's grace I found salvation;
   A meeting with the Guru
   Has led Nanak to know God.

   (Sri Rag)

2. Man! You must remember Him
   Who rules supreme.
   Man! You must remember Him
   Who saves you in the hour of your peril.
   Man! You must remember Him
   Who satisfies every hunger of your heart.
   Blessed are those who remember Him.
   Their foes and all those who find fault with them are
     defeated.
   Says Nanak, you must remember God, the Great God.
   Everyone bows before him who remembers God.

   (Sri Rag)

3. Blessed is the season in which I remember You.
   Blessed is the endeavor of your pursuit.
   Blessed is the heart in which You dwell.
   You who are the Master of us all,
   Father! You are the True Lord,
   Endless are Your nine treasures.

He is content to whom You give.
He becomes Your devotee.
Everyone looks up to You.
You dwell in every heart.
All are equal in Your eyes;
No one is a stranger to You.
You grant salvation to men of God.
The egoist is born again and again.
Says Nanak, I am a sacrifice to You.
All that I witness is Your creation.

(Majh)

4. You are my father,
    You are my mother,
    You are my relative,
    And my brother . . .
    You are my savior everywhere.
    I have neither worry nor fear.
    Blessed by You, I come to know You.
    You are my anchor,
    You are my pride.
    There is none other than You.
    It's all Your play, this world.
    Everything living is Your creation.
    You make them do what You please.
    Whatever happens is ordained by You.
    None other has anything to do with it.
    I gained the precious peace remembering Your name.
    Singing God's praises
    I am contented at heart.
    With the grace of the Guru,
    I have succeeded in the perilous task.

(Majh)

5. Brother! How does one gain happiness?
    How does one go to God and ask His help?
    Happiness doesn't lie in filial attachment,
    Nor in palatial houses and their comforts.
    Vain are such temptations, a waste of life.

He who is elated seeing the elephants and horses,
His armies, his followers, and his soldiers,
He has a noose of vanity around his neck,
He who rules over all.
Enjoying gay female company,
He is like a king turned beggar in a dream.
The True Guru has revealed to me the secret of happiness;
Whatever God does, the godly ones accept.
Nanak killed his ego and found union with God.
This is how one gains happiness, brother.
This is how one goes to God and asks His help.

(Gauri)

6. He who has God as his friend,
   He doesn't need anyone else.
   He who has endeared himself to the Lord,
   All his fears and all his dreads are shed.
   He who enjoys remembering Him,
   He does not enjoy anything else.
   He who is received in His court,
   He cares for none other than Him.
   He who submits himself to the Lord,
   Says Nanak, he is ever and ever happy.

(Gauri)

7. The big men you see around
   Are afflicted with worries and anxieties and fears.
   No one is big being rich.
   He is big who remembers Him.
   The landlord keeps on clamoring for land;
   He does not rest until his hour of death.
   Nanak has discovered a secret
   Without God's Name salvation is not obtained.

(Gauri)

8. He who shouts at the poor
   Comes to grief.
   God does justice;
   He looks after his devotee,
   Who is honored.

He who is foul-mouthed
Dies a wretched death;
He kills himself.
No one may save him.
He is talked ill of
Here and hereafter.
God saves His servants,
Holding them to His heart.
Says Nanak, submit yourself to Him
And meditate on His Word.

(Gauri)

9. I am at peace . . .
   The Guru has brought me peace.
   I am free from pain and sin.
   Daily I repeat the Name of God.
   All my ills have disappeared.
   And I've gained salvation.
   God's greatness is unfathomable.
   It is in God's company that one finds deliverance.
   I sing praises of the blemishless every day.
   My afflictions are gone and I am saved.
   I remember God in word and thought,
   Says Nanak, I am in His protection.

(Gauri)

10. O Godmen! Know this for certain in your mind:
    The True One solves all your problems,
    He defeats all your sworn enemies.
    He saves the honor of His devotees.
    Kings and king's kings are all under His sway.
    He drinks the great drink of nectar.
    Remembering His Name I became fearless.
    In the company of Godmen I gave away everything else.
    I fell at the feet of the omniscient.
    Says Nanak, His protection alone I have sought.

(Gauri)

11. On merit I have no chance of salvation,
    I commit faults every moment.

You are the forgiver; do forgive me.
And cruise Nanak across the ocean.
I am an ungrateful sinner,
A stranger with little understanding.
He who has given me life and comfort,
I don't seem to know Him.
In order to gain riches and profit
I look around everywhere.
Not for a moment do I remember the bountiful God.
Greed, falsehood, evil deeds, and worldly love,
I have collected these like a treasure.
Drunkards, thieves, and those who talk ill of others,
I live in their company.
If you please, you may forgive the false along with the
    truthful.
Says Nanak, if God so desires
Even stones may sail across the ocean.

(Gauri)

12. Where neither father nor mother,
    Neither friend nor brother
    Can help you, God does.
    Where the dreadful agent of death smothers you,
    Only God's Name abides by you.
    When you have an insurmountable difficulty,
    Remember the Name of God for a moment.
    No good deeds and ceremonials may save you.
    God's Name alone washes a million sins.
    O man of God! You must meditate on Him,
    Says Nanak, this is how you'll find real peace.

(Gauri)

13. With Whose grace you live in comfort in the world.
    You laugh with your son, brother, friend, and wife,
    With Whose grace you drink fresh water,
    Enjoy pleasant breeze and a priceless sun,
    With Whose grace you indulge in pleasures
    And live a life of luxury,
    He has given you hands and feet, ears, eyes, and tongue.

You have forgotten Him and taken to others,
Such a stupid one suffers in darkness,
Says Nanak, only God could save him.

(Gauri)

14. Forgetting the ten gifts you obtained
You chased yet another and lost your credit.
He may not give you the one you ask for
And also take away the other ten.
What would you do then, O fool?
The Master with whom one cannot argue
Must be saluted a hundred times.
Those who are devoted to the loving God
Peace comes to dwell in their hearts.
He who learns to obey Him
Acquires happiness in a heap.

(Gauri)

15. As long as he thinks he can do anything by himself,
He remains unhappy.
As long as he remains on his own
He is born and dies and is born again.
As long as he has friends and foes
His mind remains unsettled.
As long as he is drowned in filial love
He is punished by the god of death.
It's with God's grace that deliverance is obtained,
Nanak secured his salvation with the Guru's blessings.

(Gauri)

16. He covers the weakness of His devotees,
He helps His men through.
He bestows laurels on His disciple.
He makes His slave remember Him.
He protects the honor of His follower,
Nobody can know His greatness.
None can measure up to men of God,
God's servant is greater than the great.
He who has an opportunity to serve God,
Says Nanak, is known all over.

(Gauri)

17. The low-born whom no one knows
    Meditation makes him known all over.
    Lord, I seek a glimpse of You,
    Serving You many have swum across.
    He who is shunned by everyone
    The entire world washes his feet.
    He who is unwanted
    With God's grace he is welcomed everywhere.
    The mind is awakened in God's company.
    Says Nanak, he then starts loving the Lord.

                                                    (Asa)

18. He protects His devotee and makes him remember God.
    He goes posthaste where the devotee needs His assistance.
    He remains closest to the devotee.
    Whatever the devotee asks of God
    Is given to him forthwith.
    I am a sacrifice to the devotee
    Who has endeared himself to God.
    It delights one to hear about him,
    Nanak would go to meet him anywhere.

                                                    (Asa)

19. Man! Why must you worry when God Himself is bothered
       about it?
    He creates living beings in dead stones and provides food for
       them.
    He who lives in the company of men of God is saved.
    With the Guru's grace, he attains the supreme status.
    Even dry woods become green for him.
    Mother, father, friends, son, and wife
    No one can help anyone else,
    God Himself provides for them.
    What are you anxious about?
    The swallow flies away hundreds of *kos* leaving her young
       ones behind.
    Who feeds them and tends them?
    She remembers them in her heart of hearts.
    All the treasures and the eighteen powers of miracle-making

God keeps in His fist.
Nanak is a sacrifice to Him a hundred times
Whose limit cannot be known.

(Gauri)

20. Meditating on Him at heart
And repeating His name with the tongue,
Seeing the True Guru with eyes
And hearing His Name with ears,
Those who are devoted to the True Guru
Find a seat in heaven.
Says Nanak, he whom He blesses
He bestows the gift.
They are indeed the chosen ones,
There are not many like them in the world.

(Gauri)

21. God, I have one prayer to make
Out of Your generosity and grace
Make me a disciple of Your saints.
Let me sit at their feet first thing in the morning,
And remain in their company day and night.
Let me offer my body and soul
In the service of the people,
And sing Your praises with my tongue.
Let me remember God every breath of my life.
And remain in the company of holy men.
Let Your Name be my only support.
Says Nanak, this is the joy I look for in life.

(Wadhans)

22. I have found the great Guru, I am lucky.
I am enlightened.
None other is like him.
In him alone I have faith.
I am sacrifice to the true Guru.
I have happiness before me,
I have happiness behind me,
There is happiness inside me.
He who is the knower of the secrets of the heart,

He who is the maker,
He is my master.
I have become fearless sitting at his feet.
God's Name is my only support.
Seeing Him gives me satisfaction.
He is eternal.
He is there today.
He will be there on the morrow.
He protects His devotees clasping them to His heart
With love and affection.
He is honored everywhere.
His good will is enormous.
He solves every problem.
Nanak has met the great Guru
Who has rescued him from suffering.

(Sorath)

23. Like an umbrella, there are dark, rain-bearing clouds all over
And the dreadful lightning flashes.
I am all alone in bed . . .
With no sleep in my eyes.
My Lord has gone away
And there is no news from Him.
He would go a *kos* and used to send four letters.
How can I forget a lover like Him
Who is the bestower of all comforts?
I go to the top of the house and look for Him
With my eyes swimming in tears.
He is said to dwell in my heart
But the wall of ego is standing between us.
It is like the wings of a butterfly.
Without my being able to see Him,
He appears far far away.
God has been gracious,
He has swept off pain from my life.
Says Nanak, after I demolished the ramparts of the ego,
It is only then that I found the kind God,
And all my fears vanished.

My Guru gave me whatever I asked for.
He is the epitome of all virtue.

(Sorath)

24. You are the loving God, the Protector,
You are the Master of us all
I remember You every moment.
We are the children looking up to You for support.
I have only one tongue,
How can I recount Your many virtues?
You can't be measured
You are limitless
I do not know Your limits.
Forgive me my countless sins
And put me on the true path.
I am ignorant and of little wisdom.
You must save me as You have always done.
I am at Your feet,
You are my only hope.
My only good Friend
Save me, my kind Savior
Nanak is a slave in Your house.

(Dhanasri)

25. He who rules all the four quarters
Has placed His hand on my head,
He has taken kindly to me
And removed all my suffering.
The great Guru protects men of God.
Taking me into his bosom
He has washed away all my sins.
He has been gracious and forgiving.
Whatever one asks of one's master, he gives.
Says Nanak, whatever he utters from his lips
Turns out to be true here and hereafter.

(Dhanasri)

26. Not a moment of worry would he let me undergo.
He maintains His ever-loving disposition.
He protects His devotees with his own hands

And looks after them every hour.
I have given my heart to my Lord.
He helped me in the beginning,
He'll help me in the end.
He is the great benefactor.
I am overjoyed,
Seeing the surprising greatness of God.
Nanak remembered Him and was blessed
The All-powerful One has saved his honor.

(Dhanasri)

27. Those who forget God are always wretched.
    How can they be misled who have faith in Him?
    Living life without meditation is living like a snake.
    He may rule over the entire world
    And yet he would be defeated in the end.
    They alone sing praises of the epitome of virtue
    Who are blessed by Him
    Such a one is happy; his life is happy.
    Nanak is a sacrifice to him.

(Todi)

28. With God in my heart
    The messenger of death dare not approach me.
    He keeps his devotee clung to His bosom.
    This is the way of the true Lord.
    The great Guru has bestowed favors on me.
    He has punished and vanquished my foes.
    He gave me true understanding.
    God has enriched all my faculties
    And I have arrived home comfortably.
    Nanak is in His protection,
    Who has rid him of his ailments.

(Sorath)

29. I ask for the gift of Your Name
    Nothing else will accompany me.
    With His favor alone can I sing His praises.
    The raj, riches, and the pleasures
    Are like the shadows of a tree.

Howsoever you may chase them
It's all in vain.
Without God's Name whatever you may ask
Everything appears of little avail.
Nanak prays for the dust of the feet of the saints
So that he may find peace of mind.

(Todi)

30. In the company of saints
    I sing God's praises
    I wash the sins of millions of my lives.
    I get whatever fruit I want.
    In His grace He has granted me
    Whatever I had asked for.
    He has been kind,
    He has given me the gift of His Name.
    The virtue of His Name
    Has brought me every happiness.
    It's with the Guru's favor
    That I have learned the secret (of life) . . .

(Bairadi)

31. Seeing you puts life into me, O Guru!
    Be kind to me, O Lord!
    Lord God! Grant me just one favor
    Let me remember You like a slave.
    Keep me in Your protection, my kind Lord.
    With Guru's grace some do come to know You.
    God, my good Friend, listen to my prayer,
    Let me meditate on Your lotus feet.
    Nanak has only one prayer to make,
    Let me never forget You
    The epitome of all virtue.

(Suhi)

32. He who has your protection
    How can he come to harm?
    Obsessed with worldly wealth he knows not how to talk.
    He forgets that he must die one day.
    God, You belong to saints and saints belong to You.

Your devotee fears none.
The god of death dare not approach
Those who fix their gaze on You, O Master!
They are saved from the cruel cycle of life and death.
None may undo Your favors.
This is the assurance given by the true Guru,
Those who remember the Name attain peace
And they sing His praises all the while.
In Your protection and with faith in You
The five foes can be vanquished.
I am ignorant, I know not how to meditate.
I have no good deeds to my credit.
I know not You.
Says Nanak, He is the greatest of all
Who has saved my honor.

(Suhi)

33. If I err, if I make mistakes,
    I still belong to You.
    Those who are attached to others
    They are traitors.
    They die suffering pangs of separation.
    I would never leave my Lord.
    You are my ever merry Master,
    You are my support.
    You are my friend and associate.
    I am indeed proud of You.
    Be kind to me.
    Let me look to none else for help.
    I should keep this precious gift clung to my heart.

(Suhi)

34. You are the Master above temptation
    You have many a slave like me.
    You are the ocean, the mine of jewels.
    I know not You;
    You are too great to be known.
    Take pity on me.
    Be kind and give me the understanding

So that I may remember You day and night.
Man! you should not be vain;
You should be humble.
This is the way to salvation
Nanak's Master is above all.
He has several servitors like me.

(Suhi)

35. He who comes to God cannot be harmed.
    He has the protective ring of Ram around him.
    No evil may ever assail him.
    He adores the Almighty who has created the universe.
    The name of Rama is the remedy.
    It blesses man with single-minded devotion.
    He is saved by the savior,
    Killing all the evils.
    Nanak has been blessed;
    God Himself has come to the rescue.

(Bilawal)

36. The great Guru himself has protected me,
    He has blessed me with the nectar of His Name.
    It has removed the dirt of ages.
    All my foes and all my enemies have been vanquished.
    I have meditated in the manner of the Guru.
    Who dare harm me?
    My Lord is all-powerful.
    With His lotus feet in my heart
    I remembered His Name and was blessed with peace.
    Nanak the slave came to his protection
    Above whom there is none.

(Bilawal)

37. The Almighty God protects me here and hereafter.
    He helps me in ups and downs and sees me through my
       problems.
    I remember God's Name for the bliss of peace.
    I smear myself with the dust of His feet.
    No more I come and no more I go.
    I am free from the agony of birth and death.

All my fears are gone.
I am rid of the terror of death.
God has come to dwell in my heart.
Nanak has sought protection of the killer of pain.
He sees His presence all over.

(Bilawal)

38. I have found the true Guru
Exactly as I used to hear about him.
The Guru brings together those who are separated.
He leads to God's court.
He makes me remember God,
And cures the malady of vanity.
Says Nanak, they alone can meet the Guru
Who have it written in their lot.

(Ramkali)

39. You help where none other may.
You protect in the fire of the womb.
Hearing Your Name, the agents of death leave me alone.
This deep, dreadful ocean can be crossed with Your Name.
They drink the nectar who thirst for it.
The only good in the Kali Age is to sing God's praises.
The kind one looks after all every moment.
He who comes to you never goes empty-handed.

(Ramkali)

40. When You are on my side I care for none;
You have bestowed on me everything,
I am Your slave.
There is no end to Your riches;
I eat and spend.
The eighty-four lakh creatures of earth serve me.
All my foes have become friends,
None thinks ill of me.
When God favors, none may ask for the account,
Meeting the Guru, I have attained the state of bliss.
When He so desires
Everything is found in order.

(Maru)

41. I'm happy as I sit, I'm happy as I stand,
    He who understands this
    Is not afraid of anyone;
    God alone is the savior
    He knows the secret of every heart.
    Fearless I sleep and fearless I wake up.
    God is present everywhere,
    I find you at home and outside,
    Says Nanak, only the Guru may reveal this secret.

    (Bhairo)

42. He whose Name is above all
    I sing His praises ever,
    Remembering Whom all suffering ends
    The mind is at peace.
    O man! You must remember the True One,
    You will be blessed here and hereafter.
    He is the flawless Creator,
    He provides for every living creature,
    He pardons millions of sins in a moment,
    He helps them through who are devoted to Him.
    True wealth and true instruction,
    And ever true wisdom are gifts of the True Guru.
    He whom He saves in His grace
    All his sufferings end.
    He who meditates on Him
    Who is perfect, without temptation
    And found everywhere,
    He meets God shedding all doubts and fears.
    Says Nanak, he is blessed by the Kind One.

    (Bhairo)

43. I have forgotten all ill will
    Since I came into the company of Godmen.
    I have no enemy, no stranger.
    Everyone is my friend.
    Whatever God does should be accepted,
    This is what I have learned from them.
    He alone dwells in every heart.

Nanak sees Him and is in raptures.

(Kanada)

44. God, I come to Your protection
    All my name and fame I owe to You,
    I have Your support, I am at Your feet
    You are my hope, I have faith in You.
    I have Your Name in my heart.
    You are my strength, I am happy in Your company,
    Whatever You say I do.
    With Your grace I attain peace.
    God has bestowed on me fearlessness;
    I have laid my head at His feet.

(Kanada)

45. I am wretched, stone-hearted, evil-minded, given to lust,
    Master, save me howsoever You may!
    You are all-powerful,
    You save them who seek Your protection,
    You look after them.
    Meditation, asceticism, discipline, cleanliness, and correct
       behavior—
    None of these can obtain salvation.
    Says Nanak, with His grace He pulls one out of the dark
       well.

(Kanada)

46. There are three things in the tray—
    Truth, contentment, and reason.
    To this is added the nectar of God's Name
    That sustains every living creature.
    He who eats it, he who consumes it, is saved.
    It is a gift that can't be given up.
    It must be remembered every moment.
    The dark ocean of the world can be crossed by clinging to
       His feet.
    Says Nanak, God is present everywhere.

(Mundavani)

Guru Hargobind

The earlier Gurus adorned the temple; the reigning
Guru moves from place to place.
Earlier the Kings came to pay homage to the Guru,
Today our forts are attacked by them.

—*Bhai Gurdas*

"They made him sit on a red hot iron sheet. They poured burning hot sand on his body. They gave him a dip in boiling hot water."

"As serene and as calm as ever, he uttered these words:

Sweet is Your Will, O God!
The gift of Your Name alone I seek.

"Every inch of his body was burning with blisters. He suffered and he asked for a cold bath in the river close by.

"Thousands of devotees watched their Divine Master stagger to the river with helpless tears pouring from their eyes. He looked at them and said:

Sweet is Your Will, O God!
The gift of Your Name alone I seek.

"As serene and as calm as ever, he stepped into the river. The tide came to greet him. And he never emerged out of it. They waited and waited. The Master had gone. He was nowhere."

People came and informed Guru Hargobind, men and women who had seen him with their own eyes, heard him with their own ears.

This is how his revered father, the fifth incarnation of Guru Nanak, was brutally tortured to death.

It steeled his heart, the youthful son Hargobind who had succeeded his father as the sixth Sikh Guru.

It is said that when Bhai Budha, the grand old man of the Sikh brotherhood, brought him *seli*, the sacred headgear of renunciation that Guru Nanak wore and had bequeathed to his successors one after another, Guru Hargobind put it aside respectfully and asked for a sword instead. Bhai Budha who had never handled a sword brought out one and put it on the wrong side. The Guru noticed it and asked for another. "I'll wear two swords," said the Guru, "a sword of *shakti* (power) and a sword of *bhakti* (meditation)."

Guru Hargobind combined in him *piri* (renunciation) and *miri* (royalty). Henceforth the Guru's Sikhs were to carry arms and ride horses. It gave birth to a new concept of the soldier-saint.

It seems one of the most absorbing passions of Guru Hargobind's life was to steel his Sikhs against tyranny and oppression. The Hindus had become so weak that they could not contemplate any kind of resistance to the rulers of the day. It was a strange irony of fate that of all the Mughal kings, Guru Arjan's martyrdom took place during the regime of Jehangir, who was known as Jehangir the Just. It is said that he had a bell with a chain hanging outside his palace; anyone denied justice could pull it and seek the King's intervention.

No more did the Sikhs believe in self-denial alone; they grew increasingly aware of the need for assertion also. No more self-abnegation and renunciation alone, they wielded arms and lived an active life. They wouldn't frighten anyone nor were they afraid of anybody. They reared horses, rode on them, and racing and hunting became their pastimes. The Guru maintained a regular army with various cadres. The heroic youth joined him in large numbers irrespective of caste and creed. The Sikhs all over presented the Guru with the best horses and finest weapons as their offerings. The Guru built forts and battlements, donned a royal airgrette and was known as Sacha Padshah—the True King.

Bhai Budha did not quite understand this new way of life. Guru Hargobind reminded him that he himself had predicted the sort of career Hargobind had adopted. Didn't he say that he would smash the heads of the enemies? Bhai Gurdas, the poet, also could not reconcile himself to the new way of life and there was an unfortunate misunderstanding for a while in his relations with the Master.

The Guru, however, rose long before the day dawned and, after his bath in the holy tank, went into meditation. He joined his Sikhs for prayers both in the morning and in the evening. The rest of the day was devoted to parades and maneuvers, horse races and hunting. Bidhi Chand, Pirana, Paira, and Langha were some of his Sardars with a contingent of a hundred horsemen each under them. The Guru sat on a throne and received visitors and offerings like any other ruler.

All this was duly reported to the King by Chandu Shah, who still had an unmarried daughter on his hands as a constant reminder of the indignity hurled at him. He was always poisoning the King's ears against Guru Hargobind. At last, in spite of Wazir Khan, a courtier advising him to the contrary, the King decided to summon the Guru to Delhi.

It is said that the moment Jehangir saw Guru Hargobind, he was completely won over by his youthful charm and holiness. Among other questions, the King asked the Guru which religion was better—Hinduism or Islam. In his reply, the Guru quoted Kabir:

God first created light
All men are born out of it.
The whole world came out of a single spark;
Who is good and who is bad?
The creator is in the creation
And the creation in the creator,
He is everywhere.
The clay is the same,
The potter fashions various models.
There is nothing wrong with the clay or the potter.
God the true resides in all,
Whatever happens is His doing.
He who surrenders to Him gets to know Him.
He is His slave.
God is invisible, He cannot be seen.
The Guru has granted me this sweet gift.
Says Kabir, my doubts are dispelled.
I have seen the Pure with my own eyes.

(Parbhati)

The King was deeply impressed. He had also been told that the Guru was a great lover of sports. He invited Guru Hargobind to accompany him on a tiger hunt. The Guru accepted the invitation gladly. It happened that during the chase, the King was attacked by a ferocious tiger. The sportsmen accompanying the royal party lost their nerve, and their horses and elephants panicked. The bullets and arrows shot at the tiger missed the target and for a moment it appeared that the beast was going to pounce upon the monarch. At this, Guru Hargobind rushed his horse and, pulling out his sword, he engaged the tiger single-handed. The next moment, the tiger lay slain on the ground. The King was full of gratitude. He admired the way the Guru risked his life and the heroic fight he gave to save the King.

The Emperor became so fond of the Guru that he invited him to accompany him wherever he went. The Guru's tent was always pitched next to the royal tent. Once, while visiting Agra, the King happened to be relaxing under a tree. A poor grass cutter who had heard about the Guru's visit with the King came, and making an offering of a two-paisa coin, pleaded, "You are the True King. I am a poor sinner. Help me wash my sins and attain deliverance from the cycle of life and death." The monarch heard him and smiled. "The True King is in yonder tent," saying these words he directed the grasscutter to the Guru's camp. As the poor Sikh collected his coin and hurried to the Guru's tent, Jehangir realized that the True King indeed was one who gave eternal peace and deliverance.

Chandu was extremely unhappy with this new turn of events. The Guru, however, had not so far mentioned to the King the grave injustice done to his father. He was, perhaps, looking for a suitable opportunity.

While at Agra, the King was taken seriously ill. The court physicians tried their best but could not cure him. The King decided to consult his astrologers. It was a godsend for Chandu Shah. He conspired with the astrologers who told the King that his malady was due to an unfavorable conjunction of stars and that it could be remedied only if a holy man went to the Gwalior Fort and offered continuous prayers to the deity there. Who could be holier than Guru Hargobind, the King's new friend? It was therefore decided to request the Guru to go to Gwalior and undertake the penance on behalf of the

King. The Guru was aware of Chandu's intrigue; however, he readily agreed to the proposal and, accompanied by an escort of five lieutenants, he left for the Gwalior Fort. The Guru's Sikhs both at Delhi and Amritsar were unhappy to hear about it. On the other hand, the princes detained in the Fort were mighty pleased to have the great Guru with them for company. Guru Hargobind found that the princes lived in deplorable conditions. He had their living conditions improved and invited them to join him for prayers both in the morning and in the evening. In the meanwhile Chandu wrote to Hari Das, the governor of the Fort, asking him to poison the Guru somehow. He must be avenged for the indignity he had suffered owing to the Guru's refusal to accept the hand of his daughter. Evidently, Chandu was not aware that the governor was an ardent devotee of the Guru. Hari Das brought the letter and placed it before the Guru.

Several months had gone by and there was no news from Delhi. It was learned that the King had fully recovered from his ailment and yet he had no thought of inviting the Guru back. Hari Das, who was aware of Chandu's influence at the Mughal court, couldn't take the initiative in the matter. Then a stage came when the Guru started feeling as if he were also a captive, like the other princes detained in the Fort.

In the meanwhile, the Guru was visited by Bhai Budha at the head of a *sangat* from Amritsar. They remonstrated with the Guru for ignoring them for so long. The entire household and the pilgrims who came from far and near missed him badly. The Guru assured them that he would join them shortly. They should, in the meanwhile, continue to take care of his horses and feed them well in green pastures.

Soon thereafter Wazir Khan, a great admirer of the Guru in Jehangir's court, had an opportunity to mention to the King how the Guru continued to be confined in the Gwalior Fort. Now that the monarch had fully recovered, it was only proper that the Guru was invited back to Delhi and duly honored.

But the Guru would not leave the fort unless the princes detained in the fort were also released. The King could not agree to it. They were either political prisoners or had been detained for committing default in the payment of large sums of tribute due from them. Wazir Khan reminded the King that he owed his recovery from the malignant malady to Guru Hargobind's prayers. It would be the height of ingratitude if he were denied this small favor. The monarch agreed and the Guru left the fort along with all the fifty-two princes who had been languishing in the prison for years. A part of Gwalior Fort where the Guru stayed is still known as Bandi Chhor—the liberator of the detained.

When the King met the Guru in Delhi to thank him for his intervention, the first thing the Guru told him was that there was no such thing as an unfavorable conjunction of planets. It was his good deeds that saved him and that he should continue to have faith in God.

The Guru also acquainted the King with Chandu's villainy: how he had intrigued and an innocent soul was tortured to death in his name, then how he wrote to Hari Das to have Guru Hargobind poisoned while at Gwalior Fort. It seemed the King was already aware of Chandu Shah's perfidy. He lost his temper and in a fit of fury handed Chandu over to the Guru to avenge the murder of his father. Bhai Bidhi Chand and Bhai Jetha, who were accompanying the Guru, took immediate charge of Chandu Shah. His hands were tied with his own turban and he was paraded in the streets of Delhi as a perpetrator of the most heinous crime. It is said that the people hurled abuse at him and spat on his face. He was pelted with filth and rubbish. They would have done him to death but for the Guru's intervention. He wished to carry Chandu Shah to Lahore so that the people of Lahore could see his plight.

When the King heard about the Guru's desire to return home, he suggested that he might delay his departure for a few days so that they could travel together. The King wished to spend the summer in Kashmir that year.

During their journey, Guru Hargobind's tent was invariably next to the King's. It is said that Nur Jehan, the queen, took a fancy to the Guru and visited him with her confidants a couple of times. She was said to be the most charming beauty of her time. The Guru told her that the real charm of a woman was her virtue and her devotion to her husband. Nur Jehan was enchanted to hear the Guru's words and cherished his memory for long.

The royal party decided to visit Goindwal and Amritsar on their way to Lahore. At Amritsar, Nur Jehan called on the Guru's mother, who recited to her Guru Nanak's verses:

She adorns her husband's house
If she is the beloved of her husband;
If she utters false words
She is no use.
She who utters false words is no use indeed,
Nor can she ever see the lover.
She is false, forgotten by her husband
An abandoned soul
Her night passes in separation.

(Dhanasri—Chhand)

During his visit to Amritsar as the Guru's guest, Jehangir asked the Guru, "You are a handsome youth and among your devotees there are charming young women; how do you control your passions?" The Guru was amused to hear it. He replied to the monarch in a parable:

There was a king who was given to lust and sex. Once he came across a man of God and asked his help. How could he control his passions? The holy man looked at him and said, "You have just eight days more to live. You may spend them remembering God or in sin, the choice is yours." The king heard it and became panicky. He prayed day and night and fed the poor and the needy. Not for a moment did he think of lust or sin.

The emperor realized that for those who remembered death it was difficult to commit sin. The Guru then quoted Guru Nanak:

The fish forgot the net
In the vast brackish ocean.
Extremely intelligent and charming though,
She became careless
And paid for her deeds.
Death is inevitable!

(Suhi—I)

Before he left, the Emperor invited the Guru to visit him at Lahore as his guest. After staying at Amritsar for a few days more, Guru Hargobind followed the King because he had to dispose of Chandu Shah.

Crying day and night, Chandu had almost become blind. He was reduced to a mere skeleton, worrying about the fate in store for him. At Lahore, he was taken around the streets daily when the people hurled abuse at him and beat him with shoes and slippers.

Then one day when he was being paraded in the street, a grain parcher, who had seen Chandu torture the Guru with his own eyes, came rushing and hit him on his head with a pair of burning hot tongs. Chandu was knocked down. At this, the grain parcher gave him another blow, fracturing his skull. Chandu died on the spot. Nobody wept for him. His dead body was then thrown into the river Ravi. When the Guru heard about it, he said, "Chandu has suffered enough for his misdeed; may God pardon his sins!"

Chandu's death, however, did not solve Guru Hargobind's problems. Soon Chandu's son Karam Chand and Prithi's son Mehrban joined hands to malign the Guru. They went to meet Prince Khurram, who later succeeded Jehangir as Shah Jehan, and poisoned his ears. When the Guru heard about it, he tried to dissuade Mehrban but Mehrban would not see reason.

While the Guru was still in Lahore, one of his devotees in Kabul, hearing that the Guru was fond of horses, purchased for him a rare charger. It cost him a lakh of rupees. In order that the horse was not noticed on the way and stolen, he covered it in poor array and carried it along with a number of poorly bred horses. However, while crossing the river Attock, the local official noticed the elan of the horse and was fascinated. He must take possession of the horse for the King. But the Sikh would not part with him at any price. "It is for the Sacha Padshah—the True King," he said. Piqued at it, the official sent word to the Mughal court and as soon as the Sikh entered Lahore with the horses, the prize horse was captured by the King's men.

The Sikh came and told the Guru what had transpired, and the Guru said, "The horse must come to him for whom he was intended." It is said that the horse stopped eating in the royal stable. When the King tried to mount him, he would not let him. Day after day they tried but the horse would neither eat nor allow anyone to touch him. It was feared that the horse would not survive. The State Qazi, who was consulted, was of the opinion that if the holy script were read out to the horse he would be cured of the malady. Accordingly, the King handed over the horse to the Qazi. While the Qazi was leading the horse to his house he chanced to pass by the Guru's camp. The horse, who was on the verge of death, is said to have neighed as he saw the Guru's tent. It was interpreted as an appeal to the Guru to rescue him. The Guru came out and offered to purchase the horse. The Qazi was most happy to strike the deal at ten thousand rupees to be paid to him at the time of Diwali. The Qazi thought that the horse was not going to live long. But the horse suddenly turned a corner; he started eating and regained his spirit. Before long, the Guru started mounting the horse in all his glory. The Qazi felt he had been cheated. He had sold a horse worth a lakh for a sum of a mere ten thousand rupees. He started pestering the Guru for his dues long before Diwali. The Guru reminded him about their deal, but he refused to see reason. The argument was still going on when the Guru decided to return to Amritsar. As the Qazi came to know of it, he became panicky. He thought of making a complaint to the King.

Before he could do that, the Qazi had another shock. One of his daughters, who had not married, was a great devotee of Mian Mir, a divine of Lahore. She visited the dervish frequently and many a time heard him praise Guru Hargobind. He would at times recite hymns composed by the Sikh Gurus, which she had learned by heart. Young and impetuous as she was, she started talking about the Guru fondly and recited the Sikh hymns with great reverence. The Qazi was wild with his daughter and, in a fit of temper, decided to put her to death. The girl's mother became nervous and informed not only the girl but also her divine Master, Mian Mir. Mian Mir advised the girl to escape to Amritsar and seek refuge with Guru Hargobind.

The young girl came and knocked at the Guru's door. The Guru must give shelter to the shelterless. He had a special pavilion constructed for her where the girl started living. In due course, she became one of the most ardent devotees of the Guru and was called Kaulan—the lotus. A tank called Kaulsar was named after her.

For a while, the Sikhs at Amritsar feared that, instigated by the

Qazi, the Emperor's forces would attack Amritsar to recover the prize horse and the Qazi's daughter. But nothing of the sort happened. Evidently the Mughal King did not wish to offend the Guru.

The Guru had been married for quite some time but he was still without a child. During a visit to Guru Nanak's shrine, he and his mother met Baba Sri Chand, Guru Nanak's son, who had grown very old. The Guru's mother, who was anxious to see a grandson before she breathed her last, asked for Sri Chand's blessings. The Guru's wife, Bibi Damodari, gave birth to a son in 1613. The child was named Gurditta—gift of the Guru. It is said that he was the split image of Guru Nanak—the resemblance was so remarkable. Another son was born to the Guru in 1617. He was called Suraj Mal. The next year, Guru Hargobind was blessed with his third son, Ani Rai. He was followed by Atul Rai in 1620. In 1622, Tegh Bahadur, the fifth son was born.

An old woman named Bhagbhari, who lived in Srinagar, made with her own hands a fine silk robe and longed to present it to the Guru. But the Guru was hundreds of miles away in the Punjab, how would he know about it? The devotee in Bhagbhari, however, was determined that the Guru must visit her to receive the gift. Her faith was not belied; before long she had the Guru visiting her. The first thing he came and asked for was the robe that she had made after years of labor, remembering the Guru every moment.

On his way to Srinagar, Guru Hargobind spent a night with Kattu Shah, another devotee who had recently been converted. The Guru was highly pleased with him.

Hearing that the divine master was visiting Kashmir, some of the Sikhs from an out-of-the-way village came to pay homage to him. They brought with them a pot of fragrant honey to offer it to the Guru. On their way, they happened to spend a night with Kattu Shah. Hearing that they were carrying special honey for the Guru, Kattu Shah asked them again and again to let him taste it. The Sikhs, who had collected the honey for their Guru, would not let Kattu Shah touch the pot, far less allowing him to taste it. When they arrived in Srinagar and made their offering to the Guru, it was discovered that the honey had started to stink, much to their embarrassment. The Guru told them that they should not have refused Kattu Shah, the

Guru's Sikh, a taste of the honey on their way to Srinagar.

During the Guru's visit to Srinagar, Bhagbhari, who had grown very old, breathed her last. Her house was converted into a Gurdwara. It continues to be a popular place of pilgrimage.

A young boy, who had been orphaned and at a loss to know what to do, saw a party of Sikhs proceeding to Amritsar to pay homage to the Guru. He joined the party as an attendant. He listened to the Guru's hymns and served the Sikhs day and night. It so happened that during their journey, the party of Sikhs moved on while he was away to bring them water. As the youth was hurrying to catch up with them, a Pathan saw him and made him carry his luggage. The Pathan was so pleased with the boy's work that he would not release him to enable him to join the party of Sikhs. One day the youth met a Masand, to whom he communicated his longing to meet the Guru. The Masand could not help him. The Muslims ruled the country and they could be savagely unreasonable if they chose to do so. The helpless youth pulled out a *kauri* from his pocket and, giving it to the Masand, requested him to take it to the Guru as the offering of a destitute Sikh.

As the Pathan and the youth were going their way that very afternoon, they decided to rest a while under a tree which was close to an old well. After a little while the Pathan walked up to the well, and, to the youth's bewilderment, the moment he stepped on the platform it gave way and the Pathan was buried in the debris. The youth didn't know who the Pathan was and where he belonged. When he untied the heavy bundle that he had been made to carry all these days, he found that it contained jewelry and a thousand gold mohurs, rich clothes, and several other costly articles. The youth decided to carry all these to the Guru as gifts.

During his journey, he went at nightfall to a wayside house for shelter. The lady of the house welcomed the stranger. "My husband is away," she said, "I have the whole house to myself." The woman thought she could deprive the youth of his belongings when he went to sleep. The youth, used to prayers and meditation, would not go to bed till late in the night. The woman became impatient. She went to her lover next door and conspired with him to murder the stranger and loot his belongings. Entrusting the job to her paramour, the woman came and slept in her room.

In the meanwhile her husband happened to return and, finding a stranger sitting in meditation on the veranda, took him in and made him comfortable in his bedroom. And he came and slept on the veranda without disturbing his wife, who was fast asleep in her own bed. He had hardly gone to sleep when his wife's lover came and, not knowing what had happened in between, killed the husband, whom he mistook for the traveller. The next morning the woman started wailing while the youth quickly left on his journey, grateful to his Guru for saving his life. Reaching Amritsar, the youth offered the fortune to the Guru, who smiled and returned it to the youth. "This is the reward of the *kauri* that you had sent me."

Then came news that Jehangir had suddenly died in Kashmir. A few weeks after the succession of Shah Jehan, it so transpired that the King and the Guru both happened to be out hunting in the same jungle. Shah Jehan had a rare white hawk presented to him by the King of Iran. Somehow the Guru's party caught hold of the hawk and would not return it. Besides, when the King's men came to collect their hawk, the Sikhs gave them a severe beating and drove them away saying, "We will not return the hawk for fear of anyone—even the King." Bhai Gurdas heard about it and observed:

> The earlier Gurus sat in a temple
> The reigning Guru wouldn't remain at one place.
> The kings came to meet the earlier Gurus
> The reigning Guru was sent to the king's fortress.
>
> *(Var XXVI)*

The Guru heard what Gurdas had to say and didn't seem to give much importance to it.

It so happened that a party of Sikhs turned up late one evening from the far West. They had to be entertained but dinner had already been served. If the cooks prepard a meal afresh, it would be too late in the night. The Guru therefore thought of serving the visiting Sikhs the sweets stored in a room for the marriage of his daughter, for which preparations were in progress. But the key of the room was with the Guru's wife Damodari. She would not allow the sweets to be distributed to the visitors. When the Guru heard about it, he was unhappy. "My Sikhs are dearer to me than my life," he said. "If they can't be served the sweets, the marriage party too will not partake of them."

It turned out to be true. Before the wedding could take place, Amritsar was attacked by Mukhlis Khan under the orders of Shah Jehan, who wished to punish the Guru and his Sikhs for holding the royal hawk and beating the King's soldiers who had gone to retrieve it. The marriage preparations were interrupted and the Guru's household had to be evacuated to a safer place.

Mukhlis Khan, who thought that he would get the King's hawk and the Guru's head by the evening, lost his entire force, including renowned warriors such as Shams Khan, Syed Mohammed Ali, and Didar Ali. He then rushed to the battlefield. The Guru asked his warriors to keep away. He wished to engage Mukhlis Khan single-handed. The Guru shot an arrow that killed Mukhlis Khan's horse. At this, Mukhlis challenged the Guru to leave his horse and fight a duel with him with sword and shield. The Guru dismounted from his horse and invited Mukhlis to strike his blow first. Mukhlis Khan aimed a blow which the Guru parried skillfully. Mukhlis Khan's next blow was also warded off by the Guru with his shield. At this, the Guru fell upon Mukhlis Khan, saying, "You have tried twice and failed, it is now my turn." In the twinkling of an eye, he had severed his head from his body. Shah Jehan was furious to learn that the Imperial force under the command of a professional general had been completely wiped out by a dervish. He decide to teach the Guru a lesson. He was, however, dissuaded by Wazir Khan, who convinced the King that the Sikh Guru had no territorial designs. He neither frightened anyone nor was he afraid of anybody. He wished only to be left alone and to pursue his religious and social activities undisturbed.

After the conflict with Mukhlis Khan, the Guru shifted to Kartarpur where large numbers of Sikhs came to join him. He needed to replace those who had lost their lives in the fight and also to augment the strength of his force, since his relations with the Emperor continued to be strained.

While still at Kartarpur, Guru Hargobind one day went out hunting and came across an enchanting spot on the banks of the river Beas, near the ancient village of Ruhela, belonging to the Gherar tribe.

The Guru decided to found a new township called Hargobindpur
there. Bhagwan Das, the headman of the Gherar tribe, was not happy,
because he knew that the Mughal emperor did not take kindly to the
Guru and if he was friendly to him, the King might misunderstand.
However the people of the village were greatly excited; they placed
their land at the disposal of the Guru and wished him to found the
new township without delay. They thought that in this way they
would have the Guru stay amidst them. Bhagwan Das was put out.
He once tried to disturb the Guru's prayer meeting with derogatory
remarks about him personally. The Sikhs lost their temper and in the
scuffle that followed, they killed Bhagwan Das and threw his body
into the river. At this, his son Ratan Chand went to Abdullah Khan,
the Subedar of Jullundur, and instigated him to take action against
the Guru. Chandu's son Karam Chand also happened to be in
Jullundur at the time. He too joined hands with Ratan Chand.
Abdullah Khan felt that since the Guru had already displeased the
Emperor by resisting his force at Amritsar, it should be an excellent
opportunity to win his favor if he could kill or capture the Guru for
him.

No sooner was the decision taken than Abdullah Khan's soldiers
swooped down upon the Guru. They were led by noted fighters such
as Bairam Khan, Mohammed Khan, Balwant Khan, Ali Baksh, and
the two sons of the Subedar, Nabi Baksh and Karim Baksh. The
Subedar had a large contingent of soldiers as his personal bodyguard.

Guru Hargobind gave charge of defense to Bhai Kalyana, Bhai
Nano, Bhai Piraga, Bhai Mathura, Bhai Jagana, Bhai Shaktu, and
Bhai Paras Ram. Bhai Jati Mal and Bhai Molak were asked to
support Bhai Bidhi Chand. The Guru inspired his men, telling them
that it was not a fight for territorial gains but for the preservation of
their religion and their way of life. They must fight and destroy the
aggressor. But it was not an easy task. While they were a mere
handful, there were large hosts arrayed against them. However, they
fought with the conviction that since everyone born must die one day,
it was better to give up their lives in the service of the Guru; they
would attain deliverance from life and death forever and ever. And
then, one after another, the Mughal soldiers started falling in the
battlefield. Mohammed Khan was followed by Bairam Khan; Bhai

Mathura engaged Bairam Khan in a hand-to-hand fight and beheaded him. Infuriated, Bairam Khan's soldiers made mincemeat of Bhai Mathura. Balwant Khan, supported by Ali Baksh, led a fresh attack. He was shot dead by Bhai Kalyana, who was soon overpowered by Ali Baksh and killed with the Guru's name on his lips as he breathed his last. The Guru now deputed Bhai Nano to fight Ali Baksh. While Ali Baksh's matchlock missed the target, Bhai Nano's arrow pierced through his head and he fell down from his horse. However, Nano was soon overpowered and slain by Iman Baksh.

At this Bhai Piraga plunged into the fray. He was supported by Bhai Jagna and Bhai Krishan. When they were slain, Bhai Bidhi Chand sought the Guru's permission to fight the enemy. The Sikhs under Bhai Bidhi Chand's command fought with such valor that the Mughal force was routed completely and started fleeing the battlefield. At this, Abdulla Khan came forward, along with Karam Chand, and Ratan Chand and his two sons. Seeing this, the Guru threw himself into the fight and, one after the other, overpowered his enemies. The Subedar, his two sons, and all his followers were killed in the fight and the Mughal soldiers fled the battlefield in an unprecedented manner.

The completion of Hargobindpur was resumed after this conflict. The Guru made sure that, along with the Gurdwara, a mosque was also constructed in the town. New horses were purchased to replace those lost in the conflict and there were fresh recruits to strengthen the Guru's army.

A party of Masands visiting Kabul were bringing along with them Dilbagh and Gulbagh, two rare chargers, as gifts to the Guru. These horses could cross a river without the rider getting wet. They were so swift that in a race their legs didn't seem to touch the ground. On their way to Amritsar, the horses were seized by the Mughal officials and made over to the Governor.

Bhai Bidhi Chand, deeply hurt to hear about this incident, decided to retrieve the horses for the Guru. This Sikh, before joining the Guru's army, had been a notorious highwayman. While he had been completely reformed after coming to the Guru, the self-respecting and brave Sikh in him wished to restore the two horses to his Master. The Guru's Sikhs felt humiliated every time people came and talked about the beauty of the two horses and how they were prized by the Governor. Since the Mughal king continued to be hostile to the Sikhs, and the horses could one day be pressed into a fight against the Guru and his devotees, it was decided to depute Bidhi Chand to capture the horses and bring them back to the Guru. Accordingly, Bidhi Chand left for Lahore and had himself recruited as a groom in the Governor's stable to look after the horses. The devotion and industry with which Bidhi Chand served his Guru's horses endeared him to Sondha Khan, the stable-keeper, and other officials of the fort. After he had gained their confidence, Bidhi Chand got the guards and the grooms dead drunk one evening and he mounted Dilbagh and escaped from the Mughal Fort.

The Governor sent his trackers all over the country but no clue could be found of the missing horse. While everybody among the Guru's confidants was happy to have Dilbagh restored, the horse seemed to miss his companion Gulbagh. So Bidhi Chand was prepared to go and get Gulbagh. Bidhi Chand was sure that if blessed by the Guru, he would certainly succeed in his mission. This time Bidhi Chand went to Lahore in the guise of a magician. He declared that he could trace the King's missing horse provided he had an opportunity to serve the horse's companion for a few days. There couldn't be any objection to it. From the way Gulbagh greeted the magician and made friends with him, Sondha Khan and the rest felt that he was no ordinary miracle man. Bidhi Chand spent a few days in the royal stable on the pretext of reading *mantras*. Then finding an opportunity, he made good his escape with Gulbagh, this time declaring that he was the Guru's Sikh and was carrying the companion horse to his Master, to whom Dilbagh had already been restored. "I am no thief," announced Bhai Bidhi Chand at the top of his voice, "I came to claim what rightfully belongs to my Guru. Both the chargers are going to Guru Hargobind who, at present, is camping at a village called Bhai Rupa." When both the horses were presented to the Guru, he renamed them—Dilbagh as Jan Bhai and Gulbagh as Suhela.

That the Mughal army would recover the horses and chastise the Sikhs was a foregone conclusion. The Guru, therefore, at the instance of his Sardar Rai Jodh, withdrew deeper into the forest and camped near Nathana Tank, with no other source of water for miles around.

The Mughal army under Lal Beg found their whereabouts sooner than the Sikhs had imagined and launched a fierce attack. Lal Beg had his brother Qamar Beg and his two sons, Qasim Beg and Shams Beg, together with his nephew Kabuli Beg, to support him. It is said that Rai Jodh's wife would put some pearls in a tray and could read the movements of the Mughal forces with the help of the vibrations of the precious stones. While the Sikhs were only few in number, the Imperial army had fighters of several nationalities, including Ruhelas, Yusufzais, Balochs, Pathans, Ethiopians, besides soldiers of Indian origin. It was indeed an unequal fight, but with the devotion and heroism of the Sikh *sardars* and soldiers, the Mughal forces suffered crippling losses. Qamar Beg was pierced by Rai Jodh's lance, Shams Beg was struck by Bidhi Chand with his mailed fist in a hand-to-hand fight and knocked down on the ground. Bidhi Chand then, holding his enemy's two legs, tore him apart into pieces. Qasim Beg was seized by Bhai Jetha by the leg and he dashed his head on the ground. Lal Beg and Kabuli Beg were accounted for by the Guru with his own hands. The loss of life on the Guru's side was also not small. Bhai Jetha, with twelve hundred soldiers, and Gulbagh, the famed horse, also died fighting. Among the wounded were Bhai Bidhi Chand, Rai Jodh, and Jati Mal. The fighting lasted eighteen hours.

The white hawk of the Mughal Emperor was still with the Guru. Once, while his son Gurditta went out hunting, the hawk fell into the hands of Asman Khan, the son-in-law of Painda Khan, one of the most pampered sardars of Guru Hargobind. Painda Khan was not only tall and handsome, but was also the strongest man in the Guru's army. The Guru was greatly fond of him and bestowed gifts on him every now and then. He had the best dress, the best horses, and the best food to eat. It seemed that the treatment he received from the Guru had turned his head. He started feeling that he was, perhaps, indispensable and that the Guru must have him fight the Mughal forces. It was, therefore, a great disappointment for him when the Guru did not invite him to participate in the Nathana Tank battle with the Imperial forces.

After he had captured the prized hawk, rather than return it to the Guru, Asman Khan concealed the bird, hoping to restore it to the King and receive a large estate as a reward. Not only this, but Asman

Khan also started donning the special dress and arms presented to
Painda Khan by the Guru. The horse allotted to Painda Khan was
always found to be with Asman Khan.

When Asman Khan continued to maintain that he knew nothing
about the hawk, the Guru sent for Painda Khan. He came in the
ordinary dress of a common citizen, rather than in the courtly
costumes and armaments that he was used to wearing when he came
to see the Master. The Guru asked him about the hawk, his dress as a
sardar and the horse placed at his disposal. Rather than own his
mistakes, Painda Khan persisted in making false statements. The
Guru had the hawk recovered from Asman Khan and terminated
Painda Khan's services and expelled him from the *darbar.*

Painda Khan went to the Mughal court and offered to join the
Imperial army against the Guru. Since he knew all the secrets of the
Guru's forces, he received a warm welcome. Painda Khan's strength
was legendary. It is said that he could fight an elephant, and with his
thumb could pulverize a coin. Painda Khan told the King that the
Guru's army comprised the poor and the low caste, the diseased and
the disabled; they were weavers and washermen, barbers and ballad
singers.

It was decided to send a force under Kale Khan against the Guru.
He was to be supported by Painda Khan, Anwar Khan, Qutb Khan,
and Asman Khan. When word came that the Guru was again being
attacked by a massive Mughal army, Dhir Mal, the Guru's grandson,
wrote in confidence to Painda Khan, promising him his assistance. "If
you come tonight," he said, "You will find the Guru unprepared
and the fort and the treasures will fall into your hands." When
Painda Khan received the letter, the Mughals mounted the attack
immediately. On the Guru's side, Bidhi Chand, Jati Mal, Lakhi, and
Rai Jodh ranged their troops on all four sides of Kartarpur.

It was again a bloody fight with heavy carnage. It is said that Kale
Khan's entire army was wiped out in the first encounter. Kale Khan
then introduced another contingent. It, too, met the same fate and the
Pathans started retreating. At this, an arrow shot by Bidhi Chand
struck Anwar Khan in the forehead and he fell reeling to the ground.

The Sikh soldiers, who were fighting for their Guru and their faith,
were given strict instructions that they must not fire at the fleeing

forces; they must challenge the enemy and only then attack them.

The Mughal commander taunted Painda Khan and his son-in-law Asman Khan, who had assured them that they had only to launch an attack and all the treasures of the Guru would be theirs to loot. Provoked by this, Painda Khan led the next attack. In the meanwhile, Qutb Khan fired an arrow and wounded Bhai Lakhu, who fell to the ground. Qutb Khan descended upon him and severed his head with his sword. Bhai Lakhu's death boosted the morale of the Mughal forces.

Painda Khan was supported by Kale Khan, Qutb Khan, and Asman Khan. Seeing the enemy advance, the Guru deputed Bidhi Chand to engage Kale Khan; Baba Gurditta was to fight Asman Khan and the Guru himself decided to confront Painda Khan.

The Guru was riding Dilbagh, the famous charger. Painda Khan advanced, and in spite of the Guru asking him to heed reason and seek forgiveness for his misdeeds, he attacked the Guru once, twice. His first blow was aimed at the calf of the Guru's leg. The Guru moved his horse away and skillfully avoided the blow. His second blow was also parried by the Guru with his shield. It was now the Guru's turn to attack, and with frightening quickness, he struck Painda Khan with his two-edged scimitar and felled him to the ground, mortally wounded. The Guru came down from his horse and, taking his old protege in his arms, asked him to read the *Kalma* in the hour of his death. But before he could open his lips Painda Khan was dead. It is said that the Guru was deeply moved by Painda Khan's death. He took out his shield and put it on his face to provide him shade from the sun.

In another sector of the battlefield Baba Gurditta's arrow pierced Asman Khan's eye and went through his brain. At his death, Baba Gurditta also started crying since they had played together as children.

The Mughal army was greatly unnerved at the loss of Painda Khan and Asman Khan, yet Qutb Khan came forward and challenged the Guru to a hand-to-hand fight. The fight lasted one hour, at the end of which the Guru had the better of his adversary, and severed Qutb Khan's head with a fell stroke of his sword.

Finding Qutb Khan dead, Kale Khan came forward in mad fury. He showered arrows at the Guru, one of which grazed past his forehead and his face was smeared with blood. At this, the Guru shot an arrow which killed Kale Khan's horse. Seeing his enemy leave his horse, the Guru also dismounted from his steed. It was a fierce combat, their swords spitting sparks of fire. At last the Guru struck a mighty blow with his scimitar that severed Kale Khan's head from his body. At this point Qasim Khan fell upon the Guru unawares. The Guru warded off his blows one after the other and then cut him in two also.

The battle cost the Guru seven hundred of his brave soldiers, while the loss to the Mughal army was no less.

Immediately after the Mughal forces withdrew, the Guru, along with his family and close associates, left for Kartarpur. Budhan Shah, a Muslim divine, had been promised a visit by the Guru before his death. The Guru felt that Budhan Shah's end was near. Another factor that probably prevailed on the Guru to retire to an out-of-the-way quiet town was his anxiety to avoid further bloodshed. However, Dhir Mal, one of the Guru's grandsons, refused to accompany him. A spoiled young man, he was already in league with the Mughals, and he thought that if he remained behind at Kartarpur, he could style himself as the Guru. Because the copy of the *Holy Granth* was in his possession and he would not part with it, the Guru did not take any notice of him. He had already proved himself to be a traitor and alienated himself from the Guru's grace.

Budhan Shah was waiting for the Guru when he arrived. He offered him a bowl of milk and sought his blessings. He said that he had met Guru Nanak, who had promised that he would come to grant him deliverance from the cycle of life and death in the image of his Sixth successor.

At Kartarpur, the Guru maintained a small force of seven hundred horses, three hundred horsemen, and sixty artillery men, by way of his personal bodyguards. It seems the Guru had taken to heart the loss of his soldiers and sardars in wars, one after the other. He was always found remembering them.

He had not yet recovered from it, when the Guru's eldest son Bhai Gurditta passed away. Bhai Gurditta had gone out hunting when one of his companions happened to shoot a cow, mistaking it to be a deer. The villagers were furious and they caught the offending hunter and would have killed him if Bhai Gurditta had not run to his rescue. Bhai

Gurditta offered to compensate them but they would not listen to him; they must have their cow back alive. At this, Bhai Gurditta touched the cow with his cane and it is said she was reanimated. When the Guru heard about the incident, he was most unhappy. He sent for Bhai Gurditta and reprimanded him. How can anyone interfere with the ways of God? Bhai Gurditta took this to heart and retired to Budhan Shah's shrine close by, he said his prayers and, lying down with a sheet of cloth over him, he passed away, exactly the way Baba Atal, his brother, had given up his life.

The Guru was deeply shocked at Bhai Gurditta's untimely death. It pained him more when, in spite of his inviting Dhir Mal, his grandson to receive the traditional turban on the demise of his father, he refused to come to Kiratpur.

Guru Hargobind kept his grandson Har Rai always in his company. Evidently, he was grooming him for the succession. He probably wished to bestow on his grandson what was due to Bhai Gurditta, the Guru's eldest son.

Seeing this, his wife pleaded with the Guru that his sons Suraj Mal, Ani Rai, and Tegh Bahadur should be considered first. While Suraj Mal and Ani Rai were not considered fit, of Tegh Bahadur Guru Hargobind observed, "He will become the Guru and will have a son who will fight the Turks in the cause of justice. His glory will spread far and wide."

Then the Guru fixed a day for the formal consecration of Har Rai as Guru. He invited all his relatives and important Sikhs. In a grand gathering at Kiratpur, he offered prayers and then, holding Har Rai by his hand, seated him on Guru Nanak's seat. Bhai Budha's son, Bhai Bhana, applied the sacramental *tilak* and Guru Hargobind bowed before the Seventh Sikh Guru, offering him the ceremonial five paise, a coconut, and flowers.

A few days later, the Guru advised Tegh Bahadur to go to the village of Bakala in Amritsar district along with his mother and to settle there. The Guru knew that his end was close. He gave strict instructions to his family and the Sikhs not to mourn his passing. He desired that after he was gone, they should recite hymns from the *Holy Granth*. According to the author of *Dabistam-i-Mazahib*, it was a Sunday in 1645—the third of Muharram A.H. 1055. He breathed his last after a stewardship of thirty-seven years and ten months.

Guru Hargobind was a tall, handsome man of fine build and given to active life. He was fond of hunting and never evaded fighting if he had to fight. He was a leader of his men and a hero on the battlefield. Like a true hero, he avoided aggression as far as possible but when he found himself faced with evil he struck heavily; a fighter for right causes, he came out every time with flying colors. But sensitive as he was, the bloodshed and carnage on the battlefield made him unhappy. Advising his successor that he should keep only twenty-two hundred mounted soldiers for his defense, he bemoaned the loss of many a fine soldier and *sardar* and died contemplating why wars could not be eliminated from the world, why sons like Dhir Mal misbehaved, why friends like Painda Khan went astray, and why Prithi Chand and Chandu Shah refused to see reason.

Guru Hargobind's greatest contribution is that he gave a new turn to the Sikh way of life. He turned saints into soldiers and yet remained a man of God. He believed that in the times in which he lived, religion could not be separated from politics. Nonviolence is cowardice if it is resorted to out of helplessness or fear. It is the brave and the heroic who can be nonviolent. And when all other means are exhausted, there is always justification to resort to arms. Essentially a spiritual leader of a community hardly a hundred years old, he fought a number of battles with the Imperial forces and every time vanquished his foes because the truth was always on his side. It was always a fight in self-defense and never a war of aggression. The new trend he gave to Sikh polity found its finest expression in his grandson, Guru Gobind Singh, the tenth Sikh Guru.

In spite of his involvement in fighting and preparation for conflicts, however, Guru Hargobind paid a great deal of attention to social reform and the spiritual upliftment of his people. He once told his Sikhs that they must read the scriptures with understanding. Everyone present said that he did so morning and evening. At this, the Guru observed, "He who can recite the *Japji* with undivided devotion and understanding would have his wish fulfilled. It is said a Sikh by the name of Gopal volunteered to do so. He started reciting the *Japji* there and then. When he had nearly finished the text, the Guru prepared himself to offer him salvation for his feat because anything less than that would be inadequate for Gopal's piety. But as Gopal came to the last hymn but one, his mind turned away from God and he told himself that if he was rewarded with a particular horse the Guru had received earlier in the morning, he would be most happy. The Guru could read his thoughts and, sending for the horse, presented it to him. But for his slip towards the close of the recital, he would have earned his release from the cycle of birth and death.

Guru Hargobind detested miracle-making. He felt that it meant interfering with the ways of God. It is said that one of his sons, Baba Atal, had endeared himself to the Guru a great deal. Whenever he found time the Guru sent for him and enjoyed his company. Once it so happened that one of Baba Atal's playmates was bitten by a snake and died. But the playmate owed him a turn in the game that they had been playing the previous evening. When Baba Atal went to invite his companion to the game the next morning, he found his family wailing over the death of the child. Baba Atal would not believe them and in all his innocence approached the dead body and said, "Mohan, get up, you owe me a turn in the game." It is said that the dead child opened his eyes at the call and walked off to play with his companion. When Guru Hargobind heard about it, he was distressed and, sending for Baba Atal, reprimanded him. "How can anyone interfere with the ways of God?" he asked. Baba Atal heard the reprimand and withdrew from the Guru's presence. Sitting by the side of the Kaulsar he said his prayers and gave his life for the life he had saved.

Bhai Gurdas was a great intellectual and a fine poet and was respected by the Sikh Gurus. Sensitive as he was, he couldn't reconcile himself to Guru Hargobind's being on the warpath. In one of his poems, he wrote:

> Even if the Guru became a play-actor, the Sikhs should not lose their faith.
>
> *(Var XXXV)*

With a view to testing his faith, the Guru sent Bhai Gurdas to purchase two chargers for him from Kabul, at a cost of fifty thousand rupees each. It is said that after he had struck the bargain, Bhai Gurdas went into his tent to hand over the money to the horse traders. To his shock, he found that the money bags contained pieces of bricks instead of *mohurs*. Fearing the consequence, he tore the tent at the back and made good his escape. When he did not appear for an unduly long time, his companions went into the tent and discovered that Bhai Gurdas had absconded. They counted the mohurs in the money bags, which were lying intact, and disposed of the horse traders. When the matter was reported to the Guru, Bhai Gurdas went to Varanasi and settled there. It was after Bhai Gurdas realized his mistake that he was pardoned and allowed to rejoin the Guru's company.

Guru Hargobind was a man of God given to contemplation. Equally great as a man of action, he fought injustice all his life and never for a moment compromised with evil on the plea that he was a holy man devoted to a life of meditation and prayer, more interested in the life to come.

Guru Har Rai

He who has been blessed by Guru Nanak
Is lost in the praises of the Lord.
What could one teach those
Who have Divine Nanak as their Guru?

—*Guru Angad*

Once, when he was a child, a handful of flowers dropped as Har Rai disturbed a shrub accidentally. He started crying, "It must have hurt the shrub," he told himself.

Apparently he was quite the opposite of his grandfather. In fact, Guru Hargobind had himself fostered this in his successor. The bloodshed and the suffering he had witnessed in several skirmishes with the Mughal forces grieved him deeply. He retired to Kiratpur, a quiet place in the Shivalik Hills and wished Guru Har Rai to continue to stay there. He was to maintain a token force of twenty-two hundred mounted soldiers for his defense and, as far as possible, keep out of the way of the Mughals. There were several reasons for it.

Guru Har Rai was just fourteen years old when he became the seventh Sikh Guru. He was too young, in the eyes of his grandfather, to involve himself in fighting. His elder brother, Dhir Mal, was already in league with the enemies of the Guru. If possible, he should not be given an opportunity to do further mischief. Perhaps the most important factor that seemed to have prevailed with the Guru was that the Sikhs were yet a young community who could not afford to fritter away their energies in continuous warfare. After the series of battles that Guru Hargobind had to fight, they needed respite, so that the community could consolidate and prepare for the bigger and fiercer fight that was yet in store for them.

Guru Har Rai was fond of going out for *shikar* like his grandfather, but instead of hunting wild animals, he captured them and kept them as pets.

After fighting several unsuccessful battles with the Sikhs, Shah Jehan also realized that it was best to make friends with this heroic, self-respecting community. Accordingly, when his son Dara Shikoh fell seriously ill, he approached the Guru for his blessings and the young prince is said to have been cured with an herb Guru Har Rai sent to Delhi.

But this amity with the Delhi Darbar was shortlived. Aurangzeb, the third son of King Shah Jehan, usurped the throne and chased away Dara Shikoh, his eldest brother. While in flight Dara Shikoh met Guru Har Rai. He was grateful to the Guru because he had saved his life when he was on his deathbed. According to the tradition of the Guru's household, Guru Har Rai received the prince with due courtesy and gave him all help that he needed. Dara Shikoh, who was a scholar and a God-fearing person, told the Guru that he was not at all interested in the Delhi throne and that he would be happier if he were left alone for spiritual pursuits. However, Aurangzeb captured Dara Shikoh and, having got him condemned by the Qazi for deviating from the Islamic creed, had him executed.

After Aurangzeb was firmly settled on the Mughal throne, he turned his attention to the Sikhs. He was aware that the Sikh Gurus preached a new faith, which was distinct from Islam and Hinduism. He also knew that they had thousands of followers over the length and breadth of the country. Bigoted Muslim that Aurangzeb was, he thought if he could convert the Guru to Islam he would win over a large number of the Guru's devotees to his faith.

An excuse was readily available. The Guru had met Dara Shikoh, an enemy of the King, and blessed him. After Dara Shikoh was eliminated, Aurangzeb found the Guru a threat to his own power. Aurangzeb was a devout Muslim. He said his prayers regularly and led an austere life, unlike his predecessors—Shah Jehan and Jehangir. He sent word to Guru Har Rai, inviting him to his court. Aurangzeb thought that while in Delhi he would ask the Guru to work a miracle. If he did so, he would accept him as a man of God, otherwise he would treat him like an ordinary citizen and then punish him according to the law of the land.

When the King's summons were received at Kiratpur, there was a long debate. Some of the Sikhs were in favor of the Guru going to Delhi and not giving the Mughal King an excuse to take offense, whereas others felt that Aurangzeb was essentially an unscrupulous king, who had imprisoned his own father and killed his own brother. As the issue was being debated, the Guru's son Ram Rai turned up. He was definitely of the opinion that the King's invitation must not be ignored, and since the Mughal had stretched out a hand of friendship, it must be held firmly and exploited for the well-being of the community. It was therefore decided that rather than the Guru going to Delhi, Ram Rai should represent his father and find out what Aurangzeb's real intentions were. The way Aurangzeb was destroying Hindu temples at Mathura, Ajmer, and Varanasi, the Sikhs could not see any good coming out of the meeting. However, since Ram Rai was determined, everyone agreed to his visiting Delhi in response to the King's invitation.

Before Ram Rai left for Delhi, the Guru sent for him and told him specifically not to indulge in miracle-making at the instance of the King. It was against the Sikh faith. Guru Hargobind had particularly forbidden it and, as the reigning Guru, he did not approve of it. He was also cautioned that he must not allow the sanctity of the Sikh Scriptures to be compromised at any cost.

What was feared by the Guru and the Sikhs happened at Delhi. With a view to humoring the King, Ram Rai started working miracles, one after the other. Not only this, but when Aurangzeb and his courtiers took objection to one of Guru Nanak's verses,

Mitti Mussalmam ki pede pai kumhar
(The ashes of the Muslim get into a potter's clod),

Ram Rai hastened to say that it was a mistake committed by the calligraphist. What Guru Nanak had said was:

Mitti beiman ki pede pai kumhar
(The ashes of the faithless get into a potter's clod).

Aurangzeb was fully satisfied and made friends with Ram Rai, bestowing on him a robe of honor and other favors. But when this news came to Guru Har Rai he was deeply distressed. He said that he would have nothing to do with Ram Rai. He disowned him as his son and asked him not to return to him at all.

While Guru Har Rai did not go out of his way to provoke the rulers of the day, he continued the practice of maintaining and riding horses, organizing races, and going out for shikar. One day, while passing through a village, the Guru knocked at a door. It was the house of a poor widow. The moment the door opened, the woman was beside herself with joy. She rushed into the house and brought for the Guru the food she had prepared. The Guru partook of her humble meal seated on horseback, not even washing his hands, which he always did before he took his meals.

The next day the Guru's followers had taken with them plenty of food in case the Guru needed to eat during the chase. But the Guru did not need anything to eat all the while they were in the jungle.

Returning home, when his Sikhs asked the Guru about his eating at a poor widow's house uninvited, the Guru told them that rather than being uninvited he was awaited in the poor hut most anxiously. All those days the old lady would prepare her simple meal and start praying for a glimpse of the Guru. She was too old to make a journey to the Guru's place. Day after day she continued to prepare a meal for her Guru and wait for him. She never lost faith. She knew her Guru would not let her down. As last her prayers were answered.

The next time they happened to pass that village the Sikhs had the truth of what their Guru had told them verified. The poor old woman told them how she labored hard and with her earnings prepared her simple fare and longed to entertain the Guru and how he had heard her prayers and come to her place to bless her.

Similarly, Bhai Gonda, a devoted Sikh, was asked by the Guru to proceed to Kabul for the spiritual needs of the Guru's Sikhs residing in that far-off place. It was not without risk, making the arduous journey and living among aliens, but Bhai Gonda left for Kabul the moment he heard the Guru's orders. Once, while saying his prayers in Kabul, Gonda clung to the Guru's feet in his imagination. He held the Guru's feet in deep devotion all the while he was reciting his prayers.

It so happened that the Guru at that particular hour was sitting on his throne. The Sikhs marked that the Guru had been sitting in a particular posture with both his feet resting on each other for quite some time. It was time for his meal and, even then, he was sitting in that peculiar posture. The meal was announced once, twice, thrice, but he neither moved from his seat nor uttered a word. At last, after about an hour, he got up and expressed his regret at having kept his Sikhs waiting. "It was Bhai Gonda in Kabul," he told them, "he had held my feet and would not leave them. It is only after he completed his prayers that he released them and I could move away." The Sikhs were amazed to hear it. The next time Bhai Gonda came to pay his homage to the Guru, the Sikhs had the incident verified and found that every word of it was true.

The Guru was visiting Kartarpur. It so happened that a Brahmin, who had earlier been blessed by the Guru and had had a son, came wailing with the dead body of the child in his arms. His son had died of some ailment. The Brahmin said that the Guru must revive the child, otherwise he would also die sitting at the Guru's threshold. The Guru explained to him, "Everyone who is born must die. You should be grateful that your son has gone at this age; if he had been grown up, married, and had children, it would have been more painful for you." But the Brahmin kept crying and pleading for the Guru's intercession for the child. The whole day he sat at the Guru's door. Night fell and he was still there. At last a deputation of the Guru's Sikhs came to plead on behalf of the Brahmin. Their plea was that if the Guru didn't work the miracle the people of other communities would get the impression that the Sikh Guru was incapable of meeting the needs of his Sikhs. The Guru didn't appreciate their argument at all. But when the Sikhs persisted, he said, "Is there anyone amongst you who is willing to give his life for the dead child?" The Sikhs heard it and their hearts sank. The Guru repeated his question again. There was no reply. The third time he asked, one of the Sikhs in the deputation called Jiwan came out. He was willing to sacrifice his life for the Brahmin's child. It is said that at that very moment Jiwan dropped dead and the child came to life.

Guru Har Rai passed away at the early age of thirty years in 1661. Though the records are silent about the end, it must have come unexpectedly, probably owing to some fatal illness. But just before his death he had his second son Harkrishan ordained as the Guru. There was no question of considering Ram Rai, the elder son, since he had already been disinherited by the Guru because of his misconduct.

The stewardship of Guru Har Rai, as of his successor Guru Harkrishan, was a sort of interregnum in the life of the Sikh community before it set out on a new path of no compromise with injustice and waged a determined war with the unjust, corrupt, and bigoted rulers of the day.

What Guru Har Rai told Dara Shikoh, the heir-apparent to the Mughal throne, when they met on the bank of the river Beas gives an indication of the Guru's thinking. He advised the prince not to oppress his subjects, to try as far as possible to remain close to his people, and to undertake works of public welfare, like sinking wells, digging tanks, building bridges, and opening schools and hospitals.

The Guru himself remained as close to his Sikhs as possible and solved their spiritual problems and removed their day-to-day doubts. Once his Sikhs approached Guru Har Rai and asked if it was any use reciting the hymns without understanding the text. The Guru was aware that though the Sikh scriptures were in the language of the people, a large number of the Sikhs recited the hymns without understanding their meaning fully. But there was no doubting their devotion to the Holy Word. It so happened that they were then passing through the outskirts of a village. The Guru showed his Sikhs pieces of a broken pot that was used for storing butter. And now lying in the sun the little butter that had stuck to the potsherds had started melting. "It's good if one reads the scriptures with understanding. It is like holding butter," said the Guru, "but if that is not possible, it's not without virtue reading the scripture with devotion; some of it will certainly stick and when the warmth of understanding is applied to it at any time, it will surely do good."

The Guru gave great respect to the Holy Word. Once, when he was lying on his couch a Sikh turned up reciting hymns from the *Holy Granth*. The moment the Guru heard the hymn he got up in deference to the Holy Word. When asked, he told his Sikhs that the Guru himself is embodied in his hymns. Reverence for the hymns is reverence for the Guru. Guru Har Rai was a simple man of God who lived a highly simple life and valued simplicity and devotion among the followers of his creed.

Guru Harkrishan

O Nanak, the door of the heart
Does not open
Without the Guru—
He alone holds the key.

—Guru Angad

Born in 1656, Guru Harkrishan was only five years old when he was ordained Guru. It is surmised that Guru Har Rai's end, untimely as it was, must have come suddenly so that he appointed his younger son to succeed him and then passed away. His elder son Ram Rai, having alienated himself and continuing to befriend the Guru's enemies, Guru Har Rai did not wish to take any risk and leave the succession undecided.

When Ram Rai heard about it, he was wild with anger. He declared himself to be the Guru in Delhi and started appointing his own *masands* in various places and collecting donations from them. Since Ram Rai was a self-appointed guru, the masands also behaved in an unruly manner and started exploiting the Sikhs. To extract money from the poor Sikhs, they employed both threat and blackmail.

Ram Rai didn't stay quiet. He made a complaint to Aurangzeb that his father had discriminated against him because of his loyalty to the Delhi throne. He had endowed his younger brother with all the property, depriving him of his due share. Aurangzeb not only sympathized with him, but he also fanned his grievance further. He wished the brothers to keep on quarrelling so that their influence with the Sikh masses would weaken and he could win them over to Islam.

It so happened that before his passing away, Guru Har Rai had told his young son Guru Harkrishan never to see Aurangzeb. Since

Ram Rai had made friends with the Mughals, he wished him to continue to deal with the King and with state affairs. When Ram Rai learned about the injunction, he implored the Emperor to summon Guru Harkrishan to Delhi. He thought that if his younger brother met the King, he would be going against his father's wishes and thus incur the displeasure of his devotees, and if he refused to go to Delhi, the King would naturally take stern action against him.

Aurangzeb asked Raja Jai Singh to get Guru Harkrishan to see him in Delhi. Raja Jai Singh was a senior court official and known for his devotion to the Sikh Gurus. He was in a great predicament. He was aware that the Guru had been enjoined upon by his revered father not to meet the Muhgal King ever, and if he couldn't be brought to Delhi, it would annoy Aurangzeb, who was already ill-disposed towards the Sikhs and their Guru.

Raja Jai Singh, therefore, sent word to Kartarpur to tell the Guru that the Sikhs in Delhi were also as anxious to see him as the King. He assured the Guru that while in Delhi he need not see the King; his mere visit to the Capital would absolve the Raja of his responsibility.

Considering the predicament of one of the ardent devotees of the Guru's household, Guru Harkrishan's mother and other Sikhs in Kartarpur agreed to the Guru going to Delhi.

When the Sikhs came to know that the Guru was on his way to Delhi, they collected in large numbers at every stage of his journey. Seeing crowds of devotees chasing him, a Brahmin at Panjokhara near Ambala laughed at the spectacle in great arrogance. He couldn't understand the Guru's Sikhs paying homage to a "mere" child of less than eight years. Heavily weighed under his learning, he came and challenged the Guru to a debate. The Brahmin objected even to the Guru's name. He said, "The great author of the *Gita* was called Krishna and this 'child' styles himself as Harkrishan, which means he is greater than the Lord." He challenged the Guru to interpret the *Gita* for him. Among the people assembled on the occasion was a watercarrier by the name of Chhajju. He noticed how the Brahmin, in his arrogance, had not even saluted the great Guru when he came. Hardly had the Brahmin stopped talking when Chhajju came forward and said, "Before my Guru replies, I would like you to have a word with me, a humble devotee of the Guru." The Brahmin was amused to see an uncouth watercarrier in the Guru's retinue standing before him. In the discussion that followed, Chhajju gave such a splendid display of his learning of the Vedas and Shastras that the Brahmin was completely humbled. He was convinced that it was due only to the Guru's blessings that an ordinary disciple could talk about philosophical treatises with such authority and understanding. The Brahmin fell at the Guru's feet and sought forgiveness for his arrogance and discourtesy.

On his arrival in Delhi the Guru and his party were guests of Raja Jai Singh, who received them with great reverence. It is said that in order to test the Guru's insight Raja Jai Singh's wife dressed herself as a maidservant and came to pay her homage, along with other ladies. To her joy, the Guru spotted her at once and everyone present started singing the Guru's praises.

When the people came to know that Guru Harkrishan was visiting Delhi, large crowds flocked around him day and night. It so happened that during the Guru's visit, smallpox was raging in Delhi. With hundreds of devotees visiting him he could not escape contracting the fell disease. Before the King or his followers could provide proper treatment, the Guru was taken seriously ill. As he desired, he was removed to a house on the bank of the river Jamuna where he breathed his last. He was hardly eight years old when he left this world in 1664. It is said that before he passed away he indicated to his mother and all those present that his successor was in Baba Bakala, thereby referring to Guru Tegh Bahadur, who had settled there.

The Guru was cremated at a place called Tilokhari on the banks of the Jamuna in South Delhi.

A Gurdwara called Bangla Sahib came to be built subsequently at the place of Guru Harkrishan's residence in Delhi. It has, in due course, become a place of pilgrimage with a holy tank added to it recently.

It is said that Guru Harkrishan was an extremely charming child, fair in complexion and with sharp features. He had bright eyes and there was a glow on his face. Even at that early age he remembered a great many hymns of his predecessors and quoted them with amazing appropriateness. After he became the Guru, he naturally had the divine light of Guru Nanak kindled in him. Whatever decisions he made had the stamp of maturity about them. While he listened to the wise counsels of his mother and other senior members of the family, he remained steadfast in his decision not to see Aurangzeb at any cost. He agreed to go to Delhi only when he was assured that he would not have to see the king.

As a face-saving device, Aurangzeb sent his son to see the Guru, who was deeply impressed with his maturity, and he at once became a great admirer of the Guru.

Similarly, rather than enter into an argument with the Panjkhora Brahmin, he proved to him that an ordinary Sikh in the Guru's service had a sharper insight and was better informed than a vain, dry-as-dust scholar. Tender and docile, he received respect and devotion from high and low.

Guru Tegh Bahadur

Like the shadow of a cloud
Whatever you see must disappear.

—*Guru Tegh Bahadur*

"Since you have plugged the free flow of Guru's grace, . . . there will be unpleasantness and heart burning at every step." These words of Guru Amar Das to his daughter Bibi Bhani when she sought to retain the Guruship for her family proved prophetic again and again. But they were never so true as in the case of Guru Tegh Bahadur's succession. There were two reasons for it. First, Guru Harkrishan died suddenly in far-off Delhi, where the successor was not available to be formally installed. And, secondly, Guru Tegh Bahadur was essentially contemplative by temperament. As instructed by his father, he went along with his mother to out-of-the way Bakala, and lived there in seclusion for several years.

When word went around that the successor to Guru Harkrishan was at Baba Bakala it is said that as many as twenty-two aspirants from amongst the Sodhi dynasty styled themselves as Guru and started receiving offerings from the Sikhs.

The devotees coming to Baba Bakala were bewildered. A prosperous trader, Bhai Makhan Shah, met the same fate. His ship was being wrecked in a storm when he remembered the Guru for his help. The storm subsided at once and he arrived at the port of his destination safely. While caught in the storm, Bhai Makhan Shah had pledged to offer five hundred gold *mohurs* to the Guru for his blessings. And the first thing he did was to go to Delhi where the Guru was supposed to have gone. He was told the tragic news of Guru

178

Harkrishan's passing away and informed that his successor, the ninth Sikh Guru was in Baba Bakala. Bhai Makhan Shah hurried to Baba Bakala to pay his homage to the Master and make his promised offering.

When he reached Baba Bakala, he was perplexed to find a Guru at almost every step claiming offerings from the confused pilgrims. A shrewd businessman, Bhai Makhan Shah decided that rather than part with the entire amount of five hundred gold mohurs he would make an offering of two mohurs to each one of the twenty-two self-styled gurus. After he had gone around the town satisfying each one with the uniform offering of two mohurs a child told Bhai Makhan Shah that there was yet another holy man staying in a house across the street. Bhai Makhan Shah decided to visit the house pointed out to him. Guru Tegh Bahadur was busy with his prayers when Bhai Makhan Shah arrived. His people were aware that he didn't much relish meeting visitors. They would have driven Bhai Makhan Shah away but for the Guru's intervention. The Guru thought that if he did not help Bhai Makhan Shah, a devout Sikh, to identify him, he would be misled like many others and the confusion prevailing amongst the Sikhs would continue to be confounded.

Bhai Makhan Shah came to Guru Tegh Bahadur, and as he had with others, made an offering of two mohurs. The Guru smiled. Bhai Makhan Shah suddenly felt uneasy. It was the discomfiture of one who owed someone a debt. Realizing the devotee's embarrassment, Guru Tegh Bhadur said, "I thought you had pledged five hundred mohurs." At this Bhai Makhan Shah's delight knew no bounds. He clung to the Guru's feet. He kissed them again and again. In a mad frenzy, he rushed to the roof of the house and started shouting, "I have found, I have found the True Guru." The Sikhs all over the town heard it and hurried to the house of the quiet saint called Baba Tegha. They greeted him with the slogan, "Long live the Ninth Guru!" In the meanwhile, Bhai Makhan Shah brought his bag of five hundred mohurs and made his promised offering.

There were great rejoicings and celebrations at the identification of the Ninth Successor to Guru Nanak. The festivities lasted many days. The Sikhs came to Baba Bakala with their offerings from far and near. Guru Tegh Bahadur's house was full of precious gifts of all sorts.

Dhir Mal, the eldest son of Bhai Gurditta, was most unhappy. He entered into a conspiracy with a masand called Sihan and raided the Guru's house. It is said that they shot at Guru Tegh Bahadur, wounding him in the arm, and then fled with everything worth looting in the house.

Luckily Bhai Makhan Shah was still in the town. He rushed to the Guru's residence and found that Dhir Mal's men had already fled with the booty. He chased them and brought them, with hands and feet bound, for punishment. He also had all the looted property restored to the Guru. But the Guru would have none of it. He returned it to Dhir Mal, telling Makhan Shah innocently that it belonged to him. Dhir Mal heard it, and he was put to utter shame.

Guru Tegh Bahadur now decided to leave Baba Bakala and move to Amritsar. Throughout his journey the devotees lined his route to greet him. But when the Guru arrived at Amritsar, the masands shut the doors of the sanctorum and would not allow him to enter. After Guru Hargobind had moved to Kartarpur, the Amritsar temple had passed into the hands of Prithi Chand. It was now the charge of his grandson, who wouldn't allow Guru Tegh Bahadur to enter the holy shrine. The Guru waited for a little while under a tree on the premises but the misguided masands would not relent. At this, an old lady called Hariyan, belonging to a village close by, invited the Guru to spend the night in her humble house. When the womenfolk in Amritsar heard about it, they led the Guru in a big procession, chanting hymns. It is believed that the temple was thus saved for the Sikh community. It is feared that if the Amritsar ladies had not risen to the occasion, it might have ceased to remain on the map of places of Sikh pilgrimage.

Guru Tegh Bhadur's destination was Kartarpur. But he didn't find the atmosphere at Kartarpur too congenial either. Some of the Sodhis were jealous of him there also. The Guru therefore acquired a large enough tract of land from the Raja of Kahlur and founded a new town called Anandpur, about six kilometers from Kartarpur.

The Sikhs came from far and near to settle in the new town. But before the town was fully developed, the Guru had a call from the east. The Sikhs who had come to settle in Anandpur to be near the Guru were disappointed. But they had to accept the will of the

Master, who had other responsibilities on his shoulders and other duties to discharge.

Stage by stage, camping at various places, the Guru arived in Delhi, where he was received with great enthusiasm by the Sikhs, including the wives of Raja Jai Singh and Kanwar Ram Singh. Raja Ram Singh was under house arrest and Raja Jai Singh was away. It is said that the King was also away in Agra. Wherever he halted in the Punjab during his journey to Delhi, the Guru had wells sunk, tanks dug, and free kitchens established.

From Delhi he went to Patna via Allahabad. Since his wife was expecting, the Guru left his family at Patna and proceeded to Assam. During the Guru's visit to Assam, Aurangzeb deputed Raja Ram Singh with a large force of thirty thousand infantry, eighteen thousand cavalry, and fifteen thousand archers to fight the Raja of Kamrup, who had captured Gauhati. Since Raja Ram Singh was a Sikh devotee, he approached the Guru for his blessings. Aurangzeb had deputed Raja Ram Singh to lead the attack, in the hope that he would either subdue the rebel Ahom King or get killed in the fight. Either was welcome to the Emperor. Earlier, Mir Jumla, a renowned Muslim general, had failed in his attempt to put down the revolt. However, while Aurangzeb had given the command to Raja Ram Singh, he did not trust him at all. He had also deputed five Muslim generals to keep a close watch over the Raja's activities.

Situated in this unenviable position, Raja Ram Singh sought Guru Tegh Bahadur's good offices to negotiate a settlement with the Ahom King who, evidently, had great respect for the Guru. The Guru conducted the negotiations successfully. The news of the peace treaty between the contending forces pleased everybody and large crowds visited Guru Tegh Bahadur, stationed at Dhubri, to pay homage to him.

Guru Tegh Bahadur was still in Assam when news came that the Guru had been blessed with a son at Patna on the seventh day of the light half of the Indian month of *Posh* in 1666. He was given the name of Gobind Rai as suggested by the Guru before his departure for Assam. On hearing the good news, Raja Ram Singh organized grand celebrations.

Guru Tegh Bahadur had penetrated into Assam as far as Guru

Nanak had done. Hearing the news of the birth of Gobind Rai, the Guru hurried back to Patna.

After a few years' stay at Patna, the Guru decided to return to the Punjab. He left his family behind, however, because Gobind Rai was still young, and the conditions in the Punjab continued to be uncertain and unsettled. The Guru was accompanied by Bhai Mati Das and a band of his bodyguards.

The Guru arrived at Anandpur after staying at Kiratpur for some time. The people of Anandpur were most happy to have the Guru back amidst them.

Before long, the Guru sent word to Patna, suggesting that his family join him at Anandpur. The Guru devoted himself completely to bringing up Gobind Rai as best he could. He wanted him to be a great fighter as well as a great man of letters. He nurtured both his physical and intellectual talents.

The conditions in the Punjab and the rest of the country were deteriorating day by day. Guru Tegh Bahadur could see that his end was not far, and he was anxious that Gobind Rai should be able to take over the mantle from him.

Though said to be a God-fearing and pious person, Aurangzeb honestly believed that Hinduism was utterly misconceived, decadent, and corrupt. It was for the good of his people if he could rid them of their superstitions and idolatrous practices, and thereby have the gates of heaven flung wide open to them.

Another factor that contributed to Aurangzeb's ill-conceived adventure was his anxiety to improve his image. He had imprisoned his own father and starved him to death. He had his brothers Dara Shikoh and Murad murdered. He grievously insulted his son Muazzim, who later on ascended the throne as Bahadur Shah. The Islamic world thought poorly of him. He wished to please those in Mecca and Medina and secure a berth for himself in the next world. This, he imagined, he could do best by mass conversion of Hindus and bringing into the fold of Islam the entire Hindu population under his rule. He wished the country to be turned into Dar-ul-Islam, the abode of Muslims.

Accordingly, he started trying all conceivable means to achieve his objective. Where economic sanctions failed, he tried to lure people with *jagirs* and jobs. He fostered disunity and ill-will amongst the various castes and classes of Hindus. If this did not work, he threatened non-Muslims with dire consequences. And these were no empty threats. He issued instructions to his governors to launch a mass conversion drive of Hindus and ensure that not one Hindu was left in his kingdom. The Hindu temples were to be razed to the ground and mosques erected in their place instead. The Hindu idols had to be desecrated, destroyed, or buried. The King-Emperor did not want to see any *tilak* (holy mark on the forehead) or *janaeu* (sacred thread) on any of his subjects.

It is said that the sacred threads of the Hindus converted to Islam by Sher Afghan, the Governor of Kashmir, weighed a maund and a quarter. It was by design that Aurangzeb ordered mass conversions to start from Kashmir. Kashmiri brahmins were known to be most orthodox and also highly erudite. The emperor thought that if they accepted Islam, others in the country would be converted readily. The more important consideration was that Kashmir had the tribals of Kabul and Kandahar next door. If the Hindus of Kashmir mis-behaved, a *jehad* could be raised and non-believers subdued with the sword. The tribals were illiterate religious fanatics, and frightfully ferocious and wild.

Before long, the Governor of Kashmir realized that the Hindus had started fleeing his province. In this way he felt he would be left with hardly anyone to rule over. He therefore invited the leading brahmins of the community for a dialogue. He explained to them his helpless-ness in view of the firm orders from Delhi. After protracted discus-sions, it was agreed that the Hindu community of the province would be given six months to make up their mind. They were either to accept Islam or face the consequences of noncompliance with Imperial orders.

Time flew sooner than they had imagined. At last the Kashmiri brahmins decided to make a pilgrimage to Amarnath and seek intervention of the deity. It is said that while at the Amarnath temple a member of the group of worshippers, Pandit Kirpa Ram, dreamed that they could be protected only by Guru Tegh Bahadur, the ninth in succession to Guru Nanak, who was the savior in Kaliyuga. Immedi-ately they left for the Punjab under the leadership of Pandit Kirpa

Ram, and reached Anandpur via Amritsar. They lost no time and explained their plight to the Guru. He heard their tale of woe and was lost in deep thought when Gobind Rai, the young lad of nine, walked in. "What are you bothered about, dear father?" the child enquired. The Guru explained to him the situation the people from Kashmir were involved in, and said, "They can be saved only if a great soul can offer himself for martyrdom." "Then who is greater than you?" remarked the future soldier-saint of the Sikhs. The father was assured that the youth was ready to take over. He advised the visiting supplicants to go back and inform their tormentors that they would be willing to accept Islam if Guru Tegh Bahadur could first be persuaded to do so.

What could be easier than this? The King ordered the arrest of Guru Tegh Bahadur and had him brought to Delhi. The fact of the matter is, that after giving assurance to the brahmins of Kashmir, the Guru himself undertook the journey to Delhi, along with a few of his close followers. Among them were Bhai Mati Das, Bhai Dyala, and Bhai Sati Das. Before leaving Anandpur, the Guru ordained nine-year-old Gobind as the next Guru.

The Guru, along with his aides, was imprisoned as soon as he reached Delhi. There were temptations offered as well as threats of torture and death. His companions were persecuted. Bhai Mati Das was sawed into two alive. Bhai Dyala was made to sit in a boiling cauldron. Bhai Sati Das was enveloped in cotton pad and then set on fire like a torch. He was roasted before the eyes of his mentor. The Guru witnessed all this but did not flinch. At this the Mughal Emperor offered another alternative to the Guru." If you are a man of God, you must work a miracle," he said. The Guru would not purchase his release the way a juggler earns his living. Then the inevitable happened. The Qazi gave his fatwa. Jalaluddin, the executioner, sharpened his sword. Word went around the whole town and on the afternoon of 11 November 1675, the Guru was beheaded in the presence of thousands of people. It is said that the execution was followed immediately by a sandstorm, the like of which Delhi had never known before. Under cover of a blinding storm Bhai Jaita picked up the Guru's sacred head and dashed to Anandpur Sahib. Then Bhai Lakhi Shah, a Government contractor who had access to the Kotwali, picked up the remaining part of the Guru's body and, putting it in his cart loaded with sundry goods, rushed out of the town. Reaching the present site of Gurudwara Rakab Ganj, he set his house on fire along with the Guru's holy body. The search parties sent out by the Kotwal were thus hoodwinked.

Guru Gobind Singh wrote about Guru Tegh Bahadur's death thus:

He broke his potsherd on the Delhi King's head
And he left for paradise.
None else in this world can match Tegh Bahadur's sacrifice.
The people mourned Tegh Bahadur's passing away.
There was wailing in the world but rejoicing in heaven.

It was a strange irony of history. Two hundred years before, Guru Nanak, at the age of nine, had rejected the sacred thread and admonished the brahmins who insisted on his wearing it. And now when he was exactly nine years old, the tenth Guru suggested that his own father should go and give his life so that the right of a community to wear the sacred thread and practice its faith was protected. This makes Guru Tegh Bahadur's martyrdom unique in history. People give their lives for principles dear to them, ideals cherished by them, and faiths they hold. There is hardly anyone who stakes his life for other people's faith. The supreme sacrifice made by Guru Tegh Bahadur stemmed the tide of intolerance in the subcontinent and inculcated in the people respect for other religions.

Guru Tegh Bahadur was essentially a peace-loving soul. He would rather submit to aggression than resist it. But he would never compromise on principles. It was extremely easy for him to work a miracle and save his life but he didn't budge from his conviction that miracle-making was, at best, gimmickry and it did not become men of God to indulge in such activities.

Fond of a quiet life, he would have much rather liked to be left alone so that he could live a life of contemplation. He lived in absolute anonymity for twenty years in Baba Bakala, devoting himself to meditation and study of classics and philosophical works.

Guru Tegh Bahadur was a poet of keen perception. His *slokas* continue to be popular generation after generation, and they are a great solace to people in grief and sorrow.

His greatest contribution, however, is the way he groomed his son for the fearful struggle ahead. The greatest lesson he left for his followers was his own life and death.

It is said that when Bhai Jaita decided to carry Guru Tegh Bahadur's severed head to Anandpur he was in a grave predicament. In order that it not be discovered that the Guru's head had been smuggled out, it must be replaced by another head to mislead the kings' men. At this Bhai Jaita's own father volunteered to have his head substituted for the Guru's severed head. Guru Gobind Singh's father gave his head and taught Bhai Jaita's father to do likewise without flinching for a moment. Khwaja Abdulla, the *daroga* of the Kotwali in which the Guru was executed, resigned his post and went to Anandpur, where he spent the rest of his life as a recluse. Pandit Kirpa Ram Saraswati and a number of other Kashmiri pandits realized that Guru Tegh Bahadur was indeed a Messiah and they came to Anandpur and settled there. Pandit Kirpa Ram was later baptised by Guru Gobind Singh, and he gave his life heroically fighting the treacherous Mughal forces at Chamkaur along with Guru Gobind Singh's two elder sons.

However, it is not as though Guru Tegh Bahadur had never known fighting. In his youth, when the Mughal forces attacked Kartarpur, he had sought permission from his father, Guru Hargobind, and given a fearless fight to the invading forces. He rode into the thick of battle and played havoc with the enemy's ranks. He hated war because he had known what affliction and misery it caused and how meaningless it could very often be.

His words of advice, given to the people of Anandpur before leaving for Delhi, sum up his teachings: Death is a certainty, one must not set one's heart on this world. It is God who sends pleasure and pain, profit and loss, weal and woe; these must be accepted as the will of God. One must do one's duty and meditate on God. God's name alone leads to liberation. One must remember God, help the poor and the needy, and always use polite and courteous language.

Selected Hymns of Guru Tegh Bahadur

1.　Man of God, get rid of the arrogance of heart,
　　Avoid passion, anger, and company of the wicked, day and
　　　　night.
　　He who treats alike comfort and suffering
　　Honor and dishonor, happiness and unhappiness
　　Only he had understood the secret of life.
　　He disregards both respect and disrespect
　　And remains unalloyed.
　　Says Nanak, It is a difficult path,
　　Only a few men of God are aware of it.

(Gauri)

2.　It's all God's creation, oh saints!
　　One man dies and yet the other thinks he'll live forever.
　　I fail to understand it!
　　Given to passion, anger, and worldly love
　　You've forgotten God.
　　Like the dream of night
　　You treat false wealth as real.
　　Like the shadow of a cloud
　　Whatever you see must disappear.
　　Says Nanak, treat this world as a myth
　　And remain always in God's presence.

(Gauri)

3.　Man! You must fear even unconscious sins.
　　Seek support of the good and gracious God,
　　Who is the killer of all fears.
　　You must remember Him
　　Whose praises are sung by the Vedas and the Puranas.
　　Great is God's name
　　In remembering Him sins are washed away . . .
　　You'll never gain human life again.
　　It's the only opportunity for attaining salvation.
　　Says Nanak, sing praises of the kind God
　　And cross the ocean of life.

(Gauri)

4.　Whom shall I tell the agony of my heart?

Given to greed, I rush all around in search of riches.
For the sake of pleasure I suffer many a pain.
I serve man after man;
Like a dog I go from door to door.
And never think of God.
I have lived this life in vain.
I am not ashamed of people laughing at me.
Says Nanak, why don't you sing His praises?
The dirt of your body will be washed.

(Asa)

5. Everything here is for the living;
Mother, father, brother, son, relatives, and wife.
The moment life leaves the body
They call you an evil spirit,
They wouldn't have you for a half hour
And remove you out of the house.
You must understand this well,
The world is like a mirage.
Says Nanak, you should remember God
Who gives you sustenance.

(Devgandhari)

6. All worldly love is false.
Everyone is devoted to his own comfort.
Whether it's a wife or a friend
Everyone is attached to you
Because of his own selfish ends.
It's a strange truism
Nobody gives you company in the end.
But foolish men don't understand it.
I caution you day after day.
Says Nanak, those who sing the praises of God
Swim across the ocean of life.

(Devgandhari)

7. No one knows the ways of God.
The recluse who observes continence, the ascetic and the wise
All have failed in their effort.
In a moment He turns kings into beggars

And beggars into kings.
He fills those who are empty
And empties those who are full.
These are His ways.
He has created this world Himself
And Himself He looks after it.
He assumes several forms and colors
And remains distinct from all.
Uncountable, unlimited, incomprehensible and spotless.
He Himself has misled the world.
Says Nanak, one must get rid of doubts
And remain attached to His feet.

(Bihagda)

8. O man! Love God.
   Hear His praises with ears and sing them with the tongue.
   Remember Him in the company of Godmen.
   The sinner in you will be saved.
   O friend, Death roams about with its mouth open;
   You must understand it,
   It will devour one day.
   Says Nanak, you must remember God
   Or your opportunity may be lost.

(Sorath)

9. I retain in my heart what was in my heart.
   I neither remembered God nor went on pilgrimage.
   And Death has caught me by the forelock.
   Wife, friends, sons, vehicles, property, wealth, and the rest.
   Everything is a myth except the name of God.
   I wandered about for several ages
   And then obtained the human form.
   Says Nanak, it's the only opportunity to meet God,
   Why don't you remember him?

10. Man! Whose evil advice do you heed?
    Involved in another's wife, you talk ill of others,
    You never remember God.
    You know not the path of salvation.

And keep on amassing wealth.
Nothing will help you in the end,
In vain you make a slave of yourself
Neither do you remember God nor serve Godmen.
You are devoid of true understanding.
God lives in your heart
And you look for Him in the forest.
You are tired roaming from life to life,
You have not yet learned the eternal truth.
Says Nanak, now that you have gained human life,
You must remember God.

(Sorath)

11. Man! Try to understand the truth;
The whole world is like a dream.
It doesn't take a moment to undo it.
The wall made of sand doesn't last for four days,
Exactly like this are the comforts of worldly wealth.
O fool! Why are you involved in them?
Nothing is lost even now,
Sing the praises of God, says Nanak,
I tell you again and again what Godmen believe.

(Sorath)

12. Why go to the jungle looking for Him?
Omnipresent, unattached, He is within you.
Like the fragrance of a flower and the shadow of a mirror.
God lives in every heart, it's there he should be found.
The Guru has told me the secret:
He is the same inside and outside.
Says Nanak, without the understanding of the self
The shadow of doubt never disappears.

(Dhanasri)

13. Now what effort should I make
So that I am rid of my doubt
And swim across the ocean of fear?
I have done no good since I was born.
That's why I am afraid so much.
My fear is that I have not remembered Him

In thought, word, and deed.
I haven't gained understanding listening to my Guru.
Like cattle I fill my stomach.
Says Nanak—God, I can be saved
Only if You are kind as ever.

(Dhanasri)

14. Man! You must seek God's support,
    Remembering Him, the evil of the mind goes,
    And no temptation assails you.
    He is fortunate who sings God's praises.
    He washes his sins of many ages
    And goes to Heaven.
    Ajamal remembered God while dying
    He gained in a moment what devotees gain in a lifetime.
    What good deeds and acts of dharma had the elephant*
        done?
    Says Nanak, it was God's eternal grace
    That made him fearless.

(Ramkali)

15. Man! Remember God ever and ever
    Day and night, life diminishes every moment,
    Youth is lost in pleasures and childhood in ignorance.
    You have grown old and yet you don't understand,
    What bad counsel you are following!
    The Master who has given you human life
    Why have you forgotten Him?
    Not for a moment do you sing His praises,
    Remembering Whom one gains salvation.
    Why are you intoxicated with wealth?
    It never goes with you.
    Says Nanak, you should remember the Giver of all;
    He alone will help you in the end.

(Ramkali)

---

*According to the *Bhagawat*, an angel cursed by an ascetic was turned into an elephant. The elephant was caught by a crocodile but its angel soul remembered God and he was saved.

16. Mother! I have found the riches of His Name,
    My mind wanders about no more,
    It's now at rest.
    Temptation and worldly love have left
    And true knowledge has dawned on me.
    Greed and attachment don't bother me anymore.
    I have sought the support of God,
    My doubts of several lives have been removed.
    I have found the jewel of His Name,
    All my thirst has been quenched,
    I am all happiness.
    He sings His praises
    To whom the gracious God is kind.
    Says Nanak, it is the precious wealth
    That only a rare Godman gains.

                                        (Basant)

17. Except God no one will help you.
    Who is anyone's mother, father, son, wife, and brother?
    The riches, the land, and the property that you think belong
        to you,
    When you give up this body, nothing will go with you,
    Howsoever you may cling to it.
    You haven't cultivated the kind and merciful God.
    Says Nanak, this world is all myth;
    It's like the dream of night.

                                        (Sarang)

18. Remember God, remember God, this is all you need to do.
    Give up *maya* and come to God's protection.
    Treat worldly comforts as myth.
    All this act is false.
    The wealth of which you feel proud is like a dream.
    The sway over the entire world
    Is like the wall of sand.
    Says Nanak, your body will disintegrate
    The way time passes away every moment.

                                        (Jai Jaivanti)

19. You have not sung God's praises and have wasted away your
    life.
    Says Nanak, remember God, the way fish remembers water.

     ★   ★   ★

   Why are you involved in worldly passions?
   Not for a moment you miss Him.
   Says Nanak, you must remember God.
   So that you escape the noose of Death.

   Your youth went a waste
   Old age has now assailed you.
   Says Nanak, you must remember God.
   Your time is passing away.

   You have grown old, don't you see?
   Death is approaching you.
   Says Nanak, listen to me, O fool!
   Why don't you remember God?

   Wealth, wife, and property
   That you think are yours,
   None of these will accompany you,
   Says Nanak, it is the truth of life.

                                        (Slokas)

Guru Gobind Singh

I tell the truth that all may hear
He who loves, he alone has found God.
　　　　　　　　　　　　—Guru Gobind Singh

Guru Tegh Bahadur's execution in Delhi in public outraged the conscience of the entire Sikh brotherhood. After Guru Arjan Dev's martyrdom in Lahore, the slaughtering of another peaceloving, non-violent man of God like Guru Tegh Bahadur gave a severe jolt to the young community. The Sikhs streamed towards Anandpur from far and near to be with the nine-year-old Gobind Rai, who succeeded his father.

Born in Patna in 1666 and brought up for the grim struggle ahead, the young Guru, rather than being overwhelmed with his tragic loss, evinced firm determination and tenacity of will to fight the forces of evil and bigotry in defense of the poor and Dharma. The disconsolate Sikhs who flocked to Anandpur saw in Gobind Rai the promised savior and a man of the hour.

A soldier of destiny, Gobind Rai started consolidating his resources and preparing himself and his people for a gruesome fight, until the poison that had permeated the body politic of the country had been completely rooted out. Guru Gobind Rai realized the need to give the new religion a distinct identity. Islam, under rulers like Aurangzeb had become rigid, narrow-minded, and uncompromising, and Hinduism had been severely enfeebled by ritualism.

As a first step, it was necessary to consolidate the resources and manpower, which necessitated a discreet pause, during which links were forged with Sikhs spread all over India and abroad, including Kabul and Kandahar, Bulkh and Bokhara.

The young Guru started practicing archery, going out on shikar, and playing mock battles with his companions. In spite of advice to the contrary from his mother and *masands*, he had a huge drum made, and made it a practice to collect his people, whenever he required them, with drum beats. It was feared that the beating of the over-sized drum called Ranjit (the victorious), would offend the neighboring hill rulers, particularly Bhim Chand of Bilaspur. But the drum had become the symbol of the rallying of the Sikhs, and the Guru was determined to pursue his path.

In the meanwhile, the Guru continued to be visited by his followers, who brought for him highly precious gifts, which were the envy of the neighboring hill chiefs. Duni Chand, a Sikh from Kabul, brought for the Guru a canopy that was worth rupees two and a half lakhs. During his visit to Assam, Guru Tegh Bahadur had blessed a ruler who was issueless. As a result, a son was born to the ruler. While the Raja had died, his queen came with the prince, called Ratan Rai, to pay homage to the Guru with various gifts, including an elephant of uncanny intelligence. He carried out various commands to the delight of the spectators. He washed the Guru's feet with water and then wiped them with a towel. He fetched the arrows discharged by the Guru. At night he showed the way with lighted candles held in his trunk. He performed several other interesting feats.

Once the Raja of Bilaspur came to visit the Guru. He was wonderstruck to see the grandeur of the tent that the Guru had been presented with by his Sikh disciple from Kabul. He had hardly recovered from it when he was shown the elephant from Assam. Raja Bhim Chand was even more struck by the clever feats the elephant performed. He must possess the elephant by any means, fair or foul, the Raja told himself. Before long, the chief found an excuse to ask for the elephant. His son was to be engaged to the daughter of the Raja of Srinagar (Garhwal). Raja Bhim Chand sent word to the Guru to lend his elephant for the entertainment of his guests. He thought once the elephant came to him, he would retain it for good. The Guru was a mere child who would not dare protest and moreover he was not in the good books of the Mughal Emperor. The Guru, who knew the

Raja's mind, declined to oblige. Bhim Chand was wild with rage.

The Guru's *masands* advised the Guru not to annoy the Raja but the Guru would not compromise with arrogance and deceit. Both the parties started making preparations for the inevitable showdown. In the meanwhile, the Raja of Nahan, who was a great devotee of the Guru, invited the Guru to visit his state. The Guru's people found it a welcome opportunity and persuaded the Guru to accept the invitation, hoping that it might help the tension subside.

The Guru went to Nahan with his family and five hundred Sikhs. The Raja gave the Guru an excited welcome. He made lavish arrangements for his hospitality. During his visit to his state, the Raja persuaded the Guru to build a fort that came to be known as Paonta Sahib, in due course. It is said that with the help of the Guru's Sikhs, the fort was raised in a matter of days. It is situated at a picturesque spot on the banks of the river Jamuna.

The period the Guru spent at Paonta was primarily devoted to research and literary and artistic activities. The Guru had fifty-two eminent poets working with him; poetic symposia were held frequently. The Guru, who was a scholar in Sanskrit and Persian, participated in them. His writings are a clear break with the tradition of his predecessors. He wrote powerful verse which is replete with images of wars and warriors from ancient mythology and folklore. He worshipped God; he also had an unmistakable love for the sword.

While the Guru was still in Paonta, Raja Fateh Singh of Srinagar (Garhwal) came to pay homage to him. He was advised by his ministers that it was best to make friends with the Guru. The Guru received him with due courtesy, and suggested to him that it would be advisable if he made up with Raja Nahan also. Raja Fateh Singh was willing to do as counselled by the Guru. Both the Rajas were brought together and made to embrace each other.

As this meeting was taking place, a panic-stricken villager came and reported that there was a man-eating tiger in the jungle close by. The tiger had lifted cattle and had become a terror to the villagers. The villager knew where the tiger's lair was. The Guru, along with the two Rajas, left for the forest immediately. The tiger, hearing the tramp of the horsemen, came out of its lair and sat on his haunches in readiness. The Rajas wished to shoot the tiger with a matchlock or an arrow. The Guru forbade them, and alighting from his horse, he advanced toward the tiger with his sword and shield. Seeing this, the tiger roared and pounced upon the Guru. The Guru held him at bay wih his shield and in the twinkling of an eye severed his head with his sword. The two Rajas accompanying the Guru marvelled at his courage and prowess.

Syed Budhu Shah of Sidhaura, a Muslim devotee of the Guru, was approached by a contingent of five hundred Pathans in uniform, saying that they had been disbanded by Aurangzeb on a trivial charge and, fearing the Emperor, no one would employ them. The Syed thought of Guru Gobind Rai and sent them to him at Paonta. The Guru listened to their story and employed them in his service without any hesitation. The contingent consisted of well known fighters like Hyat Khan, Kale Khan, Nijabat Khan, and Bhikan Khan.

The offers of friendship made by Raja Fateh Shah of Srinagar (Garhwal) were, however, dubious, as were the Pathan contingent's solicitation of recruitment in the Guru's forces. Fateh Shah's daughter was engaged to be married to Raja Bhim Chand's son, who was a sworn enemy of the Guru. He threatened to break the engagement. Fateh Shah, therefore, not only decided to have nothing to do with the Guru but also joined Bhim Chand's forces poised for an attack on the Guru. When the Pathan contingent heard that the hill chief had joined hands to humble the Guru, they lost no time in quitting the Guru's service and went over to his enemies. No appeal to their good sense and tradition of loyalty prevailed with them. When the sovereigns of the hill states were arrayed against the Guru, the Pathan contingent was prominent among them. Syed Budhu Shah of Sidhaura, who had recommended the Pathan contingent to the Guru for employment, was mortified to hear it. With a view to making amends, he rushed to the Guru's aid, along with his two sons and seven hundred men fully equipped to engage the enemy. Besides them, there were just eight men who could be called professional soldiers. They were the Guru's five cousins, the Guru's uncle Kirpal, Bhai Dyala, and Nand Chand. The rest were what the enemy called "the dregs of the populace," but they were deeply devoted to the Guru and anxious to lay down their lives for him.

It is said that during the fight, a barebodied *mahant* came to the

Guru and asked his permission to challenge Hayat Khan. He had just a simple club in his hand. The Guru was amused and blessed him. It was a spectacle to see a naked godman riding a horse with his matted hair tied in a bun on the top of his head. Hayat Khan felt slighted and would not attack an unarmed enemy. At last, when challenged again and again, he pulled out his sword and aimed a blow at the mahant. The mahant received it on his club. Hyat Khan's blow was so severe that his sword broke into pieces. At this the mahant pounced upon him and hit his head, breaking his skull into smithereens.

Similarly, in the thick of fighting, a cook called Lal Chand came to the Guru and offered to plunge into the enemy ranks. But he had never handled a weapon all his life. The Guru marked the determination in his eyes and, giving him a sword and shield, told him how to handle them. Even the Guru's soldiers laughed at the cook going to fight fully armed. It is said that to everybody's astonishment, Lal Chand engaged no less a warrior than Amir Khan. Amir Khan was the first to attack with his sword. Lal Chand warded off the blow with his shield. The next moment he gave a return blow with his sword and Amir Khan, the renowned hero, was found collapsing to the ground.

A mechanic from Varanasi called Ram Singh made a cannon for the Guru which played havoc with the enemy.

Budhu Shah and his men fought heroically. One of his sons fell victim to an arrow shot by Raja Gopal.

The Guru himself engaged Hari Chand. He has described his combat in his autobiography, *Bichitar Natak:*

> Enraged Hari Chand shot his arrows, one of which hit my horse. He then discharged another but God protected me; the arrow simply grazed my ear. The third arrow pierced through the buckle of my waistband and just touched my body, though it didn't harm me. God Himself protected His slave. When Hari Chand's arrow touched my body, it angered me, and picking up my bow, I started showering arrows all over. Seeing this, the enemy fled. I took an aim and hit Hari Chand. As he collapsed, my brave soldiers pushed forward and annihilated them completely. The Chief called Karori was also finished. At this the men belonging to the hill chiefs took to their heels in terror. It was the mercy of God Almighty that gave

us victory. Having won the battle, we started singing songs of victory. I rewarded the victorious soldiers generously. There was rejoicing all around.

After the battle of Bhangani the Guru did not return to Paonta, since he found that the Raja of Nahan was afraid of making enemies of other hill chiefs. The Guru came to Anandpur, visiting Kiratpur en route. Realizing his mistake, Bhim Chand sued for peace and made friends with the Guru. He came to Anandpur and was presented by the Guru with a robe of honor.

It was about this time that a son, Ajit Singh, was born to the Guru in 1687. He was followed by Jujhar Singh in 1691, Zorawar Singh in 1697, and Fateh Singh in 1699.

As the children grew up, the Guru gave them training in riding horses and handling arms and reading and interpreting the classics. In the meanwhile, the scholars engaged by him were busy translating other philosophical treatises from Sanskrit into the popular language of the common people.

In Raipur, near Ambala, there lived a rich couple, Sohina and Mohina. They were idol worshippers. They rose early in the morning, went to a well nearby, brought fresh water and gave a ceremonial bath to the idol, and then worshipped it. One day as they were bringing water for their deity, they saw a stranger reeling on the road and asking for water. It was the time for them to say their morning prayers. Ignoring the thirsty wayfarer, they went home. But while they were worshipping the idol, the couple felt uneasy. The cry of the helpless stranger on the roadside rang in their ears again and again. Helpless, they went back to the stranger on the roadside with water to serve him. But before they could arrive, the man had died. Sohina and Mohina came to know that he was a Sikh and had been wounded in an encounter with bandits who were trying to waylay a party of unarmed travellers. Sohina and Mohina returned home but could not forget the helplessness with which the stranger had asked them for water. It continued to haunt both husband and wife day and night. They could neither eat nor sleep. They lost all peace of mind. At last they decided to visit Anandpur and seek the blessings of the Guru. But while they tried their best, they couldn't have access to the Guru. It seemed the curse of the dying Sikh continued to haunt them. At last they met Kesra, the Guru's gardener, and living with Kesra, they started tending the Guru's garden with devotion. Before long the garden became a feast for the eye. The Guru was extremely happy and he complimented Kesra for it. An honest Sikh, Kesra told the Guru the secret of the improvement he had noticed in the garden. The Guru still did not take any notice of the strangers.

It so happened that the Guru's birthday was approaching. Sohina and Mohina had special flowers laid for the Guru on the auspicious occasion. A dervish called Roda Jalai saw these and wanted to pluck them. Sohina and Mohina would not allow it. The entire flowerbed had been tended for the Guru. Jalai's intention was to win the Guru's favor with those flowers. Roda Jalai stole into the garden early in the morning when it was still dark and stole the flowers. When the young couple Sohina and Mohina saw what had happened to their flowerbed, they were heartbroken.

In the morning Roda Jalai offered the flowers to the Guru.

"Why did you have to pluck such lovely flowers?" the Guru asked Roda Jalai, "A dervish need not stand on such ceremony."

"I didn't wish to come empty-handed on this auspicious day and dervish that I am, I had nothing else to offer," and saying this, Roda Jalai bowed before the Guru in obeisance. The moment he lowered his head, as ill luck would have it, his cap fell down, and along with it, a handful of gold mohurs that he had stored in it, and he was ridiculed by all those present. Knowing as he did wherefrom Roda Jalai had stolen the lovely flowers, the Guru picked up the blossoms and went over to the forlorn Sohina and Mohina and blessed them. "You may ask for anything and it will be given to you," said the Guru. They did have a moving request to make.

"If you are gracious, my Lord," said the young couple, "kindly grant pardon to Roda Jalai also."

The Guru was aware that most of the masands were corrupt and oppressed the Sikhs. They extracted money from the poor people, threatening them with the Guru's displeasure. The Guru was aware of what was going on. In a festival gathering, he got folk artists to depict how the masands exploited the innocent people. However, reports about the villainies of the masands continued to pour in. At last, the •

Guru discontinued the practice of appointing masands and told his Sikhs to send their offerings directly to the Guru at Anandpur.

Bhai Nand Lal Goya, a poet and an erudite scholar of Persian and Arabic, was in the service of Prince Bahadur Shah, the heir-apparent, who resided at Agra. Bahadur Shah, who was a poet himself, had collected several artists and scholars around him. Bhai Nand Lal had come to India after the death of his father, who was the principal scribe at the court of the ruler in Ghazni. Before long, Bhai Nand Lal distinguished himself amongst the learned men in the employment of the Prince. The communications he drafted for the royal court on behalf of the Prince began to be noticed and appreciated in Delhi. Because of his hard work and devotion, he rose to be the chief scribe of the Prince. It is said that in the royal court at Delhi a controversy was raging in respect to the interpretation of a verse from the Holy Quran. Several explanations were offered by the learned Muslim scholars, but somehow, none could convince Aurangzeb. When Bhai Nand Lal heard about it, he ventured his interpretation of the controversial verse. The Emperor read it and was fully satisfied. He decided to honor the scholar responsible for the interpretation with an award. But when he came to know that it was a Hindu who was responsible for the brilliant interpretation, the King ordered that the author should be persuaded to embrace Islam. If he didn't agree, the King indicated that they might also use force. When Bhai Nand Lal learned of it he escaped from Agra with the help of one of his Muslim admirers, Ghiasuddin. The only asylum he could think of was Anandpur, where he arrived and received a warm welcome. Bhai Nand Lal, "Goya," emerged in due course as a great poet of Persian and admirer of the Guru. He presented the Guru with his collection of verse called *Bandgi Nama* (The Book of Prayer); the Guru read it and renamed it as *Zindgi Nama* (The Book of Life). Bhai Nand Lal's poetry is overflowing with devotion and love for the Guru. He admired his person as a beloved adores her lover.

For the next Baisakhi festival in 1699, the Guru issued a general invitation to his Sikhs throughout the length and breadth of the country to visit Anandpur. The Guru advised his Sikhs to come with unshorn hair. Several thousand Sikhs came to participate in the fair in response to the Guru's call.

On the morning of the main fair day, after the hymn-singing had concluded, the Guru appeared on the dais with an unsheathed sword dazzling in his hand and asked the audience, "My sword is thirsty. It needs the blood of a Sikh to quench its thirst. Is there anyone in the audience who is willing to offer his head?" There was consternation amongst those present.

"Is there no one who is willing to present his head to satisfy my sword?" the Guru repeated.

The gathering grew more uneasy. "Do I understand that there is none amongst my Sikhs who is willing to sacrifice his life for his Guru?" As the Guru repeated his call the third time a Sikh called Daya Ram, a Khatri from Lahore, about 30 years of age, rose from the crowd to offer his head. "It is yours in life and death," said the Sikh humbly. The Guru caught hold of him by his arm and led him to a tent pitched adjacent to the dais. There was a thud of the sword.

A moment later the Guru appeard, with his sword dripping with blood. "I want another head," shouted the Guru. There was panic in the audience and they even doubted if their leader was sane at all. Still, before the Guru could repeat this call, another Sikh, this time a Jat from Haryana, rose and placed his head at the disposal of his Master. The Guru pulled him into the tent in a strange frenzy. Again there was the thud of the sword followed by a stream of blood flowing out of the tent. And as before, the Guru came out of the tent with blood dripping from his sharpedged sword.

"I want another head, the third." He stood, glowing with fiery eyes. Even at his first call, Makhan Chand, a Sikh from far-off Dwarka, hurried to the scaffolding, apologizing for his not offering himself earlier. The same frightful thud of the sword followed; and red blood squirted out of the sacrificial tent. The thirst of the Guru's sword was still not quenched. He came out the fourth time demanding yet another head. The blade of his sword was stained with blood. Some people from the astounded crowd started running away. "I want the fourth head," the Guru looked around, and before he finished speaking, Himat Chand, who had come all the way from Jagannath Puri in Orissa, rushed to the Guru. He was a sacrifice to the Guru. His head was at his Master's disposal. Like the other three Sikhs, he was also led to the tent. The thud of the sword was repeated and the stream of blood flowing from the tent was augmented with fresh blood. Emerging from the tent, with blood dripping once again, the Guru asked for yet another head! By now, the crowd had thinned considerably. Sahib Chand of Bidar rushed to the dais and fell at Guru's feet for not responding to his call all the while. The Guru led the fifth Sikh into the tent also. Terror-stricken, some Sikhs ran to inform the Guru's mother, others thought of seeking the intervention of the Guru's senior advisers. They had gathered to celebrate the festival of Baisakhi and here the Guru had started butchering them. They were on the horns of a dilemma. They did not know what to do when suddenly, from behind the tent, they saw the five faithful Sikhs emerge one after the other, radiant and glorious, like five resplendent stars descended from heaven. They were followed by the Guru glowing with a new confidence. The audience burst into spontaneous joy. They hailed the Guru with slogans, "The Guru is great," "Long live the Guru," "Glory to the Guru." Shouting such slogans, they were going crazy when the Guru raised his hand and silenced them. "Great are these five faithful! Glory to them! They are the chosen ones. They have found immortality. Those who know how to die, only they win deliverance from the cycle of birth and death," said the Guru.

The Guru, it is said, had killed only goats; every time he took a Sikh inside the tent, he slaughtered a goat and came out with its blood dripping from the blade of his sword.

The Guru, then, had a steel vessel brought and poured water into it. The five faithful Sikhs were asked to recite hymns from the sacred scriptures each by turn, while the Guru stirred the water with a double-edged dagger. The Guru was preparing *amrit*—nectar—to baptize Nanak's Sikhs to turn them into *khalsa*—the elect. As the five faithful Sikhs were reciting the Holy Word, clad in their blue robes of divine angels, the Guru's mother Mata Sahib Devan came in with *patashas*—sugarcandy—as her offering. The Guru was most happy. "It is a timely gift," he said and, taking the patashas from his mother, put them into the vessel. "It is marrying valor to compassion," said the Guru. "The dagger was to turn my Sikhs into heroes; the sugarcandy will foster in them the milk of human kindness."

When the recitation from the predetermined text of the scriptures was over, the Guru baptized the five beloved faithful with the nectar, the draught of immortality, and knowledge sublime.

After the Sikhs had been thus baptized, the great Guru stood before them with hands folded and prayed to them to baptize him in return. Thus the Guru turned himself into a disciple. It was for the first time in the annals of history that the Master sat at the feet of his disciples asking them to be blessed with a draught of nectar. The moment he had the sublime sip, from Guru Gobind Rai, he became Guru Gobind Singh. So were the five faithful Sikhs and thousands of the Guru's devotees who had gathered at Anandpur. According to a report of a diarist of the Mughal court to the Emperor in Delhi, twenty thousand Sikhs were anointed on that blessed Baisakhi day. This was the birth of a new nation, the reincarnation of Guru Nanak's Sikhs. A draught of amrit—and every Sikh became a Singh, a lion. Everyone had to sip amrit from a common vessel, thereby joining them in eternal brotherhood and casting away the barriers of caste and creed.

The Guru then enjoined those who had been blessed with amrit to wear long hair (Kesh). The hair is sacred. It is the symbol of the *khalsa*—the pure. They were also to wear a steel bangle (*Kada*) on their wrist. It should serve as a reminder of their commitment to truth. An anointed Sikh must also wear short pants (*Kachcha*) to ensure cleanliness. The Sikh should have a comb (*Kanga*) in the hair to keep it tidy. Also he should always carry a dagger (*Kirpan*) as a weapon of defense as well as hope.

The Guru was aware that the need of the hour was an army of soldier-saints who could effectively fight the forces of evil, exploitation of the poor, and communal hatred in Indian society.

The anointed Sikh was not to smoke or take any other intoxicants. He must not eat Kosher meat. He must be loyal to his spouse and not covet other women. All Sikhs were equal; there was no high or low caste amongst the khalsa. The khalsa believed in One God, said his prescribed prayers daily, and did not worship idols or images. The khalsa must help the needy and protect the poor.

The Sikhs who adopt the prescribed way of life are as good as the Guru. The Guru is the khalsa and the khalsa is the Guru.

After the grand baptism, the Guru declared that all his Sikhs were to be known as Singhs (lions). The baptism had turned jackals into tigers. The khalsa must fight all oppression. It is maintained that having been anointed with amrit, a single Sikh could fight a hundred thousand enemies.

The Guru invited the hill chiefs to take amrit and join the forces of the khalsa. "Aren't you ashamed of yourself?" he exhorted them, "The Mughals carry away your daughters and wives and you dare not utter a word of protest. The Hindu temples of worship have been desecrated and mosques put up in their place. Thousands of Hindus are converted to Islam every day. The only solution is to unite under the banner of the khalsa and fight for truth and annihilate evil."

Not only did the Guru's call have no effect on the hill chiefs, they duly communicated it to the Mughal Emperor, pledging their loyalty to him. When the Guru was out hunting in a forest, Balia Chand and Alam Chand, two hill chiefs, thought it to be a God-sent opportunity for them to attack the Guru's party and capture him. The Guru had only a few bodyguards with him, while the hill chiefs had a substantial force of several thousand. After initial reverses, the Sikhs asked Guru Gobind Singh to lead them himself, and a small party of hunters defeated a regular army deputed to attack them. While Alam Chand managed to escape, Balia Chand, his companion, had to pay with his life.

When this humiliating defeat occurred, the hill chiefs were convinced that they were no match for the Guru. His strength increased every day. They must appeal to the Mughal Emperor in Delhi to put an end to the potential danger that the Sikhs posed for the whole lot of them in the region. There were as many as twenty hill chiefs, and yet they were scared of the Guru's Sikhs, more so after their baptism on Baisakhi day. They found a vast change in them. Barbers and washermen, weavers and carpenters styled themselves as Sardars and behaved like lions—Singhs, as they started calling themselves. Every one of them carried a sword. In their smithies they had started manufacturing arms of all sorts. They brought weapons and the finest horses for presentation to the Guru from far and near. With a single sip of amrit, the Guru had created a militia who were always willing to stand up and fight for their Guru and causes dear to him.

In order that their case appear convincing, the hill chiefs first asked the Guru to pay them large arrears of tax for land around Anandpur that he occupied in their territory. The Guru reminded them that the land had been purchased by his father and there was no question of his paying any dues on that account. He also took this opportunity to explain to them that it was in their own interest to make friends with the Guru and the Sikhs. United, they could keep the Mughal forces in check, otherwise, sooner or later, they would sweep them away and no trace would be left of either their states or their faith.

Still, the hill chiefs approached the Mughal Emperor for assistance. Aurangzeb being away in the Deccan, the Subedar of Sirhind came to their rescue, but only after they had paid a large sum as expenditure for the fighting force to be drafted to deal with the Guru. It was most humiliating for the hill chiefs to purchase assistance; it was even more disgraceful for the Mughal soldiers to attack the Guru as mercenaries. The Guru's Sikhs, fearless as they had become, accepted the challenge readily.

The ten thousand strong Mughal forces were led by Painde Khan and Dina Beg, the hill chiefs giving them support. The battle was fought at Rupar. The Guru always tried to do the fighting as far away from Anandpur as possible. The Sikhs were far outnumbered, yet their self-confidence was enormous. Painde Khan had protected himself completely with a coat-of-arms. The Guru challenged him but found that he was invulnerable. Then the Guru discovered that Painde Khan's ears alone remained uncovered. He lost no time in aiming an arrow at the vulnerable target and the enemy lay dead on the battlefield. In the meanwhile Dina Beg had also been injured severely. The hill chiefs panicked and took to their heels.

The Guru had once again emerged victorious. At this, the hill chiefs from Jammu, Nurpur, Mandi, Bhutan, Kullu, Kainthal, Guler, Chamba, Srinagar (Garwal), Dadhwal, and others met in council and decided to blockade the Guru, closing all supply routes to the Sikhs collected in Anandpur. The siege lasted two months. The Sikhs had entrenched themselves by the thousands in Fatehgarh and Lohgarh, the two forts in Anandpur, and had given a sustained fight. All the efforts of the combined hill armies did not seem to prevail. At last, as a face-saving device, they approached the Raja of Basali, who was an ardent devotee of the Guru, to invite the Master to his state as his guest, to which the Guru agreed and the siege was lifted. In this way, while the Guru's men had a welcome respite to muster their forces, the hill chiefs could tell the world that they had obliged the Guru to vacate Anandpur and flee to Basali.

But they could not deceive themselves and their people for long. Having spent a little time at Basali, the Guru returned to Anandpur. In the meanwhile, the Sikhs had started enlisting in the Guru's forces from far and near. They came equipped with bows and arrows, swords and spears, daggers and dirks, muskets and pistols, and above all, with the desire to die fighting for their faith and their Guru.

When the Guru was on his way to Basali, in spite of their pledge not to attack the Guru's men, the hill chiefs started sniping, for which they paid dearly. However, when the Guru returned to Anandpur, they advisedly took no notice of it. The Guru came and stayed in Anandpur as before and continued with his activities, looking after the spiritual and temporal needs of the Sikhs.

In the meanwhile, realizing his helplessness, Raja Ajmer Chand, the leader of the hill chiefs, sued for peace with the Guru, followed by the rest of the chiefs trying to make friends with him. They sent him costly gifts in token of good neighborliness. The Guru also responded in the same spirit.

During the respite Guru Gobind had the embattled city of Anandpur and its two forts attended to. The Sikhs, being aware that Aurangzeb would avenge the defeat the Mughal forces had suffered at the hands of the Guru, prepared for the inevitable. In the meanwhile, the Guru himself was preoccupied with the quality of men his Sikhs must turn out to be.

There was a Sikh by the name of Joga Singh on the personal staff of the Guru. He had been in the service of the Guru since his childhood. He belonged to Peshawar where his parents were still living. His people found a bride for him and asked him to come to Peshawar to get married. The Guru could ill-afford to relieve Joga Singh when preparations were afoot for meeting the imminent attack from the Mughals. But Joga Singh had to go, for all the arrangements for his marriage had been finalized. "If there is anything untoward, a word from the Master and I will return that very instant," Joga Singh promised the Guru.

With a view to gauging the devotion of his Sikh, the Guru sent a message (*hukamnama*) to be delivered to Joga Singh in the midst of the actual marriage ceremony, asking him to return forthwith. It is said that Joga Singh had circumambulated twice along with his bride, and had yet to take two more ritual rounds when the Guru's message was delivered to him. He suspended the marriage ceremony there and then and left for Anandpur. All those present were amazed, but such was the sense of devotion of Joga Singh to his Guru that he heeded nothing else.

On his way back to Anandpur, Joga Singh happened to spend a night at Hoshiarpur. After his evening meal, as he was strolling in the bazaar, he saw a dancing girl and was allured by her.

But every time Joga Singh tried to go into the house, a chowkidar at the gate stopped him. Joga Singh tried again and again the whole night, though without any success. And then day dawned. Joga Singh was suddenly reminded of his Guru and he left for Anandpur.

Joga Singh presented himself before the Guru and was pained to find a stern look on the Master's face. He had seen this very scorn somewhere else. Yes, it was only the previous night. The frown that the Guru wore was writ large on the face of the chowkidar guarding the house of the dancing girl who would not allow him to enter time and again.

"It was the Guru himself," Joga Singh suddenly realized and he fell at his Master's feet. The Guru had saved his Sikh from sin by standing guard at the dancing girl's quarters the whole night long.

Joga Singh, who had been feeling conceited for having carried out the Guru's command in the midst of the marriage rites and for having returned to his Master without consummating the marriage, now felt humbled.

A Jain monk called Hans sought audience with the Guru but every time he tried he was refused. He was a great scholar and also a fine artist. One of his paintings, in which he had depicted sunrise, was a superb piece of art and it was admired by everyone including the Guru himself. But to everyone's surprise, the Guru would not see Hans. At last, Senapat, one of the poets in the Guru's court, intervened on his behalf and pleaded for an audience for Hans. Senapat felt that Hans was a scholar and it would enhance the prestige of the Guru's cell of poets and learned men if he could join them. "He is a sensitive artist and it would be an asset to have him among us," Senapat said again and again. At last, the Guru lost patience and told Senapat, "Your artist friend is callous. He is stonehearted." Senapat was shocked to hear these words. He begged the Guru to enlighten him. He had known Hans only for a brief period.

At this, the Guru asked Daya Singh to go to a cave in a hill close by, where he would find a young ascetic. Daya Singh was to bring him to the Guru. The Guru cautioned Daya Singh that he would have to carry the ascetic, since he was too feeble to walk the distance.

The next morning, the ascetic was presented to the Guru. He was just a skeleton on the verge of collapse. The Guru fed him with his own hands and made him sit with him. Senapat was then asked to call his learned friend Hans to appear before the Guru. Hans was very happy to get an audience with the Guru and came at once.

"Do you recognize this young man?" the Guru asked Hans, pointing to the ascetic.

Hans couldn't, for the young ascetic was so reduced to a bundle of bones that recognition was impossible. But the young man recognized Hans all right. At the Guru's bidding to do so, he narrated his tale.

He was a child when Jain monks visited their village. He saw them and, like many other children, was fascinated by their way of life. He decided to become a monk. Several years later, he came across a nun from their village in one of the monasteries. They used to play together as children and were greatly fond of each other. In fact, the girl had turned a nun only after she learned that he had become a monk. In the surprise meeting that winter afternoon in the monastery, they were delighted to see each other. They sat in a secluded corner under the warm sun and talked about their childhood days back in the village. As they were thus engaged in recalling happy memories of days gone by, they were seen together by the chief of the monastery. A monk and a nun must not be alone together. The chief ordered that the eyes of the girl should be plucked out and the young monk was handed over to Hans for his reformation. He was ridiculed day and night in spite of assuring them that they were innocent. At last, Hans ordered him to undergo penance for twelve years in a cave to atone for his sin.

"Isn't it cruel?" The Guru asked Hans. The realization of what he had done dawned on Hans and he fell at the Guru's feet.

The Guru had the girl located and got the young couple united once again. It is said that in his benign mercy, the girls's eyes were also restored by the Guru and they lived a happy married life.

Har Gopal's father Bishambar Das was an ardent devotee of the Guru. They belonged to Ujjain. They were well-to-do traders. Bishambar Das was keen that Har Gopal should also lead a pious life and seek the Guru's blessing. Accordingly, he persuaded Har Gopal to visit the Guru. The young man was cynical and attached to worldly ways. He had little faith in holy men. But since his father had asked him again and again, he agreed to visit the Guru.

When Har Gopal arrived at Anandpur, he was amazed to find the splendor in which Guru Gobind Singh lived. Everything about him was royal and grand. He felt he had been misled. Guru Gobind Singh was essentially a man of the world, a great fighter who lived a kingly life. He found nothing godly about him. He regretted having listened to his old father and undertaken the arduous journey all the way from his hometown.

Unhappy as he was, he came indifferently to attend the Guru's morning congregation, where hymns were sung and prayers held. And much to his surprise, Har Gopal went into ecstasy, listening to the singing. Such a sublime experience he had not known before. After the prayers Har Gopal went up to the Guru and fell at his feet and sought his blessings.

Har Gopal stayed on at Anandpur for a few weeks but he could not reconcile himself to the Guru's fondness for *shikar*, the keenness with which he trained his horses, and the maintenance and manufacture of all sorts of weapons of destruction. Unlike other holy men, the Guru was a non-vegetarian. He relished eating meat of all varieties.

On the eve of his departure, he went to the Guru to take leave of him. Guru Gobind Singh happened at that time to be sitting on the river bank. Har Gopal presented a pair of gold bracelets to the Guru. While admiring the bracelets, the Guru started playing with one of them. He would toss it into the air again and again and then catch it with his right hand. As the Guru did this, the bracelet slipped from his hand and rolled down into the river. Har Gopal, who happened to witness all this, jumped into the river but it was of no avail. The bracelet was lost. As he came out, he said, "Sir, if you could only point to the exact spot where the bracelet fell, maybe I can fish it out." At this, the Guru also threw the other bracelet into the river in order to indicate the spot. Har Gopal was distressed. But the very next moment realization came to him that the worldly riches to which he attached so much importance had no meaning for the Guru. It was vain of him to have felt that he was making such a costly gift to the Master. The Guru attached little significance to it.

When he was leaving, the Guru made a return gift of a steel bangle (*Kada*) to Har Gopal. This fact again put off the young man. Here he had come all the way from Ujjain, spending a fortune to visit the Guru. He had brought several costly gifts for him. A little while earlier, he had presented the Guru with two gold bracelets studded with diamonds and in return for all this the Guru had given him just a steel bangle!

On his way home Har Gopal happened to stay with Bhai Dhyan Singh, a devotee of the Guru, residing at Chamkaur. While talking about the Guru, Har Gopal mentioned the steel bangle cynically. He was also heard grumbling about the gold bracelets, which were worth not less than five hundred rupees.

Bhai Dhyan Singh's wife, who was an ardent devotee of the Guru, was enraged. Har Gopal obviously didn't realize how priceless the steel bangle gifted to him by Guru Gobind Singh was. She went to the bazaar and, mortgaging her personal jewelry, obtained six hundred rupees and hurried back to offer the amount to Har Gopal. "It is a little more than what your bracelets were worth. Kindly accept this in exchange for the steel bangle the Guru presented to you." Har Gopal was most happy at the bargain.

Reaching home, he narrated the clever manner in which he had used the faith of a Guru's Sikh to retrieve the loss of his bracelets. Bishambar Das was deeply grieved.

As feared by his father, his all-too-clever son started losing in business. He became bankrupt before long.

His father reminded him how he had denied himself the blessings of the Guru. Har Gopal realized his folly and begged his father to take him to the Guru again, so that he could ask his forgiveness.

On their way to Anandpur, they broke journey at Chamkaur again. Bishambar Das purchased back the steel bangle and, accompanied by Bhai Dhyan Chand, they went to Anandpur. When the Guru saw them all together, he smiled knowingly and blessed each one of them with his mercy and grace.

The hill chiefs, in the meanwhile, collected at Rawalsar and invited Guru Gobind Singh for peace negotiations. The Guru went to Rawalsar. The chiefs and their consorts, who accompanied them, were deeply impressed with his integrity and love for peace and amity. However, while he was still in Rawalsar, the hill chiefs, having learned that Aurangzeb was planning to attack the Guru again, dropped the peace efforts. A princess of Nahan called Padma, who knew of it, was distressed and communicated to the Guru in confidence the secret designs of the hill chiefs and the Mughal forces.

The Guru hastened back to Anandpur. He was attacked by a large Mughal army under General Syed Khan. It so happened that General Syed Khan's sister was married to Pir Budhu Shah. Since she had lost two of her sons in an earlier battle, he went to condole with her. He was under the impression that his sister's sons had died fighting the Guru. But he was shocked to learn that Pir Budhu Shah and his sons had fought on the Guru's side. Still, his sister Nasiran continued to be an ardent devotee of the Guru.

While there was no running away from the mission on which Syed Khan had been deputed, in his heart of hearts he started nursing a longing to meet the Guru on the battlefield. And he was not disappointed. He did see the Guru in a man-to-man encounter. He saw him on his blue horse, moving amidst myriads of swords and weapons but no harm seemed to come to him.

The General shot an arrow at the Guru. It missed him. Then he pulled out his musket but his aim, which was known to be flawless, let him down again. It appeared to the General that his sister Nasiran was standing close to him and every time he shot at the Guru she made his aim falter.

Since the General had failed in his aim twice, the Guru invited him to a hand-to-hand fight with swords. When he had a glimpse of the Guru from closer quarters, rather than attacking him, he came down from his horse and put his head on the Master's stirrup. All his soldiers were amazed to see this strange happening on a battlefield.

General Syed Khan was blessed by the Guru. Instead of going back to fight, he retired to Kangra hills for meditation. It is said that he remained in meditation for several years until the Guru went to the Deccan where he joined him.

General Syed Khan's surrender to the Guru was taken as a defection. It annoyed both Aurangzeb and the Mughal soldiers. He ordered General Ramzan Khan to take over the command of the forces against the Guru and capture him alive, or bring him dead to Delhi. The Subedars of Sirhind and Lahore were to give him support as were the hill chiefs of Bilaspur, Kangra, Jaspal, Kullu, Kainthal, Mandi, Jammu, Narpur, Chamba, Guler, Srinagar, and a number of other states.

On the other hand, besides his normal army, the Guru had Sikhs from Majha and Malwa who had joined him recently and had received training in warfare. Several of the Guru's Sikhs put on saffron-colored uniforms, declaring that they had but a few days left to attain salvation.

Not satisfied with the way the war was being fought, the Emperor entrusted the supreme command to Wazir Khan, a ruthless soldier. Such odds the Sikhs had never encountered before. After a heroic fight on the battlefield and the loss of many a valiant soldier, the Guru felt it expedient to withdraw into the town of Anandpur. He gave the charge of Kesgarh fort to his son Ajit Singh and that of Lohgarh fort to Nahar Singh and Sher Singh.

Finding that the Sikh forces had withdrawn into Anandpur, the Mughal armies laid seige to the town from all sides in collaboration with the hill chiefs.

As the Guru was busy reinforcing his defense, it was brought to his notice that one of his Sikhs called Kanaiya had been offering water to the Mughal soldiers wounded on the battlefield along with Sikh soldiers. The Guru sent for Kanaiya to find out the truth about it. Kanaiya heard the charge and pleaded with folded hands, "Master, since I have come in touch with you, I see God above me and the entire creation as His children. Amongst the wounded, I fail to distinguish between the Hindus and the Muslims." The Guru was highly pleased with his Sikh. He blessed him and bade him to continue serving the suffering soldiers as he had been doing, irrespective of caste or creed. The followers of Kanaiya have ever since continued to serve people in the same spirit and are known as *Seva-panthis*.

It was a relentless fight. The siege was protracted. It lasted three long years. The allied forces were successful in cutting off even the water supply to the town. The ration stores were empty. The Sikhs faced starvation and certain death. The Guru's favorite horses died for want of food. The famous elephant Prasadi also met the same fate. The Sikhs ground the dried bark of trees and ate it. They made daring forages on the Mughal army surrounding the town and plundered their rations at grave risk to themselves.

The Guru had to starve. So did his family, including his mother and children. But he would agree to the suggestion that they should flee Anandpur and seek refuge elsewhere. While the Sikhs dared not approach the Guru, they went to his mother and suggested to her that it was an unequal fight. If they continued to remain at Anandpur, they would die of starvation, all of them. But the Guru refused to listen to anyone. He was determined to hold on and fight till the last. The mother was helpless.

At this juncture, Aurangzeb sent a message under his own seal inviting the Guru to Delhi. The King swore that no harm would come to the Guru. If he did not wish to go to Delhi, he could go anywhere else. But he must surrender the town of Anandpur with the two forts. The envoy who brought the message assured the Guru that Aurangzeb was highly impressed with the courageous fight he had given to the imperial forces. The hill chiefs, too, had sworn that if the Guru and his Sikhs vacated Anandpur and left the town, they would provide them safe passage through their territory.

The Guru did not believe a word of it. But in view of the assurance from the King himself, his mother and some of his close advisers pleaded with him again and again not to lose the opportunity offered to them to evacuate with their lives.

At last, under heavy pressure, the Guru relented and said that he would first send his treasure and other precious articles and if these could pass through the enemy forces safely, he would follow them. The Mughal envoy gave a solemn promise and retired.

The next day the Guru had rubbish and cowdung packed in large bags and, covering them with costly brocade shawls, sent the first consignment out of the town. The moment the caravan reached the Mughal army, the soldiers could not resist the temptation of plundering it. They fell upon the mules carrying the huge bags only to find to their chagrin that it was nothing but rubbish and cowdung! Thus the Guru proved to his mother and the Sikhs that the enemy could never be trusted and that they would be risking their lives if they left the town.

But remaining any longer in the town was no less risky. The misery and destitution were turning people insane. At last, forty Sikhs approached the Guru to allow them to escape. They could not bear the travail of hunger and want any more. The Guru told them that if they wished to go against his wishes, they must disclaim him. The desperate lot of disciples were prepared for it. Accordingly, they wrote a disclaimer and left the Guru. It is said that when they reached their homes, their mothers and wives disclaimed them. They did not know where to go.

After the forty apostates had left the Guru, he started destroying everything that could be burned or demolished in Anandpur. What he could not burn he had buried. He then left Anandpur with the remaining few Sikhs on the night between the fifth and sixth of December 1705, never to return to his beloved city again. There was much pain, but a stage had come when it couldn't be helped.

The Guru and the party had not gone far when the day broke. It was time for them to say their morning prayers. They halted on the banks of the Sirsa and started singing the morning hymn, *Asa Di Var*. They barely concluded their prayers when the enemy, violating all pacts made, attacked them. A bloody fight ensued. Bhai Udai Singh, the commander of the Guru's forces, and three out of the Five Faithful, along with several devoted Sikhs, were killed in the battle. Quite a few of the Guru's family accompanying him lost touch with him.

The Guru succeeded in crossing the river Sirsa, and along with a handful of his brave fighters and two of his elder sons, rushed to Chamkaur near Rupar and occupied the fort. They were duly chased by the Mughal forces who surrounded the fortress from all four sides.

The Mughal forces were determined to annihilate the Guru. On the other hand, the Guru, having lost several of his brave fighters, precious manuscripts, and valuable arms in the battle at Sirsa, and knowing the fate that was in store for the rest, was desperate. He installed himself on the balcony of the fort and decided to fight the enemy till the last drop of his blood. It is said that he had just forty men, including two of his elder sons. The arms he had were limited, the rations were scanty. It was indeed a fight with his back to the wall.

While the besieged Sikhs showered arrows on the advancing enemy forces, causing havoc in their ranks, their sheer number was overwhelming. They were closing in on the battlements of the fort. At this, the Guru sent out his brave soldiers one after the other to give the enemy a hand-to-hand fight and stem their advance as far as possible. Every hero who left the fort had certain death awaiting him. But one after the other the brave Sikh fighters were making it difficult for the enemy to get too close to the fort to capture it finally.

After a number of Sikhs had been martyred, Guru Gobind Singh's eldest son, Ajit Singh, approached his father and volunteered to go out and fight the enemy. The Guru was most happy and he blessed him. But the Sikhs got agitated, he was the Guru's own son, and could not be allowed to risk his life. "All of you are my own sons," said the Guru and, overruling their objection, directed his eighteen-year-old child to go out of the fort and face the enemy several thousand strong.

From the balcony the Guru saw with his own eyes the most heroic way in which his firstborn fought the Mughal army and then was overpowered by them. They tore him to pieces with their swords and spears.

Finding that his elder brother had been martyred, the Guru's second son, Prince Jujhar Singh, came forward and offered to follow his brother. He was only fourteen years old. The Sikhs would not permit it. "In the absence of any news about the younger princes, he is your only surviving son," they pleaded with the Guru. "All of you are my sons!" The Guru was determined, and patting Prince Jujhar Singh on the back, he bade him good-bye. The Prince had hardly stepped out when he retraced his steps and asked for a little water. He was feeling thirsty. "There is no water left with us for you, my son. Go and face the enemy. Your elder brother awaits you with a goblet of nectar in his hand.'' The child heard his father's command and plunged into the enemy's ranks. He killed a number of his foes before he fell dead, pierced with spears, and hacked with swords.

Having lost two of his sons, the Guru decided to challenge the enemy himself. The Sikhs would not allow this at any cost. Instead they collected and, after offering solemn prayers, passed a resolution (*Gurmatta*) that the Guru, along with the remaining two Faithful should leave the fort under cover of night while the rest of the Sikhs would continue to give fight to the enemy till the last.

The Guru had already divested himself of all authority. He had declared at the birth of the *Khalsa* at Anandpur that the Five Faithful were supreme. They had assembled and decided to request the Guru to leave the fort. The Guru had to bow before the mandate and left the fort under cover of night, accompanied by Bhai Daya Singh. Dharam Singh, and Man Singh. Before he left the fort, he sprayed arrows in all directions, creating confusion amongst the enemy hordes, and made good his escape.

However, while doing so he lost touch with the three Sikhs who were accompanying him out of the fort. He was left alone. Guru Gobind Singh was all alone, without a horse, without any arms, with no attendant. Having wandered through hostile jungles, his clothes were torn. Walking day and night his shoes were worn out. With thorns pricking his feet, lonely and forlorn, it is said he reached Machhiwara jungle. He lay down on the bare earth with a stone for his pillow. It was here that his companions found him. As they approached him, he sang out what is now one of his most famous hymns:

Go tell the plight of his devotees to my beloved Lord.
The luxury of soft beds is agony without Him,
It is like living in a snakepit.
The goblet is poison and the cup a dagger,
Life is like receiving the punches of a butcher's dagger.
I would rather live in hiding, with my Beloved;
It's hell living with strangers without Him.

The Guru's feet were full of blisters. He could barely walk. He had to be physically carried by his Sikhs. Rai Kalha, the Muslim chief of the town, welcomed the Guru and gave him shelter in his town in spite of the risk involved. It was here, while recouping his health, that the Guru received the tragic news of how two of his younger sons were slain and how his old mother died from shock.

It was the most shameful crime on the part of Nawab Wazier Khan, the Governor of Sirhand, to have killed the two innocent children, of whom the elder was nine years old and the younger was just seven years.

It is said that not long after Mata Gujri, the Guru's mother, and the two young princes got separated from him in the fighting at Sira, they were betrayed by Gangu Brahmin who had served them as a domestic servant once upon a time.

The Nawab of Sirhind was very glad to have the two sons of their sworn enemy in his custody. Then with a view to gaining favor with the Mughal King, he decided to execute the two children. In spite of advice to the contrary by friends like the Nawab of Malerkotla, he carried out the executions in the most cruel way.

The choice before the children was death or conversion to Islam. The young cubs of the lion frowned at their persecutors. They would not give up their faith, come what may. It was therefore decided that with a view to overawing the youth, they should be buried alive in the city's wall. It should also serve as a deterrent to the rest of the community.

Accordingly, a portion of the old wall was demolished. The children brought up with utmost affection and care were made to stand in the breach. And it is said that the masons walled them up alive. This most heinous crime took place on 12 December 1705. Barely five years later, Banda Singh Bahadur razed the entire city of Sirhind to the ground, killing Wazir Khan in the fight.

Guru Gobind Singh had lost all his four sons, both his parents and innumerable brave Sikhs in his struggle against the oppression of the Mughal ruler. He who lived like a king, with royal splendor, was rendered homeless. He was being chased by the enemy forces from town to town, from wilderness to wilderness. Even then he was not demoralized. While camping at the village of Dina, the Guru wrote a letter to Aurangzeb, in response to his invitation to see him. The Guru's letter is known as *Zafar Nama,* the Epistle of Victory.

The Guru told the King that he had taken up arms because he had exhausted all other means of redress. The Guru continued:

> If I had not believed your word and your oath on the Quran, I wouldn't have left my town. If I had known that you are deceitful and crafty like a fox, I wouldn't be here today . . .
>
> Every soldier of your army who left his defenses to attack us was slaughtered . . . Many were done to death on either side with arrows and bullets showered on them. The whole earth was smeared with red blood. Heads and legs lay in heaps. The arrows whizzed and the bows twanged. The clamor all over reached the heavens. My heroic soldiers fought like lions. But how could forty men, even the bravest of soldiers, succeed against countless odds? . . .
>
> You are faithless and irreligious. You neither know God nor Muhammad. A religious man never breaks his promise. Had the Prophet been here, I would make it a point to tell him about your treachery . . .
>
> What if my four sons have been killed, I live to take their revenge. It's no heroism to extinguish a few sparks. You have only excited a devastating fire . . .
>
> You have the pride of your empire, while I am proud of the kingdom of God. You must not forget that this world is like a caravanserai and one must leave it sooner or later.

The Guru had his letter sent to Aurangzeb through Daya Singh and Dharam Singh.

In the meanwhile, he started contacting his Sikhs and making preparations for his defense. Since the Mughal forces were still in pursuit, rather than cause embarrassment to his hosts, he camped on a site near Khidrana in Ferozepur district, where his followers started flocking to him. One such contingent was under the command of Mai Bhago. It consisted of all the unhappy Sikhs who had disclaimed the Guru at Anandpur and had come away. They had been feeling miserable all this time. They had been abandoned by their kith and kin for having been disloyal to the Guru. Mai Bhago had collected them and was bringing them to the Guru for his pardon when they were attacked by the Mughal forces. All of them died fighting. When the Guru heard about it, he rushed to the battlefield. He found the brave Sikhs lying dead all over. Among them he saw one who still seemed to have life in him. The Guru picked him up. He was Mahan Singh. The moment Mahan Singh saw the Guru, he fell at his feet and asked his forgiveness. The Guru pulled out the disclaimer that he had carried all these days and tore it to pieces. Seeing this, Mahan Singh breathed his last peacefully.

In the meanwhile, the King had received the Guru's letter. He read it and was struck with remorse. He removed all restrictions on the movement of the Guru and gave orders that Guru Gobind Singh and his Sikhs should no longer be harassed. Aurangzeb's conscience seemed to prick him for the cruelties inflicted on the Guru and his Sikhs. It is said that Aurangzeb took to his bed and soon thereafter he died.

The Guru came to Talwandi Sabo, now known as Damdama Saheb. The local chief, Dalla, came to him and condoled with him on the martyrdom of his four sons. Dalla led a contingent of four hundred men and said again and again that if he had known it, he would have placed his men at the Guru's disposal. "Each one of them would have died fighting for you." As he was talking, a Sikh came and presented a gun to the Guru. The Guru asked Dalla to go and get one of his men so that he could check his aim. Dalla was astounded to hear it. But when the Guru insisted, he went over to his people and, as he had feared, not one of his men came forward to serve as the Guru's target. Dalla was greatly mortified. He returned to the Guru, his head hanging in shame.

The moment the Guru saw him, he asked one of his attendants to go and tell the two young Sikhs tying their turbans at a little distance that the Guru wanted one of them to serve as a target to test the new gun that he had been presented with. The moment the young Sikhs heard it they came running to the Guru. They vied with each other for the honor. They happened to be brothers. The elder brother said that he had a better claim to serve his father, the Guru, while the younger one said he must have his share of the "father's" property.

Dalla was astonished to see this devotion. The Guru told him that it was amrit which made such heroes of men. It made sparrows challenge hawks and turned jackals into lions. At this, Dalla and his men offered themselves for amrit and they were duly baptized.

It was at Damdama Saheb that the Guru's consort joined him. It is said that when she arrived the Guru was in a congregation.

"Where are my children, my four dear sons?" the bereaved mother cried in agony.

"Here are scores of them, all your children," was what the Guru told her, pointing to the congregation.

It was again at Damdama Saheb that Guru Gobind Singh found time to redictate the *Holy Granth,* incorporating in it Guru Tegh Bahadur's hymns. But he didn't include his own poetry in the *Holy Granth.*

Aurangzeb did not live long after the receipt of the *Zafar Nama.* He died in 1707, a disconsolate and frustrated man, utterly disillusioned with life. As usual, there was a scramble for succession. Aurangzeb's eldest son Bahadur Shah was in Peshawar; therefore his younger brother Azam proclaimed himself King. Bahadur Shah knew Guru Gobind Singh through Bhai Nand Lal, who had served the Prince at Agra. He sought the Guru's assistance. Since he was the rightful successor and the Guru was keen to ensure that, like his father, Bahadur Shah was not misled, he placed a detachment at his disposal. Bahadur Shah was victorious and invited the Guru to his coronation, when he gave him a robe of honor and several precious gifts.

Bahadur Shah became so fond of the Guru that he persuaded him to accompany him to the South. Guru Gobind Singh agreed, since it would give him an opportunity to preach his gospel and meet the Sikhs in distant parts of the country, which he had not been able to do owing to constant conflict with Mughal power.

On his way to the South the Guru happened to pass the *samadhi* of Dadu, a great saint of the Bhakti Movement. Dadu was also a fine poet. It is said that the Guru, out of respect for the poet-saint, lowered his arrow before the samadhi. The Sikh accompanying him took objection to it, for had the Guru himself not told them that they must not worship anyone excepting the great God? They must not worship gods and goddesses nor visit mausoleums and samadhis. The Sikhs passed the *Gurmata*—a resolution of the faithful—and fined the

Guru for his lapse, which he accepted with grace. The Guru was proud of his Sikhs for their respect for the principles laid down for the *Khalsa*.

During his sojourn in the South, the Guru sighted a picturesque spot on the banks of the river Godavari at Nanded. It was the hermitage of the *tantrik,* Madho Das. When the Guru arrived at the hermitage, Madho Das happened to be away. The Guru made himself comfortable and his Sikhs slaughtered a goat and started cooking meat. When Madho Das returned, he was furious. How could anyone cook meat on the premises of a strict vegetarian like Madho Das? However, the moment he looked at the Guru, he was a changed person. They had a brief dialogue and he became a devotee of the Guru.

Since the Guru was fascinated with the beauty of the place, he decided to camp at Nanded. The Guru told Madho Das, who had been named Banda Singh Bahadur after his baptism, how the Mughal Governor of Sirhind had tortured his innocent sons to death and how he had to fight many a battle with the Mughals and hill chiefs. Banda, who was now no longer a recluse, collected the Guru's Sikhs around him and decided to punish the Mughal Governor of the Punjab and the hill chiefs.

In the meanwhile, Wazir Khan, the Governor of Sirhind, who feared Bahadur Shah's growing friendship with the Guru, sent a party of assassins to put an end to the Guru's life before he poisoned the King's ears and embittered his relations with him.

The assassins came disguised and one afternoon, when the Guru was resting, they attacked him unawares. In the encounter, the Guru and his bodyguard put both of them to death but they succeeded in inflicting a deep wound in the Guru's side with a dagger.

It is said that the wound was attended to by a surgeon sent by the Mughal King, and it seemed that it had started healing and that the Guru was well on his way to recovery when he happened to tug a bow and the wound opened up again.

In spite of the best treatment possible, this proved fatal. When the end came on 7 October 1708, Guru Gobind Singh addressed his Sikhs thus:

As ordained by God, the Lord Eternal,
A new way of life is evolved.
All the Sikhs are asked
to accept the Holy Granth as the Guru.
Guru Granth should be accepted
As the living God.
Those who wish to meet God
Will find Him in the Word.

The Guru henceforth was to be found in the Divine Word. The Sikh community had to be guided by the decisions of the Five Faithful—*Panj Piare*—chosen from among the devotees. Thus, Guru Gobind Singh gave Sikhism a democratic orientation of the most modern form amongst the religions of the world.

Selected Hymns of Guru Gobind Singh

1. He who has no form, features, class, or caste,
   He who belongs to no community,
   He who has no color, no complexion, no mark, no garb,
   No one knows what He is like.
   Immovable, self-refulgent and all-powerful,
   He is the Indra of millions of Indras,
   He is the king of kings,
   He is the sovereign of the three worlds—of demigods, human
       beings, and demons.
   The jungle and the woods remember Him every moment.
   How can one call Him by all His Names?
   The wise give Him Names according to His manifestations.

   (Jap)

2. How does it help if you shut your eyes
   And like a crane sit and meditate?
   You wander and wander bathing in the seven seas;
   You've lost this world as well as that.
   You remained in the company of the evil-minded
   And wasted your life in vain.
   I tell the truth that all may hear,
   He who loves, he alone has found God.

   (Swaiyya)

3. Some carry the stone-deity on their head,
   Some suspend *lingam* from their neck.
   Some see God in the South,
   Some bow towards the West,
   Some worship images,
   Some go to propitiate the dead.
   The whole world is lost in empty rituals,
   No one knows the secret of God.

   (Swaiyya)

4. He helps the helpless every moment
   Exhorts saints and kills their enemies.
   Birds and beasts, snakes and serpents and their kings.
   He looks after them all the while.

He protects those in water and those on earth every moment.
He ignores the evil of the Age of *Kali*
He is the benefactor of the poor,
He is the source of all kindness.
He is aware of evil deeds.
And yet he ceases not to be bountiful.

(Swaiyya)

5.   Give me Your hand and protect me.
Let me fulfill the desire of my heart,
That my thoughts should remain with You.
Help me as the one belonging to You.
Vanquish all my enemies and all my evils.
And save me with Your own hands.
Let my people live in peace, O God!
And all my servants and all my Sikhs.
With Your own hands help me
And destroy all my enemies today,
Let my heart's desire be met.
And I should continue to long to sing Your praises,
I should remember none excepting You,
Let all my servants and Sikhs attain salvation
And defeat my foes, each one of them.

(Chaupaee)

6.   What God has told me Himself
I tell the world.
Those who meditate on Him
Only they will go to Heaven in the end.
God and Godmen are one
There is no difference between them—
Like the tide that rises from water
And subsides in water again.

(Doha)

7.   When I came of age
The Guru talked to me—
Son, my only advice is,
As long as you live
You may sleep with your own wife every day

But never go to the bed of another's wife even in dreams.

(Chhand)

8. Give me a boon, O God!
I should not deflect from good deeds,
I should not fear those with whom I fight,
I must make my success a certainty.
In my heart of hearts I should long
To sing Your praises like a Sikh,
And when the hour of reckoning arrives
I should die fighting on the battlefield.

(Swaiyya)

9. If I ask for wealth
It comes from every country.
My heart doesn't care for
Divination or magic.
Asceticism and penance that I hear about
I wouldn't torture my body with.
I ask only one boon of You, O God
That I should die a fearless death fighting on the battlefield.

(Swaiyya)

10. Man, let your asceticism be like this:
Treat your dwelling like a forest,
And remain a recluse at heart.
Your matted hair should be your continence
And the holy bath, your search for God.
The discipline be your growth of nails
And the Guru's teachings your guide.
Smear the body with the ashes of His Name.
With frugal food and scanty sleep,
Compassion and forgiveness should be your attainments.
Practise mildness and forbearance
In this way you'll gain more than the three cardinal virtues.

(Shabd Hazare)

Guru Granth Saheb

As ordained by the Lord Eternal
A new way of life is evolved.
All the Sikhs are asked
To accept the Holy Granth as the Guru.
Guru Granth should be accepted
As the living Guru,
Those who wish to meet God
Will find Him in the Word.

—*Guru Gobind Singh*

Guru Gobind Singh, the tenth Sikh Guru, handed over the stewardship of the *Sikh Panth*—the Sikh way of life—to the *Holy Granth*. Those who wish to seek God, Guru Gobind Singh said, can find Him in the Holy Word.

The *Holy Granth* came to be compiled with a view to insulating the text of the compositions of Guru Nanak and his successors against the wild adventures of Prithi Chand, Guru Arjan's eldest brother, who started composing his own verses and passing them on to the Sikhs as the scriptures.

Guru Arjan went about the project of the compilation of the *Holy Granth* in a scientific way. As a first step, he sent scribes to the various places visited by Guru Nanak and his followers to contact those whom the Gurus had met and obtain from them the authentic version of the hymns. A Sikh was deputed even to Sri Lanka. When it was reported that Mohan, the eldest son of Guru Ram Das, would not part with the hymns in his custody, Guru Arjan visited him personally at Goindwal and placated him to cooperate in the noble undertaking. On his way back, Guru Arjan also visited Datu, Guru Angad's son, and collected whatever manuscripts were available with him.

227

Considering the importance of the work, Guru Arjan had a special cell set up in a quiet corner of Ramsar, one of the holy tanks in Amritsar. Bhai Gurdas, the eminent Sikh litterateur, was entrusted with the job of preparing the master copy, Guru Arjan dictating the text himself. When ready, it was installed with due ceremony at the Har Mandir and Bhai Budha appointed the first custodian of the *Holy Granth*. Guru Arjan offered to include the compositions of Bhai Gurdas, but out of modesty the Sikh scholar denied himself the great honor.

The *Holy Granth* was redictated by Guru Gobind Singh towards the close of his life, when he had a little respite at Talwandi Sabo called Damdama Saheb. He had Guru Tegh Bahadur's compositions incorporated in the body of the text. Again Guru Gobind's greatness as a poet made him opt to remain out.

The unique catholicity of Guru Arjan is evidence in the fact that, along with the hymns of the Sikh Gurus, he incorporated the compositions of as many as thirty-six men of God belonging to various castes and creeds, regions and avocations. Among them were Jaidev of Bengal, Surdas of Awadh, Namdev, Trilochan and Parma Nand of Maharashtra, Beni, Rama Nand, Pipa, Sain, Kabir, Ravidas and Bhikhan of Uttar Pradesh, Dhanna of Rajasthan and Farid of Multan. Kabir was a weaver, Sadhna a butcher, Namdev a seamster, Dhanna a jat, Pipa a king, Sain a barber, Ravidas a tanner, Farid a Muslim divine, Bhikka a learned scholar of Islam and Sivdas, a Hindu mystic and poet.

The hymns compiled in the *Holy Granth* have been arranged in various *Ragas* according to Hindustani music. They hymns under every musical measure are led by Guru Nanak and other Sikh Gurus in chronological order, the compositions of the Bhaktas following them. There are about six thousand hymns in the *Holy Granth* in thirty-one ragas.

It is said Kahna, Chhajju, Pilu and a few other contemporary poets approached Guru Arjan and offered their verses for inclusion in the *Holy Granth*. The Guru duly considered their compositions but regretted his inability to include them in the volume for one reason or another.

Some of the bards who subscribed to the Sikh faith had composed several panegyrics in praise of the Sikh Gurus. At their representation the Guru agreed to include them in the Holy Book.

The scripting of the text was completed in 1604, the Guru providing an epilogue in *Mundawani:*

Three things are there in the vessel:
Truth, contentment, and intellect.
The ambrosial Name of God is added to it,
The Name that is everybody's sustenance.
He who eats and enjoys it
Shall be saved.
One must not abandon this gift,
It should ever remain dear to one's heart.
The dark ocean of the world
Can be crossed by clinging to His feet.
Nanak, it is He who is everywhere.

This was followed by an apologia in utmost modesty:

I can't measure Your grace;
You've made me worthy of You.
I am full of blemishes;
I have no virtue,
You have been compassionate.
Compassionate You have been and kind,
Thus I met the True Guru.
Nanak, I live on the Name alone,
It pleases my heart and soul.

The Rag Mala following this does not tally with the *ragas* in the *Holy Granth* and its inclusion continues to be a subject of controversy.

It is said Bhai Banno, a Sikh belonging to Mangat, a village in the present-day Gujarat district of West Punjab, was keen to have a copy of the Holy Book. When the volume was being bound in Lahore, he had a copy made for him. He got some hymns originally omitted by the Guru also included in his volume.

Prithi Chand bore a grudge against Guru Arjan. Rather than being happy at the completion of a monumental work like the *Holy Granth* after years of hard labor, he had a complaint made to the Mughal Emperor Akbar that the work compiled by Guru Arjan had compositions that maligned Islam and Hinduism. Akbar happened to be touring the Punjab in those days. He summoned the Guru along with a copy of the *Holy Granth*. While the Guru did not consider it necessary to go personally, he sent Bhai Budha and Bhai Gurdas along with the compilation. It is said the King had a hymn read out to him at random. It was a composition of Guru Arjan himself:

From clay and light God created the world.
The sky, the earth, trees, and water are made by Him.
I have seen men pass away.
Forgetting God in avarice is like eating carrion
The way the evil spirits kill and devour the dead.
One must restrain oneself,
Hell is the punishment otherwise.
The miracle man, the riches, brother, courtiers, kingdom, and palaces
None will come to your rescue at the hour of departure
When the messenger of death comes to carry you away . . .
God the Pure knows what's in store for me.
Nanak, my appeal of a slave is to you alone.

(Tilang)

The King heard the hymn and was deeply impressed. However Prithi Chand contended that it was on purpose that Bhai Gurdas had read a piece that was not objectionable. At this, the King himself pointed out a hymn and had it read out to him. This, too, was found least offensive to anyone. Wicked as he was, Prithi Chand maintained that since none of them knew the Gurmukhi script, Bhai Gurdas had read the hymns from memory rather than the text indicated by the King. At this, Akbar had one Sahib Dyal sent for to read out a piece pointed out by the King himself. The text read out was:

You don't see God who dwells in your heart,
And you carry about an idol on your neck.

A non-believer, you wander about churning water,
And you die harassed in delusion.
The idol you call God will drown with you . . .
Ungrateful sinner!
The boat will not ferry you across.
Says Nanak, I met the Guru who led me to God,
He who lives in water, earth, nether region, and firmament.

(Suhi)

The Emperor heard it and said that it was a great work, worthy of reverence. He made an offering of fifty-one gold *mohurs* to the *Holy Granth* and awarded robes of honor to Bhai Budha and Bhai Gurdas. The King complimented Guru Arjan on the compilation and promised to visit Amritsar personally in the near future to pay homage to the Guru. He remembered to keep his promise.

The *Holy Granth* having been installed in Har Mandir, its reading was already considered sacred. When the news of Guru Arjan's martyrdom reached Amritsar, Guru Hargobind had Bhai Budha read out the *Holy Granth* for ten days. When Guru Hargobind decided to retire to Kartarpur, his grandson Dhir Mal wished to stay on in Kartarpur. He was friendly with the Mughal Governor at Jullundur. He took charge of the entire property at Kartarpur including the *Holy Granth*. Bhai Bidhi Chand, a Sikh, had started making a copy of the *Granth* and had covered up the portion up to Rag Bilawal. He wished to carry the original with him, so that he could complete copying the rest of the text. But Dhir Mal would not agree to it. He was aware that the Sikhs would continue to come to Kartarpur on pilgrimage. Kartarpur being out of the way, hardly anyone would go there. If he had the custody of the *Holy Granth*, he would be entitled to offerings from the Sikhs and could also style himself successor to the Guru, in due course. When the Guru heard about it, he remarked, "Let the *Granth* remain with him. A time will come when the Sikhs would reclaim it." Accordingly, for a long time, the Guru and his Sikhs made do with the incomplete copy prepared by Bhai Bidhi Chand. Dhir Mal was so petty that he wouldn't part with the *Granth* even when his own father, Baba Gurditta, died and Guru Hargobind wished to organize a reading of the *Holy Granth* in his memory.

Once Aurangzeb invited Guru Har Rai to his court. The Guru was not inclined to oblige the King. At this, his son Ram Rai volunteered to go to Delhi on the Guru's behalf. He, in fact, wished to make friends with the Emperor. It is said that in spite of his father advising Ram Rai not to perform any feat at the court, he worked a number of miracles. Not only this, but when Aurangzeb pointed out a couplet in the *Holy Granth* which according to him was derogatory to the Muslims, Ram Rai misread the original to please the King. It was indeed sacrilegious. When this fact was brought to the Guru's notice, he sent word to Ram Rai never to return or show his face to his father, the Guru.

The text of the *Holy Granth* has utmost sanctity accorded it since its compilation. No change of even a syllable was permitted. For a long time, the Sikhs would not permit the words in the text to be written or printed separately; they continued to be copied as a continuous text following the original as per the practice prevailing when Bhai Gurdas had prepared the volume.

It is said that once, when Guru Har Rai was resting, a Sikh came reciting hymns from the *Holy Granth*. The moment Guru heard him, he rose and sat upright in reverence to the Holy Word. Later, when Guru Tegh Bahadur left Baba Bakala finally for Kartarpur, the Guru's Sikhs's took possession of the *Holy Granth* from Dhir Mal by force. However, while crossing the river Beas, the Guru learned about it. He had the Holy Volume restored to Dhir Mal.

It was left to Guru Gobind Singh to secure the original copy and bring it up-to-date, with Guru Tegh Bahadur's compositions appropriately incorporated in it.

The *Holy Granth* is the most ambitious compilation of devotional verse. It is also the most representative of its times. It has a grand design and a highly scientific manner of presentation. The pattern adopted by Guru Arjan was such that it permitted incorporation of later compositions without interfering with the text of the works already compiled. Guru Gobind Singh didn't have to disturb the arrangement while adding Guru Tegh Bahadur's compositions to the compilation.

The *Holy Granth* opens with the mool mantra, the basic postulate:

There is but one God:
His name is Truth;
He is the creator;
He fears none nor does He hate anyone.
He is in the image of the Eternal.
He is beyond birth and death;
He is self-existent.
He can be attained by the Guru's grace.

This is followed by the *Japji* and the *Rahras*. The latter comprise *Sodar*, consisting of five hymns and *Sopurkh*, consisting of four hymns. *Sohila* comes at the end of this section. It contains five hymns. While the *Japji* is recited in the morning, the Sikhs are ordained to recite *Rahras* in the evening and *Sohila* at night before going to bed.

The main body of the *Holy Granth* is arranged according to the Hindustani ragas or musical measures. There are thirty-one ragas included in the *Holy Granth*. The *Japji* is intended to be recited and not sung. The various hymns figuring in *Rahras* and *Sohila* are written to musical measures and are repeated in their respective ragas, as they should be.

The ragas included in the *Holy Granth* are: Sri Rag, Majh, Gauri, Asa, Gujri, Dev Gandhari, Bihagra, Wadhans, Sorath, Dhanasri, Jaitsri, Todi, Bairadi, Tilang, Suhi, Bilawal, Gaund, Ramkali, Nat Narayan, Mali Gauda, Maru, Tudhari, Kidara, Bhairo, Basant, Sarang, Malhar, Kanada, Kalyan, Parbhati, Jaijaivanti.

Following the compositions figuring under the various ragas, there are a number of other hymns, like Sanskrit *slokas*, (e.g. the slokas of Kabir, Farid, and Guru Tegh Bahadur), the *Gatha*, and the *Swaiyyas* of Guru Arjan and others.

The order of hymns usually followed under each raga is as follows: *shabd*, Ashtpadis, Chhand, Var and hymns contributed by the Bhaktas. The *shabds* of Guru Nanak come first, followed by the other Gurus in chronological order. In order that there is no risk of interpolations every shabd and every verse is numbered and recorded throughout the Holy Book. The numbering also helps in locating the hymns conveniently.

The *Holy Granth* comprises compositions of six Sikh Gurus: Guru

Nanak, Guru Angad, Guru Amar Das, Guru Ram Das, Guru Arjan, and Guru Tegh Bahadur. Since it was the spirit of Guru Nanak that travelled from one Guru to the other Guru, the Gurus following Guru Nanak use Nanak as their nom de plume at the end of their respective hymns.

The Bhaktas whose hymns qualified to be included in the *Holy Granth* are: Kabir, Namdev, Ravidas, Trilochan, Farid, Beni, Dhanna, Jaidev, Bhikha, Surdas, Prama Nand, Sain, Pipa, Sadhna, and Rama Nand.

In addition, some of the panegyrics composed by *bhats*, minstrels in the employ of the Gurus, written mainly in praise of the Gurus, are also included in the *Holy Granth*. They are: Kalshar, Jalap, Kirat, Bhikha, Sallh, Bhallh, Nallh, Bullh, Gyand, Mathura, and Harbans. Baba Sundar, though not a *bhat*, also figures along with them.

Apart from the five Sikh Gurus whose compositions are included in the *Holy Granth*, Guru Hargobind, Guru Har Rai and Guru Harkrishan do not seem to have composed any hymns. It is not understood why Guru Gobind Singh, who was a prolific author and a highly powerful poet, chose not to figure in the Holy Book. The only reason appears to be his modesty or perhaps practical considerations, since the inclusion of his works would have made the Holy Book too unwieldy, Guru Gobind Singh's compositions being varied and voluminous.

As a literary work, the *Holy Granth* has some superb pieces of poetic excellence both from the viewpoint of form and of content. The language varies from Sanskrit and Persian to the Punjabi spoken in those times in the form of various regional dialects. The poetic forms are as varied as they are original. They invariably reflect the mood of the text and succeed in communicating it eminently. The Gurus and the *bhaktas* take ample liberties with the form and do not seem to observe the rigidities of the traditional poetic molds. In order that their compositions become popular, the Gurus preferred the measures and the tunes of the folk ballads and folksongs. It must have helped the Sikhs to sing the hymns in their proper tunes. The Hindustani music having an oral tradition, it is a great pity that most of the tunes prescribed by the respective authors are lost with the times.

The poetry of the *Holy Granth* is a mine of philosophic thought. It is highly revealing and reflects a way of life which is as simple as it is ennobling. Every word of it inspires and elevates. It has equal appeal for the erudite scholar as for the least literate reader. What is needed is an attitude of devotion.

It must, however, be understood that paper and the printed word are not the Guru. They are only a vehicle. The Guru is what is contained in it; what one imbibes by reading the text; the revelation, the vision, the ecstasy. However, the fact remains that while the container that holds the nectar may not be nectar itself, it is no ordinary container.

About the Author

Kartar Singh (K. S.) Duggal, born in 1917, began writing while still a student. He is an author of repute in Punjabi, Urdu, Hindi, and English. His works have been translated into many other languages, and are used in literature classes in a large number of colleges and universities throughout the world. His published works include twenty-one collections of short stories, seven novels, seven plays, and two collections of poetry.

He has received numerous awards and prizes for his writing, including the Ghalib Award for Urdu Drama (1976), the Soviet Land Nehru Award (1981), the Fellowship of the Punjabi Sahitya Academy (1983), and the Bharatya Bhasha Parishad Award (1985).

His short story, "Come Back My Master" is included in the *Greatest Short Stories of the World*. He was recognized by both the Punjabi government (1962) and the Delhi Administration (1976) as a distinguished man-of-letters and awarded a "Robe of Honour." His collection of short stories, *Ik Chhit Chanan Di*, won the Sahita Academi award in 1965.

Mr. Duggal also served as Director of the All-India Radio from 1942 to 1966, as Director of the National Book Trust from 1966-1973, and was an Advisor (Information) to the Planning Commission from 1973 to 1976.

He has worked to encourage and promote literature and the arts throughout his life. He also served as a columnist for *The Indian Express*, *The Tribune*, and *The Indian Book Industry*, as a commentator on books, authors, radio, and television programs and the contemporary publishing scene in India.

Glossary

Amrit: Nectar
Ang: A limb
Arati: A form of Hindu worship
Bani: Holy utterances
Baoli: A dug-in tank
Bhakta: A devotee
Bhakti: Devotion
Bhang: Hemp
Bhat: A professional singer
Chatrik: An Indian bird symbolizing thirst
Darbar: Court
Dharmasala: A Sikh place of worship
Daroga: Guard
Fatwa: An injunction given by a Muslim religious chief
Ghazi: Invader, one who fights against infidels
Gurbani: The Guru's word
Gurdwara: Sikh temple
Gurmatta: Decision taken in a Sikh congregation
Gursikh: A devotee of the Guru
Harmandir: The Golden Temple at Amritsar
Houries: Fairies
Hukamnama: Religious commandment
Jagir: Landed property
Janaeu: Hindu sacred thread
Jehad: Crusade
Jhalli: Crazy
Jizia: Tax levied on those not belonging to the State religion
Kachcha: Underwear—trunks

Kada: Bangle
Kaliyuga: The dark age
Kartik: A month according to Hindu Calendar—advent of winter
Kesh: Hair
Khalsa: The pure
Kirpan: Sword
Koel: An Indian bird known for its sweet call during the summer months in the mango groves
Kos: A mile and a half in distance
Langar: Community eating
Lota: A vessel for ablutions
Madrasa: Muslim school
Mahant: Manager of a place of worship
Maktab: School
Manji: A diocese, a Sikh religious administrative division
Mantras: Incantations
Masand: A Sikh priestly cadre
Maya: Illusion
Miri: Royalty
Mlechchas: Bad characters
Mohur: A gold coin
Nath: A sect of Hindu yogis
Pathshala: Hindu school
Patwari: A revenue official
Pir: A Muslim divine
Piri: Spirituality
Posh: A month according to Hindu calendar—peak of winter
Qazi: An administrator of Muslim Law
Rabab: A string instrument
Sacha Padshah: The true king
Sadhu-kkari: Alms collected by a recluse
Sahj: A state of beatitude
Samadhi: Meditation
Sangat: Congregation
Sarang: An Indian bird symbolizing pangs of separation
Sardar: Leader
Satnam Sri Vahguru: God is truth

Seli: A head gear signifying spiritual order

Shabd: The divine communication

Shakti: Power, here potency of a god

Shikar: Hunting as a sport

Shudra: The lowest of the four major Hindu castes

Siddha: Hindu ascetic

Singh: Lion

Slokas: A metric form

Tantric Yoga: Shakti-worship

Tilak: Hindu mark worn on the forehead

Udasi: Recluse

Vaishnav Bhakti: Devotion to Vishnu, the preserver of the Universe

Zimmies: Inferior citizens

Select Bibliography

Ahluwalia, Rajinder Singh, *Founder of the Khalsa*, Chandigarh: Guru Gobind Singh Foundation, 1966.

Ahuja, N.D., *Great Guru Nanak and the Muslims*, Chandigarh: Kirti Publishing House.

Ahuja, N.D., *Islam and the Creed of Nanak, A Comparative Study*, Chandigarh:Vee Vee Publishers.

Ahuja, N.D., *Muslim Sikh Relations, the Truth*, Chandigarh: Vee Vee Publishers.

Ahuja, N.D., *Nanakism, Message of the Master*, Chandigarh: Vee Vee Publishers.

Anand, Balwant Singh, *Guru Tegh Bahadur*, New Delhi: Sterling, 1979.

Archer, John Clark, *Sikhs in Relation to Hindus, Moslems, Christians and Ahmediyas*, 1946.

Ashta, Dharam Pal, *Poetry of the Dasam Granth* 1959.

(Ayyangar) Iyengar, K.R. Srinivasa (Ed.), *Guru Nanak—A Homage*, Calcutta: Sahitya Academy, 1973.

Bal, Surjit Singh, *Guru Nanak in the Eyes of the Non-Sikhs*, Chandigarh: Publication Bureau, Punjab University, 1969.

Bal, Surjit Singh, *Life of Guru Nanak*, Chandigarh: Publication Bureau, Punjab University, 1969.

(Banerji) Banerjee, Anil Chandra, *Guru Nanak And His Times*, Patiala: Punjab University, 1971.

(Banerji) Banerjee, Anil Chandra, *Guru Nanak to Guru Gobind Singh*, New Delhi: Rajnesh Publication, 1978.

Banerji, Indubhushan, *Evolution of the Khalsa*; Vol. 1. *The Foundation of the Sikh Panth*, 1963; Vol. 2. *The Reformation*, 1962.

Bedi, Gursharan Singh, *Psalm of Life*, an English translation of Guru Nanak's *Japji Sahib* in Verse, 1950.

Doabia, Harbans Singh, *Shri Guru Tegh Bahadur Saheb, Life, History, Sacred Hymns and Teachings*, Amritsar: Singh Bros., 1975.

Field, Dorothy, *Religion of the Sikhs,* Delhi: ESS Publication, 1976.

Fripp, Peter, *Mystic Philosophy of Sant Mat,* 1964.

Gandhi, Surjit Singh, *History of the Sikh Gurus,* Delhi: Gurudas Kapur & Sons, 1978.

Gill, Pritam Singh, *Trinity of Sikhism,* Jullundur: New Academic Publishing, 1973.

Greenless, Duncan, *Gospel of the Guru Granth Sahib,* 1960.

Grewal, J.S., *Guru Nanak in History,* Chandigarh: Publication Division, Punjab University.

Grewal, J.S. and Bal, S.S., *Guru Gobind Singh, A Biographical Study,* Chandigarh: Dept. of History, Punjab University, 1967.

Gupta, Hari Ram, *History of the Sikh Gurus,* New Delhi: U.C. Kapur & Sons, 1973.

Gupta, Hari Ram, *Life-Sketch of Guru Nanak,* Delhi: National Publishing House, 1969.

Guru Granth Ratnavali, Patiala: Punjab University.

Jain, Nirmal Kumar, *Sikh Religion, Philosophy,* New Delhi: Sterling 1969.

Johar, Surinder Singh, *Guru Gobind Singh, A Biography,* Delhi: Sterling, 1967.

Johar, Surinder Singh, *Guru Nanak, A Biography,* Jullundur: New Book Company, 1969.

Johar, Surinder Singh, *Guru Tegh Bahadur, A Biography,* New Delhi: Abhinav Publications, 1975.

Johar, Surinder Singh, *Hand Book of Sikhism,* Delhi: Vivek Publishing Company, 1977.

Johar, Surinder Singh, *Sikh Gurus and Their Shrines,* Delhi: Vivek Publishing Co., 1977.

Karam Chand, Dharamdas, (Tr.), *Origin and Growth of Udasis.*

Khan, Mohammed Waliullah, *Sikh Shrines in West Pakistan,* 1962.

Kohli, Surinder Singh, *Critical Study of Adi Granth,* Delhi: Motilal Banarsidas, 1976.

Kohli, Surinder Singh, *Outline of the Sikh Thought,* Delhi: Munshiram Manoharlal, 1978.

Kohli, Surinder Singh, *Philosophy of Guru Nanak,* Chandigarh: Publication Division, Punjab University, 1969.

Kohli, Surinder Singh, *Sword and the Spirit,* New Delhi: Ankur Publishing House, 1977.

Kohli, Surinder Singh, *Travels of Guru Nanak,* Chandigarh: Publication Division, Punjab University.

Kumar, H.C., *Guru Nanak as An Occultist—On the Philosophy of Japji,* 1926.

Leohlin, C.H., *Sikhs and Their Scriptures,* Delhi: I.S.P.C.K.L.P.H., 1974.

Mecauliffe, Max Arthur, *Sikh Religion, Its Gurus, Sacred Writings and Authors,* 6 Vols.

Mansukhani, *Gobind Singh, Guru Nanak the Apostle of Love,* New Delhi: Hemkunt, 1969.

Mansukhani, *Gobind Singh, Guru Nanak—World Teacher,* New Delhi: India Book House, 1968.

Mcleod, W.H., *Evolution of the Sikh Community,* Delhi: Oxford University Press, 1975.

Mcleod, W.H., *Guru Nanak and the Sikh Religion,* Bombay: Oxford University Press, 1968.

Nanak Dev—Guru Nanak's Japji, tr. by Gurdip Singh & Charanjit Singh, New Delhi: Navyug Traders, 1970.

Nanak Dev, Hymns of Guru Nanak, tr. by Man Mohan Singh, Punjab Language Dept., 1972.

Nanak Dev, Hymns, tr. by Khushwant Singh, Orient Longman, New Delhi: 1969.

Narang, Gokul Chand, *Glorious History of Sikhism,* New Delhi: New Book Society of India, 1972.

Narang, Gokul Chand, *Transformation of Sikhism,* 1950.

Ray, Niharranjan, *Sikh Gurus and Sikh Society,* New Delhi: Munshiram Manoharlal, 1975.

Singh, Attar, (tr.) *Sakhee Book or the Description of Gooroo Gobind Singh's Religion and Doctrines,* Benares: Medical Hall Press, 1873.

Singh, Daljeet, *Sikhism, A Contemporary Study of its Theory and Mysticism,* Sterling, 1979.

Singh, Darshan, *Religion of Guru Nanak,* Ludhiana: Lyall Book Depot, 1970.

Singh, Fauja, *Guru Amar Das,* New Delhi: Sterling, 1979.

Singh, Fauja, et al., *Sikhism,* Patiala: Punjab University, 1969.

Singh, Fauja and Gurbachan Singh Talib, *Guru Teg Bahadur, Martyr and Teacher,* Patiala: Punjabi University, 1975.

Singh, Gopal, *Prophet of Home, Life of Guru Gobind Singh,* Delhi: Sterling, 1967.

Singh, Gopal, *Religion of Sikhs,* New Delhi: Asia Publishing House, 1971.

Singh, Gopal, *Sri Guru Granth Sahib,* Vol. 4.

Singh, Gurmukh Nihal (Ed.), *Guru Nanak, His Life, Time and Teachings,* New Delhi: Guru Nanak Foundation, 1679.

Singh, Harbans, *Guru Gobind Singh,* Chandigarh: Guru Gobind Singh Foundation, 1966.

Singh, Harbans, *Guru Nanak and Origin of the Sikh Faith*, New Delhi: Asia Publishing House, 1969.

Singh, Harbans, (ed.) *International Seminar on the Life and Teachings of Guru Nanak*, (Papers), Patiala: Punjabi University, 1975.

Singh, Jagjit, *Guru Gobind Singh, A Study*, 1967.

Singh, Ishwar, *Nanakism, A New World Order*, New Delhi: Ranjeet Publishing House, 1976.

Singh, Ishwar, *Philosophy of Guru Nanak*, New Delhi: Ranjit Publishing House 1969.

Singh, Joginder and Daljit Singh, *Guru Nanak the Great Humanist.*

Singh, Kahn, *Encyclopaedia of the Sikh Literature*, 4 Vols.

Singh, Khazan, *History and Philosophy of the Sikh Religion.*

Singh, Khazan, *Miracles of the Sikh Gurus.*

Singh, Khushwant, *Sikhs Today*, edited by Rahul Singh, Bombay: Orient Longman, 1976.

Singh, Khushwant, *A History of the Sikhs*, London: Princeton, Vol. 2, 1963.

Singh, Khushwant, *Japji: The Sikh Prayer.*

Singh, Khushwant, *The Sikhs*, London.1953.

Singh, Manjeet, *Gurubani and Science*, Delhi: Educational Publishers, 1973.

Singh, Mehr, *Sikh Shrines in India*, New Delhi: Publications Division, Ministry of Information and Broadcasting, 1975.

Singh, Narain, *Our Heritage*, Chief Khalsa Diwan, Amritsar.

Singh, Puran, *Book of Ten Masters*, Lahore: Sikh University Press.

Singh, Puran, *Guru Gobind Singh, Reflections & Offerings*, Chandigarh: Guru Gobind Singh Foundation, 1968.

Singh, Ranbir, *Glimpses of the Divine Masters*, 1965.

Singh, Ranbir, *Guru Tegh Bahadur*, Chief Khalsa Diwan, 1975.

Singh, Ranbir, *The Sikh Way Of Life*, New Delhi.

Singh, Shanta Sarabjit, *Nanak the Guru*, New Delhi: Orient Longman, 1970.

Singh, Sher, *Philosophy of Sikhism*, New Delhi: Sterling.

Singh, Sher, *Social and Political Philosophy of Guru Gobind Singh*, New Delhi: Sterling.

Sikhism and Indian Society, Transactions of the Institute of Advanced Study, Simla: 1967.

Singh, Teja, *Growth of Responsibility of Sikhism*, 1957.

Singh, Teja, *Japji or Guru Nanak's Meditations*, 1920.

Singh, Teja, *Sikhism, Its Ideals and Institutions*, 1951.

Singh, Teja, *Psalm of Peace*, English translation of Guru Arjan's *Sukhmani*, 1950.

Singh, Trilochan, *Guru Nanak, Founder of Sikhism, a Biography*, Delhi: Gurdwara Prabandhak Committee, 1967.

Singh, Trilochan, *Selections from the Sacred Writings of the Sikhs*, Re. by George S. Fraser, London: Allen & Unwin, 1960.

Singh, Wazir, *Humanism of Guru Nanak, a Philosophic Enquiry*, Ess Ess Publications, 1977.

Talib, Gurbachan Singh, *Guru Nanak, His Personality and Vision*, Delhi: Gurdas Kapur & Sons, 1969.

Talib, Gurbachan Singh, *Bani of Sri Guru Ram Das*, New Delhi: Sterling, 1979.

Talib, Gurbachan Singh, *Guru Granth Sahib, Selections from the Holy Granth*, New Delhi: Vikas, 1975.

Trumpp, Ernst, (tr.) *Adi Granth, the Holy Scriptures of the Sikhs*, 2nd edn., Munshiram Manoharlal, 1970.

Varma, Sharad Chandra, *Guru Nanak*, Gurdwara Prabandhak Committee, 1969.

Vaswani, T.L., *Prophet of the People*, Poona: Geeta Publication House.

Index